TOTALITY AND INFINITY AT 50

Totality and Infinity at 50

edited by
Scott Davidson
and
Diane Perpich

DUQUESNE UNIVERSITY PRESS
PITTSBURGH, PENNSYLVANIA

Published in the United States of America by
DUQUESNE UNIVERSITY PRESS
600 Forbes Avenue
Pittsburgh, Pennsylvania 15282

Library of Congress Cataloging-in-Publication Data

Totality and infinity at 50 / edited by Scott Davidson and Diane Perpich.
        pages cm
    Summary: "Essays by 14 Levinas scholars provide a fresh acount of argument and
purpose of Emmanuel Levinas's major work, Totality and Infinity, drawing parallels between Levinas and other thinkers; considering Levinas's relationship to other
disciplines such as nursing, psycotherapy, and law; and bringing this seminal text to
bear on specific, concern issues of present-day concern"—Provided by publisher.
    Includes bibliographical references and index.
    ISBN 978-0-8207-0452-4 (pbk. : alk. paper)
    1. Lévinas, Emmanuel. Totalité et infini. I. Davidson, Scott, 1970–editor of
compilation. II. Perpich, Diane, editor of compilation.
    BD396.L433T68 2012
    111—dc23

                                                                              2011046660

∞ Printed on acid-free paper.

If it was sometimes difficult to understand [Levinas], it was because his thought was more rapid than his diction. His writing was also nervous, often difficult to decipher. If you had only seen the scraps that *Totality and Infinity* or *Difficult Freedom* were written on! He wrote on the backs of envelopes, the bottom halves of bills, or on the smallest bits of unused paper. Often I had to turn the page in all directions to reach the ends of sentences. He used his refillable fountain pen—but certainly not the kind with cartridges, they ran out too quickly! He wrote a lot, corrected a great deal, crossed things out, cut and pasted like a collage. He only stopped when the text translated his thoughts with exactitude.

He gave me his manuscripts, I typed them, then he corrected them. He was never satisfied with what he had done. One day, he even dared to ask me if I thought it was good!

I found in his writing a kind of musical rhythm, like a metronome. When I heard this rhythm while I was typing, or reading the manuscript over, I knew that it was good; I knew that he had finished, that he wouldn't correct it further. I said to him: now it's musical, it's good.

—*Thérèse Goldstein*

Thérèse Goldstein was Emmanuel Levinas's assistant at the Ecole Normale Israélite Orientale. She typed the manuscript of Totality and Infinity *as well as the bulk of Levinas's work between 1953 and 1980. These remarks are extracted from her presentation at the Centre Communautaire Juif de Paris on January 23, 2006, at a conference entitled, "A Century with Levinas: A Humanism for the Future." They also appear in an unpublished interview given to Joëlle Hansel in August 2009.*

Contents

Works listed are primary texts by Emmanuel Levinas. Any other abbreviations used are indicated in the endnotes of the individual essays.

AT   *Alterity and Transcendence*. Trans. Michael B. Smith. New York: Columbia University Press, 1999.

BPW   *Basic Philosophical Writings*. Ed. Adriaan Peperzak, Simon Critchley, and Robert Bernasconi. Bloomington: Indiana University Press, 1996.

BV   *Beyond the Verse: Talmudic Readings and Lectures*. Trans. Gary D. Mole. Bloomington: Indiana University Press, 1994.

CPP   *Collected Philosophical Papers*. Trans. Alphonso Lingis. Pittsburgh: Duquesne University Press, 1998.

DEH   *Discovering Existence with Husserl*. Trans. Richard A. Cohen and Michael B. Smith. Evanston: Northwestern University Press, 1998.

DF   *Difficult Freedom: Essays on Judaism*. Trans. Seàn Hand. Baltimore: Johns Hopkins University Press, 1990.

EE   *Existence and Existents*. Trans. Alphonso Lingis. Pittsburgh: Duquesne University Press, 2001.

EI   *Ethics and Infinity*. Trans. Richard A. Cohen. Pittsburgh: Duquesne University Press, 1985.

EN   *Entre Nous. Thinking-of-the-Other*. Trans. Michael B. Smith and Barbara Harshav. New York: Columbia University Press, 1998.

GCM   *Of God Who Comes to Mind*. Trans. Bettina Bergo. Stanford: Stanford University Press, 1998.

IR   *Is It Righteous to Be? Interviews with Emmanuel Levinas*. Ed. Jill Robbins. Stanford: Stanford University Press, 2001.

ITN   *In the Time of the Nations*. Trans. Michael B. Smith. Bloomington: Indiana University Press, 1994.

OB   *Otherwise than Being or Beyond Essence*. Trans. Alphonso Lingis. Pittsburgh: Duquesne University Press, 1998.

OE   *On Escape*. Trans. Bettina Bergo. Palo Alto: Stanford University Press, 2003.

OS   *Outside the Subject*. Trans. Michael B. Smith. Stanford: Stanford University Press, 1996.

PN   *Proper Names*. Trans. Michael B. Smith. Palo Alto: Stanford University Press, 1996.

TI   *Totality and Infinity*. Trans. Alphonso Lingis. Pittsburgh: Duquesne University Press, 1969.

TIH   *The Theory of Intuition in Husserl's Phenomenology*. Trans. André Orianne. 2nd ed. Evanston: Northwestern University Press, 1973.

TO   *Time and the Other*. Trans. Richard A. Cohen. Pittsburgh: Duquesne University Press, 1987.

UH   *Unforeseen History*. Trans. Nidra Poller. Urbana: University of Illinois Press, 2004.

On a Book in Midlife Crisis

Scott Davidson and Diane Perpich

The year 2011 marks the fiftieth anniversary of the publication of Emmanuel Levinas's *Totality and Infinity,* a work widely regarded as one of the most significant philosophical texts produced in the second half of the twentieth century. Originally, Levinas submitted this work as a book manuscript to the French publisher Gallimard and seems to have come close to tearing it up when it was turned down for publication.[1] Jean Wahl encouraged Levinas instead to submit it as the main thesis for the *Doctorat d'Etat,* with his essays on phenomenology serving as the secondary, historical thesis.[2] Fifty-five when he submitted his two theses, Levinas thus came late to a university career, a circumstance due in part to the war and its aftermath, and in part to Levinas's position as a relative outsider to French academic circles.[3] The examining committee included Jean Wahl, Gabriel Marcel, Georges Blin, Vladimir Jankélévitch, and Paul Ricoeur. Merleau-Ponty was to have been on the committee as well but died of a stroke several weeks before the oral defense took place.[4] At the defense, Levinas's work was celebrated by the committee: Wahl predicted this would be a dissertation that other dissertations would be written about,[5] while Jankélévitch is reported to have said that Levinas deserved to be seated in his own spot as an examiner, rather than being the one examined.[6] *Totality and Infinity* was subsequently published in the well-respected *Phaenomenologica* series under the auspices of the Husserl Archives at the University of Leuven and established Levinas as a significant philosopher with a unique and original voice.[7] His first university appointment was at the University of Poitiers in 1964; he subsequently went on to positions at the newly established University of Paris-Nanterre (1967), and then at the Sorbonne (1973) where he taught until his retirement in 1976.[8]

One year after the publication of *Totality and Infinity* a conference on the book was organized at the University of Leuven. Adriaan Peperzak credits this event with introducing Belgian and Dutch philosophers to the revolutionary character of Levinas's thought and, indeed, there are more essays devoted to Levinas's thought in Dutch publications than in either French or English ones during the 1960s and 1970s.[9] In France, Levinas remained somewhat outside the philosophical mainstream until the early eighties when there was a surge of interest in his work.[10] A collection of essays entitled *Textes pour Emmanuel Levinas* appeared in 1981 and contained contributions by such luminaries as Blanchot, Derrida, Jabès, Lyotard, and Ricoeur, among others. By the mid-eighties, book-length monographs discussing Levinas's thought were regularly appearing in French and, in 1986, the Centre Culturel International de Cerisy-la-Salle hosted a two-week conference devoted to Levinas's thought. The proceedings from this conference remain one of the most significant bodies of secondary literature in French on Levinas's thought. By this point, it is safe to say that Levinas had established himself as a major figure in French philosophy.

As for Levinas's reception in the United States and Britain, Alphonso Lingis, who did his graduate studies in Belgium, translated *Totality and Infinity* into English in 1969, and as early as 1970, Levinas visited the United States to receive an honorary doctorate from the University of Loyola in Chicago.

Nonetheless, a full decade and a half would have to pass until the first significant collection of essays on his thought—*Face to Face With Levinas* (1986)—would appear in English.[11] In the intervening years, the rise of Derrida's popularity with British and American philosophers working in the continental tradition brought new attention to Levinas's work. Derrida's long essay, "Violence and Metaphysics," was translated into English in 1978 and its impact on the first wave of Levinas scholarship was significant enough that the editors of *Re-Reading Levinas* complain (already in 1991!) that the reception of Levinas's thought in the English speaking world had been too completely dominated by *Totality and Infinity* (to the neglect of Levinas's later work, especially *Otherwise than Being or Beyond Essence*) and too thoroughly shaped (or misshapen) by a particular understanding of Derrida's essay—which many read as a devastating critique of Levinas rather than a deconstructive engagement with his thought.[12]

What ties the various receptions of Levinas's thought together is the manner in which the concept of the Other came to dominate the landscape of late twentieth century French philosophy. Whether it was Lacan, Deleuze, Foucault, Derrida, Levinas, Lyotard, or the French Feminists Cixous, Kristeva, and Irigaray, the themes of otherness, difference, and *alterité* were never far from the center of discussion. Moreover, the rise of a new concern with ethical and political questions in the late works of these same figures helped push Levinas's thought to the forefront during the final decade of the century. Without doubt, it is the convergence of these themes that explains the explosion of interest in Levinas's work some three decades after the publication of his major treatise. By the late 1990s, interest in Levinas's thought was at its height in the English-speaking world as well as in France, Germany, Italy, and Belgium. The number of dissertations, conference presentations, essays, and books devoted to Levinas's work increased exponentially both within continental philosophy circles and in a host of disciplines ranging from literature and religious studies to education, nursing, and law. The interest in Levinas's thought remains unabated to this day and his relevance to an understanding of contemporary French thought is unquestionable.

Nonetheless, as *Totality and Infinity* reaches the half-century mark, the question is where do things stand with Levinas scholarship and with this text in particular? Our diagnosis, with the arrival of this fiftieth anniversary, is that the relation between this book and its readers is suffering a textual midlife crisis. A certain stagnation seems to have set in, both in the kinds of questions readers are asking of the text and in the general tenor of the interpretations being offered. In its first half century, Levinas scholarship tended to focus on basic tasks: surveying the philosophical development of his thought; tracking down significant philosophical, literary, personal, and religious influences on his work; expositing key terms such as alterity, infinity, the face, eros, or fecundity; and making a case for the overall relevance of his work for contemporary philosophy. The value of this work cannot be underestimated as it laid the necessary groundwork for an understanding of Levinas's thought and of *Totality and Infinity* in particular. But at the same time, the questions and approaches that initially helped guide readers through the admitted complexities and difficulties of Levinas's text now seem more often to preclude them from asking new questions or bringing new perspectives to bear. As a result, the growing body of scholarship on Levinas sometimes seems to do little more than plow familiar terrain, remaining stuck in the rut of well-worn interpretations and overused phrases.

The current collection is conceived both as a *Festschrift* for a book that has changed the landscape of contemporary philosophy and as a rescue operation of sorts, meant to save Levinas and his readers from a relationship that seems to have fallen into a dull routine. A number of the essays here strike out along unexplored pathways, showing us how to pursue the ideas advanced in *Totality and Infinity* in new directions or disciplines. Other essays put Levinas in conversation with thinkers or traditions that may initially seem foreign to his work but which show the possibilities of his thought in a new light. Still others focus our attention on themes that have been overlooked or ignored by the habits of reading established in the first half-century of Levinas scholarship. Most of the essays here do several of these things at once as they shift and resituate the way we read Levinas's major works.

The organization of essays follows the more organic path of family resemblances rather than a strict categorization in terms of themes or topics. This approach is dictated by the fact that the essays here seek to go beyond the ways in which Levinas studies, and the interpretation of *Totality and Infinity* in particular, has traditionally been framed and thus do not fit neatly into a set of predetermined boxes. Nonetheless, the reader will find many familiar topics treated: self and other, ethics and politics, responsibility, vulnerability, the welcome of the other, futurity, and fecundity. If we have achieved our aim even partially, however, the treatments here will cast those terms in new forms.

The collection begins with a reflection shared by Thérèse Goldstein, Levinas's long-time secretary at the Ecole Normale Israélite Orientale (ENIO). Commenting on Levinas's habits as a writer and giving us a glimpse into the day-to-day life of her friend and employer, Goldstein's account poignantly brings to life the literal construction of this text, which had such an impact on the course of twentieth century philosophy. While many have noted the poetic quality of the language in *Totality and Infinity*, Goldstein calls our attention in a different way to the text's musicality.

The first full chapter situates *Totality and Infinity* within the context of a philosophical tradition that associates the origins of philosophy with the feeling of wonder. Levinas, as Silvia Benso shows, at once belongs to and breaks free from these Greek origins of philosophy. While *Totality and Infinity* is a work that inspires wonder, the basis for this feeling does not come from the discovery of our ignorance and the search to gain knowledge, as it does for the Ancients. A philosophy that is solely preoccupied with the self, as Levinas observes in the text's closing line, cannot escape from the tedium and boredom of life. Benso examines *Totality and Infinity,* accordingly, as an attempt to alleviate boredom in a philosophical tradition that has been largely self-preoccupied, and in so doing, to rekindle a sense of novelty and surprise within the philosophical life.

Stacy Bautista and Adriaan Peperzak remind us that *Totality and Infinity* is fundamentally a defense of subjectivity, specifically one depicting the subject fundamentally not in terms of thought but the affective dimension of need and desire. One of the limitations of this account, however, is that Levinas draws a sharp distinction between the centripetal movement of need which draws back to the interiority of the self and the centrifugal movement of a desire that goes out to the exteriority of the other, but he does not integrate these two affects into a unified self. As a result, he is able to account for the ways in which others disintegrate our lives as in torture or violence but not so easily for how others can integrate them as in parenting or care giving.

Asher Horowitz further develops our understanding of the relationship of the self to others through an engagement with Marx's conception of the social nature of the self. Although scholars have recognized an affinity between Marx and Levinas, their relation has not been explored yet in significant detail. Horowitz suggests that both Marxians and Levinasians have much to gain from an engagement of their respective social ontologies. Marx's social ontology can gain a richer understanding of the alienation that occurs in the interpersonal relationship, while Levinasians can gain a richer sense of the way in which the forces of historical production shape the interpersonal domain.

Michael Morgan adds further interpretive insight into the self by presenting Levinas as a philosopher of the ordinary, though one for whom ordinary life turns out to be extraordinary. A philosophy of the ordinary, influenced by figures like Heidegger, Wittgenstein, and Austin, has been a prominent theme in the work of the contemporary American philosopher, Stanley

Cavell. To show how Levinas can be considered a philosopher of the ordinary, Morgan juxtaposes Levinas with Cavell and specifically with Cavell's use of some claims that Peter Brooks makes about melodrama. By considering what Cavell has to say about melodrama and the way in which melodrama figures in Cavell's film criticism and in his philosophical disclosure of the everyday, Levinas's philosophy is shown to employ the tactics of the melodramatic imagination, which is to say that our everyday ordinary lives become the basis for building meaningful relationships with others.

Georg Bertram engages the question of normativity that governs interpersonal relationships in *Totality and Infinity*. Instead of presenting an ethics, Bertram takes Levinas's philosophy as a theory of normativity which provides an account of what it means to be obligated—to be obligated, for Levinas, necessarily contains a reference to alterity. This account of normativity, as Bertram shows in considerable detail, is developed in contrast with Husserlian intentionality, such that it takes on precisely its opposite characteristics. After establishing this contrast, Bertram goes on to explore what it means for consciousness to be structured in terms of both intentionality and normativity, and thus to be bound both to the world and to others.

If Levinas has become known for his normative theory of ethics, Diane Perpich's essay attunes us to some of the difficulties that arise for attempts to apply his work to professional settings. Perpich examines recent efforts of this kind in two particular fields: nursing and psychotherapy. The nursing profession, as she shows, has been in search of an ethical framework that gives meaning to the care-giving activity of nurses, and in this context, some theorists have looked to Levinas. Psychologists, too, have been in search of an ethical framework to guide the clinical setting, where the therapist would be oriented to the good of the patient. But, on her view, neither field can get the sort of ethical clarity or certainty that they would like to find in Levinas. After showing why this is the case, she then provides some suggestions about what applications and uses Levinas might provide to professional ethics.

Taking up one such professional setting, Desmond Manderson examines some of the implications of Levinas's thought for the study of law. The field of tort law deals with a set of concepts—harm, negligence, responsibility—that resonate with Levinas's account of ethical responsibility. The temptation in tort law, as Manderson shows through a study of important cases, has been to establish a standard of reasonable care in which responsibility becomes something that can be limited, weighed, and calculated. Yet, there is a tension within tort law itself, such that it does not always adhere to or accept these limits. Levinas's notion of an infinite responsibility, according to Manderson, provides a good account of why this happens and why it is good that it does.

A similar dynamic guides the notion of human rights, insofar as they are codified into law and at the same time challenge the codified law. Ethical responsibility, to be sure, is front and center in Levinas's thought, but Scott Davidson suggests that human rights, construed as the rights of the other, are implicit as the other side of Levinasian responsibility. Davidson suggests that although the face-to-face encounter forms the basis for ethical responsibility for the other, it is also reread by Levinas as the basis for a "phenomenology of the rights of the other." By showing this interconnection between responsibility for the other and the rights of the other, there emerges a new way to address the common charge that Levinas transfers all rights over to the other and leaves the self defenseless. In addition, Levinas's account of human rights should also be welcomed by contemporary human rights theorists because it provides a compelling response to the typical charges against human rights—that they are egocentric and antagonistic. The Levinasian account overcomes the charges of egoism and antagonism by presenting human rights as for-the-other.

Joëlle Hansel takes up the key theme of the master in *Totality and Infinity*. The French term *maître* has a dual sense that is exploited by Levinas but that does not translate smoothly into English. First, it is associated with the figure of the Other who is at once the poor *par excellence* and the master who commands my servitude, albeit without violence. But, the French term also has a second sense which is associated with the teacher. The Other, in this sense, is the one who teaches me the idea of the Infinite. Through the dual sense of the word "master"—the one who commands me and the one who teaches me—transcendence becomes a concrete reality. From this starting point, Hansel then goes on to examine the difference between Levinas's philosophical conception of the teacher and his religious conception of the Talmudic master.

Claire Katz develops a related issue by examining the importance of education in Levinas's thought. Taking his years as the Director of the ENIO as her cue, Katz argues that Levinas was deeply concerned about the task of education. His understanding of this task was associated with what he perceived to be the crisis of humanism. The essays written in the 1950s and collected in *Difficult Freedom* suggest that Levinas saw Jewish education as playing a key role in preserving Jewish humanism. But, can the same be said of education in *Totality and Infinity*? By carefully examining the different references to teaching contained there, Katz suggests that education is fundamentally tied to his ethical project and to the meaning of fecundity.

John Drabinski compares the role of history and memory in Levinas with their role in the postcolonial thinker Edouard Glissant. Drabinski reads *Totality and Infinity* as a work about beginning after catastrophe. The problem of futurity and the notion of fecundity are, according to him, essential for resolving the theoretical and existential problem of how to make the world meaningful *again* or *for the first time*. And yet, through the comparison with Glissant, Drabinski highlights how the actual way of thinking about catastrophe is bound up with the history of Europe and with Glissant's own experience of loss. What Glissant adds, then, by thinking from his own experience from a postcolonial perspective is another set of insights into what it means to begin after a catastrophe and thus a different sense of futurity.

In the final essay of the collection, Robert Bernasconi challenges an established tendency in the secondary literature on *Totality and Infinity* that takes Levinas to present an ethics, that emphasizes the section "Ethics and The Face," and that takes the section to stand on its own. Such readings give a certain picture of Levinasian ethics that, as Bernasconi shows, is preempted by Levinas himself. In support of this point, Bernasconi calls our attention to the fourth section of the book, with its analyses of eros and fecundity. A proper understanding of Levinas's ethics, he argues, calls for a much more complex and nuanced understanding of how those two sections of the book work together.

We can only speculate on how far the essays in this collection will succeed in challenging the current terms of debate, but that these terms need to be challenged and that we need to see *Totality and Infinity* with fresh eyes can hardly be questioned. This volume thus invites readers here to look to the future and to renew and reinvigorated their relationship with this text. Indeed, it is only by opening up a new relationship with the book, that we can go back and recapture some of its original attraction, thereby ensuring that it can be as a vital a companion to us in the next half-century as it was in the preceding 50 years.

ONE

Joy beyond Boredom

Totality and Infinity as a Work of Wonder

Silvia Benso

"On s'amuse mieux à deux."
— Levinas, "Dialogue with Emmanuel Levinas"

Totality and Infinity has been presented variously as a metaphysical treatise; as a book on the primacy of ethics over ontology, on ethics as first philosophy, and on the Other; as a critique of intentionality, a defense of subjectivity, and an essay on hospitality. The subtitle of the book reads: *An Essay on Exteriority.* The theme of exteriority reappears in the title of the third section of *Totality and Infinity,* "Exteriority and the Face," as well as in the title of two chapters in the "Conclusions." There, the final yet not unexpected claim is that "being is exteriority" (*TI* 290) and that it produces itself in language, in which "the interlocutor . . . is forever outside" such that "the exteriority of discourse cannot be converted into interiority" (295). In a claim reminiscent of ancient philosophical remarks, Levinas announces that "exteriority is...a marvel" (292)—*une merveille:* a miracle, astonishment, wonder.

It is my contention that *Totality and Infinity* is, in fact, a work on, of, and by wonder—altogether, a wondrous work. In this sense, the book retrieves the highest inspiration guiding ancient philosophy and, in so doing, restores this metaphysical sentiment to a philosophical tradition that for the most part has forgotten how to wonder. Through an intertwining of boredom and wonder, this essay engages Levinas with the originary inspiration of Western philosophy as expressed in the work of Plato, whom Levinas credits with the notion, fundamental for his own thought, of "the Good beyond being" (*TI* 102–03). Performed in the Levinasian register of a critique of ontology, a brief analysis of the notion of wonder and the related concept of philosophy that it originates in Plato will prepare for Levinas's restoration of wonder, which remains in accordance with, yet goes beyond its Platonic inspiration.[1] In this move beyond the tradition from within the tradition, the novelty, that is, the wondrous character, of Levinas's text *Totality and Infinity* emerges in its full force. And *Totality and Infinity* proves itself a wonderful work, that is, a work of renewed wonder inspired by the conviction that "on s'amuse mieux à deux."[2]

SOME QUESTIONS ABOUT AN ANCIENT MOTIF

Levinas's evocation of wonder as the theme of his first major book—an essay on exteriority where exteriority is said to be a marvel—does not stray from the philosophical tradition with which Levinas so often otherwise contends. As is well known, the association between wonder and philosophy is ancient and is reasserted in various registers across the centuries. In his *Theaetetus,* Plato has Socrates remark that "this feeling of wonder [*thaumazein*] shows that you are a philosopher, since wonder is the only beginning of philosophy."[3] Years later, Plato's words are echoed by Aristotle's claim that "it is through wonder that men [*sic*] now begin and originally began to philosophize."[4] Centuries later, in a completely different geographical, historical, and cultural context, Kant asserts that "two things fill [his] mind with ever new and increasing admiration and awe...: *the starry heavens above and the moral law within.*"[5] This sense of wonder thus originates Kant's philosophy.

In spite of this widespread agreement on wonder as the origin of philosophy, questions remain as to its source: Where does philosophical wonder originate? What is its inspiration? In other words, what is the origin of the origin of philosophy? The answer to these questions will prove fundamental for assessing Levinas's book, which will turn out to be wonderful precisely for its identification of the source of wonder.

According to Heidegger, who is one of Levinas's major interlocutors in *Totality and Infinity,* the fundamental philosophical question is: "Why are there beings rather than nothing?"[6] It is ultimately disputable (and it is certainly so for Levinas) whether the ontological question is, or should be, the question motivating philosophy. For instance, Nietzsche's remark that "everything has become: there are no *eternal facts,* just as there are no absolute truths" compels one to reconsider the possibility that being may in fact provoke wonder.[7] Can there be wonder if there are no beings to wonder about? Pre-Socratic philosophy, for example, is arguably born out of wonder not at being, but rather at the multiplicity and seemingly disparateness of such beings—out of wonder at the variety and variation or changeability of things. Can there be wonder, one might ask, where there is no change, no becoming, no history, but only being(s), if they indeed are, rather than nothing? Would becoming, that is to say, change, fluidity, difference, discontinuity, and separation, perhaps even instability and chaos rather than being, be a better, more plausible candidate for the source of wonder? What should philosophy truly wonder about? Is its wondering about being genuinely wondrous, or does it rather produce the opposite sentiment from wonder, namely, boredom?

BOREDOM AND WONDER

The theme of tedium (*ennui*), "fruit of the mournful incuriosity that takes on the proportions of immortality," is evoked by Levinas (through the quotation of Baudelaire) in the very last sentence of *Totality and Infinity*. The triumph of boredom is a specter that haunts the "heroic existence, the isolated soul" (*TI* 307), that is, the subjectivity that has not let itself be touched by the Other's exteriority. Without this exposure to exteriority, the subject ends up in boredom.

That self-absorption produces a devastating form of boredom is already clear to Kierkegaard, probably the first philosopher to provide an extensive philosophical analysis of such a sentiment.[8] "How terrible tedium is—terribly tedious," Kierkegaard writes in *Either/Or,* in the context of a discussion of the aesthetic life and of the individual concerned with bringing constant novelty and amusement to his life precisely as an antidote to the monotony of boredom. Absorbed by a quest for novelty that originates within oneself, the aesthetician however only encounters the same, that is, himself and his own loneliness—each experience becomes the same as any other, in a dialectical confirmation of the boredom that the aesthetician wishes in fact to escape. The section in question is significantly subtitled by Kierkegaard "ad se ipsum."[9]

An analogous triumph of boredom manifests itself in the history of Western philosophy, which, according to Levinas, has followed "the *way* of the Same" (*TI* 38). In *Of God Who Comes to Mind,* a book published several years after *Totality and Infinity,* Levinas acknowledges the devastating effects of boredom as well as its connections with the ontology of the same: "Nothing, in effect, is absolutely other in the being served by knowledge wherein variety turns into monotony.... The unknown is immediately made familiar and the new customary. Nothing is new under the sun. The crisis found in Ecclesiastes is not found in sin but in boredom. Everything is absorbed, sucked down and walled up in the Same" (*GCM* 12). The fullness of an all-encompassing self and its way of being turns into the emptiness of a "nothing new under the sun" (that is, into boredom) when it establishes a complete familiarity, transparency, and/or adequation between the wondering subject and the object of its wonder. What causes boredom is the sameness, that is to say, the lack of variety and difference, through which the self ensures its identity as an I (*TI* 36).

What is the cure for boredom? How can one overcome, or even better, prevent it? "We can only annul boredom by enjoying ourselves—*ergo*, it is our duty to enjoy ourselves," Kierkegaard's aesthetician, a great (albeit unsuccessful) expert in both boredom and amusement, suggests. It has already been remarked that the aesthetician's search for entertainment is self-defeating and only produces more boredom. Commenting on Kierkegaard's philosophical protest against Hegel's totalization, Levinas observes that "it is not the I who resists the system, as Kierkegaard thought; it is the other" (*TI* 40), because "the level of [the I's] purely egoist protestation against totality" (26), in its being dictated by the I, still belongs to the sphere of the I, or what Levinas names "the economy of the Same." Applied to boredom, this means that the attempt to overcome boredom, in order to be successful, cannot come from the self's own quest for enjoyment but from elsewhere. Wonder counteracts and moves beyond boredom, yet the dispelling of boredom cannot be the primary motive or inspiration of wonder but only one of its consequences, albeit a fundamental one. If *Totality and Infinity* defeats boredom and leaves only the specter of it at its conclusion, I argue that this is because it is a book not on overcoming boredom but on realizing (an albeit very peculiar form of) wonder.

What antidote could both inhibit the "cry[ing] out for change"[10] of the one who feels bored as well as the subsequent boredom resulting from aesthetic enjoyment? What would it mean, in philosophical terms, to enjoy oneself successfully—or, in Levinasian terms, to enjoy oneself ethically rather than aesthetically? Can wonder provoke positive enjoyment and thus

provide the powerful remedy to boredom? If not all wonder
is wondrous, and if it, as the Platonic wonder will reveal, may
itself be boring, what kind of wonder would this be?

PLATO AND THE BOREDOM OF THE RETURN

The first evocation of the connection between philosophy
and wonder occurs in Plato. Plato, inspired by Socrates, situates wonder within the epistemological context. Mindful of
the Delphic oracle, which associates wisdom with knowledge
of one's ignorance, the Socratic philosopher wonders at what
he or she does not know *because* he or she does not know it,
and knows of this lack of knowledge. This way, ignorance is
turned into the measure of knowledge. As Meno recalls in the
dialogue that bears the same name, knowledge of one's own
lack of knowledge is fundamental to the search for knowledge.
The philosophical adventure is thus the attempt to dispel ignorance, in the conviction, still of Socratic descent, that wisdom
equals knowledge equals virtue. Legitimately, then, philosophy
is defined as "love of wisdom": it is the desire for a complete
unity with the principles of knowledge allowing all shadows of
ignorance to be diffused.

This implies that wonder originates *within* the ignorant
subject. Wonder is provoked not by what is (that which is out
there and faces the I in incommensurability and surprise), but
by what the I ignores. It is the I that dictates the boundaries
of its own ignorance, knowledge, and wonder; it thus defines
the extent and boundaries of the I's philosophical adventure.[11]
Again, in accordance with the Delphic oracle, to philosophize
means, first of all, to "know thyself." Not only the measure but
also the object of philosophy is thus located within the self, in
whose intimacy the truth can be found.

No wonder, then, that for Plato philosophy proceeds in a
conversation of the soul with(in) itself. As Socrates emphasizes
in the *Apology,* the maieutic teacher can only bring forth a truth
that is already there, within the soul of the inquirer; a teacher

thus acts as a "midwife to a mind already pregnant with its fruit" (*TI* 98). This leads Levinas to say that "the primacy of the same was Socrates's teaching" (43). Philosophical education is not a matter of being taught in the sense of "receiv[ing] from the Other beyond the capacity of the I" and being offered a content that "comes from the exterior and brings me more than I contain" (51). Rather, based on the assumption that "sight is there but that it isn't turned the right way,"[12] education is a matter of guiding the soul, turning it around and redirecting it appropriately.

Accordingly, Plato's dialogues are arguably not dialogues at all, but monologues. The dialogical characters, very few of whom possess a truly philosophical nature and the ability to enter a genuinely philosophical conversation with Socrates, are mere spectators of Socrates's own search for the truth. As such, they leave the scene of the dialogue for the most part untouched by Socrates.[13] Without any meaningful encounter between the self and the other, there is only an imitation of dialogue in which, as Levinas would say, there is a representation of the other *relative* to the I but there is no Other. Platonic wonder is born out of the philosophizing self, not out of the encounter with the interlocutor. Although Socrates bends his rhetoric to meet the needs of his counterparts and searches for an agreement with the interlocutor, the constant presence of the Socratic speaker to his discourse guarantees authorial control. Like the statues of Silenus to which Alcibiades compares him, Socrates is full of hidden resources.[14] However, the surprises he stores inside—his inner weapons of enchantment—are only surprising for the interlocutors, not for Socrates himself, whose theoretical arsenal is never endangered. Socrates remains altogether self-possessed (that is, in constant touch and continuity with himself) and untouched by the encounter with the Other.

In the great myth of the winged souls in the *Phaedrus,* a fundamental commonality (*kekoinoneke*) is said to exist between the wings of the soul and that which nourishes the soul—the Forms.[15] It is this common belonging to a same originary place that initially enables the soul to recognize what is similar to itself and that consequently spurs the soul to embark in the project of knowledge, that is, in the erotic ascent toward contemplation of the Forms.[16] Plato's philosophy is spurred by nostalgia for a land of origin to which the soul originally belongs—not a foreign land. As Heidegger remarks, quoting Novalis, "'philosophy is really homesickness, an urge to be at home everywhere.'...To be at home everywhere—what does that mean?...[It] means to be at once and at all times within the whole."[17] For Plato, likewise, philosophy is the desire to recognize the common belonging of all things to being, and that is what dialectic achieves: a network of relations whose interconnections grant simultaneously the whole of being and a home for the soul within the whole.

Now, if one is to take seriously Socrates's repeated claim of ignorance in the so-called early Platonic dialogues, one is led to conclude that complete knowledge can be obtained only at the moment of death, after the dissolution of the self and its bodily limitations. At the moment of supreme unity with the source of being, all ignorance is over but so is all wonder. The gods, those who know everything, do not philosophize or wonder. In the *Symposium*, Love, the philosopher *par excellence*, is not a god, but a demigod. Unlike the gods, Love does not know but wishes to know, and therefore acts as the mediator for the return to there from where all human souls come.[18] Do the gods, to whose omniscience the Platonic philosopher aspires, live in a situation of intellectual boredom, stemming from this lack of wonder? Aristotle coherently claims that God is thought that only thinks itself, void of all movement and desire, including the metaphysical Desire that according to Levinas marks infinity. What can be more boring, one could ask, than the monotony of the constant repetition of a thought that already knows what it is thinking, namely, itself? If it aims at divine knowledge, does philosophy lead to boredom? In this vein, it would seem that the more one philosophizes, the more one becomes bored. Complete knowledge is the complete transparency of being to the self, but is also the complete transparency of the self to itself, and thus the resolution of reality, both internal and external, in a coincidence and intimacy that dissolve the space for the discrepancy and strangeness from which alone wonder can arise. The complete transparency of the fullness of being turns into the ethereal inconsistency of an emptiness with no thickness.

One could contend that the divine condition of omniscience does not apply to humans who indisputably remain *philo-sophoi* and never become *sophoi*. Human finitude would prevent the transformation of philosophical wonder into boredom because human omniscience is never possible. Yet death only affects the body, not the soul, Socrates reminds his interlocutors in the *Phaedo*.[19] Omniscience may be precluded to the soul in its embodied dimension, but not to the soul once it has released itself from the shackles of earthly existence. If that is the case, is anything left for the philosophically inclined soul except eternal boredom?

Moreover, if all knowing is reminiscing, that is, introspection into the remote interstices of one's soul, as Plato argues, is the philosophical project anything else except rhetorical questions (questions whose answers are already known but forgotten), repetition, and, thus, boredom?[20] Reminiscence, Platonic memory, as well as the substitute for memory in the later dialogues, that is, dialectic, are anchored in a past that can be controlled. Knowledge is not inventiveness, creativity, fabrication, or new discovery but rather retrieval and restoration. The future toward which memory and dialectic strive is the reinstitution of an originary situation of familiarity and belonging, that is, a synchronization in the present of the past from which the soul comes. Anamnesic necessities and not unexpected contingencies pervade Platonic wonder. In the cosmic myth in the *Timaeus*, time is circular. The future is the return to where the soul has already been. Nietzsche names such a concept "the eternal recurrence of the same," and Levinas employs the figure of Ulysses as the image of the Western philosophical self for whom every adventure is a return home (*TI* 102).

But if it is the same that returns, is there any novelty, marvel, and wonder as to the future? Is there any unaccounted possibility? Is there any future for philosophy? If what causes philosophy is also what terminates philosophy, is there any future *in* philosophy? Even more radically, is there any *event* of philosophy? Or does philosophy defined as love of a wisdom born out of ignorance annihilate the very project of philosophy as wondrous questioning? Is philosophical wonder, as conceived by Plato when interpreted in the Levinasian register of a critique of ontology, wonder about nothing (because wonder about what I am already familiar with, that is, being)—is it an empty wondering that entails no wondering whatsoever, and is it not therefore necessarily boredom?

Levinas and the Wonder of the Other

A wondrous conception of philosophy capable of avoiding its drifting into (whether metaphysical-epistemological or ontological-existential) boredom comes from *Totality and Infinity*. For Levinas, it is not from within the deepest folds of self-consciousness, from its being or even, in a Heideggerian mood, from its being-toward-death that wonder arises. Being can only inspire horror and shame, for Levinas: horror at existing, at being unable to escape what Levinas calls the *il y a* (see *EE*), and shame at one's inability to undo the tie to oneself and one's self-identification (see *OE*). The death of the self, which some might invoke as the possibility of self-annihilation and therefore of escaping one's own being, for Levinas is merely the return to that being that is the ground of existence (*TI* 146). As such, death, especially my death, can provoke no wonder because it does not interrupt the continuity of being that saturates it. "What tragedy! What comedy!," writes Levinas, "The *taedium vitae* is steeped in the love of the life it rejects" (146). As Kierkegaard's aesthetician knows, boredom has a duplicating effect: it confirms that which it wishes to deny. Like death, boredom too is tied to being, and to a certain way of being, namely to a self that is riveted to itself. It has already been noticed for Levinas how boredom is a dimension of the self stemming from the fact that there is "nothing new under the sun" (*GCM* 12). Stated otherwise, boredom arises because there is no discontinuity, extraterritoriality, or difference between the self and what it may wonder about.

Where does wonder come from then, for Levinas? Philosophical questioning comes for Levinas not from the self, the soul, or (in Heideggerian terms) the Sein of Dasein, but from the presence of another who *questions* the self, that is, who puts it into question. As Levinas writes, "questioning is not explained by astonishment [*étonnement*] only, but by the presence of him to whom it [that is, questioning] is addressed" (*TI* 96). Wonder is neither autogenous (generated by/within the self) nor autonomous; it is rather heterogeneous and heteronymous, and works toward displacing the autochthony, the feeling at home of the self. When asked "How does one begin thinking?," Levinas replies that thinking "probably begins through traumatisms or gropings to which one does not even know how to give a verbal form: a separation, a sudden consciousness of the monotony of time" (*EI* 21). Wonder is brought about by the shock provoked within the monotonous terrain of familiarity by that which remains alien, unassumable by the I and its abilities for speech and categorization. Wonder is provoked by the excess, the surplus that the I cannot recuperate to itself. Marvel is something that upsets, destabilizes, and displaces the self, but also reveals to the self the monotony of a conception of temporality that is in fact stuck in the present of self-concern, in a time that, as Levinas claims in *Existents and Existence* and in *Time and the Other,* is not time because it is void of past and future—hence, the monotony and boredom of the present and its eternity.

Wonder ultimately comes from the always transcendent, never present, absolutely heteronomous face of the Other, the only being that the self will never be able to possess, the only being that can repeatedly face the self with the novelty of an ever new,

never boring change, with a constant, unexpected, and unfore-
seeable surprise. Wonder is the "marvel of the idea of infinity"
(*TI* 27). It is the marvel of the appearance, within the cognitive
abilities of the self, of something or someone that goes beyond
and exceeds the self's capacities for knowledge. Wonder is not
about what the self does not know, as it is for Plato, but rather
about that which cannot be known—the Other. Wonder thus
is about neither being nor nothingness. Neither epistemological nor ontological, wonder is about the otherwise than being;
it is the "traumatism of astonishment" revealed in discourse as
"the experience of something absolutely foreign" (73). It is
only with the appearance of the Other in his or her absolute
alterity that the future is made possible, according to Levinas.
It is the Other who destabilizes the total presence, the total
immanence of the self to itself, and the complete boredom that
ensues from it. The Other thus constitutes the origin of wonder. "Vanity of vanities," writes Levinas, "everywhere we have
fallen back upon our own feet, as after the ecstasies of a drug.
Except the other whom, in all this boredom, we cannot let go"
(*GCM* 12). The Other saves the self from boredom by restoring
the contingency of wonder—on conditions that wonder comes
from the Other who *is* a marvel. For brevity's sake (and not to
cause boredom), I will not repeat Levinas's characterization of
the Other, instead I will focus on the features of wonder, its
effects on the self, and the concept of philosophy that follows
from the wonder of the Other.

Wonder itself is the shock, the break, or the trauma brought
about by the approaching of the Other. It refers to a surplus, an
excess that goes beyond, upsets, uproots the self in its innermost
existential, ontological, and cognitive structures. The proximity
of the Other cannot be recuperated by the I, whether within a
temporal or a spatial framework. Ultimately, this is because the
I and the Other are separate. They are "terms that suffice to
themselves," and separation is not a diminution, lack, or " 'fall'
of the Infinite" (*TI* 103) that requires redemption as if it were
an evil. Noticing "how ruinous boredom is for humanity,"

Kierkegaard observed that "boredom is the root of all evil."[21] If the self-consciousness that ensues from self-reflection (*ad se ipsum*) is boring, one could ask, also on a Levinasian account, whether such a self-consciousness is, if not itself evil, at least the source of evil. The moral possibility of evil would then be rooted in an ontological self-concern that, while establishing the self's own identity, also generates evil as exclusion of the other. Yet, it is not the self-concern of the I and its process of individualization that constitutes evil, for Levinas. Nor is boredom the source of evil, as Kierkegaard suggests. Evil emerges, instead, only after the Other appears on the scene, appeals to the I in its egoism, and is met with neglect, refusal, and rejection — that is, once the wonder of the Other goes unrecognized. It is the Other that gives meaning to evil and opens the possibility of the future. Hence, the Other brings wonder into an existence that otherwise remains trapped in the structures of identification of the self — a boring existence, an existence folded upon itself. The wonder of the Other brings in the possibility of opening up self-absorption and conclusively defeating boredom — not in enjoyment (*jouissance*), which is "the satisfaction and egoism of the I" (94–95), but in what I would call "joy."

THE JOY OF WONDER; OR, HOW TO ENJOY ONESELF ETHICALLY

Far from being the egoistic contentment of fulfillment with which the self loses itself in the sensible world of elements and nourishments in order to strengthen itself and reassert its own separation and mastery, joy is, I argue, "the austere happiness of goodness" (*TI* 292) brought about by the possibility of the encounter with the Other, by the possibility of social multiplicity.[22] This happiness is austere because its parameters are dictated by the necessity "not to welcome empty-handed the face and its voice coming from another shore" (216). "Life is *love of life*" (112), writes Levinas, accentuating the dimension of the self's happiness to which enjoyment yields ("to live is to enjoy life") and which life substantially is ("originally life is happiness" [114]). Yet, this situation of material contentment also displays the boredom of happiness; boredom pervades such happiness because it occurs in solitude. If solitude is boring, then "*within the very interiority* hollowed out by enjoyment there must be produced a heteronomy that incites to another destiny than this animal complacency in oneself" (149). Rather than denying such happiness, which is in fact "a withdrawal into oneself, an involution" (118), the encounter with the Other (referred to in terms of "a shock" occurring "in the course of this descent into [one]self along the path of pleasure" [149]) reaffirms and increases the self's happiness through service and hospitality, that is, through the self's ability to open its interiority, its happiness, its home to the Other (its ability to "be for the Other" [304]) and become a host. All this does not necessarily occur in sacrifice and ascetic renunciation, as a too severe and unilateral reading of Levinas might emphasize. Instead, it occurs in joy—the joyfulness of plurality and conviviality that is aroused through the presence of the Other (because "war presupposes peace" [199], which is exactly the joy of the presence of the Other).

What needs to be overcome is not happiness but solitude; as a consequence, an increment in happiness that elevates happiness beyond boredom will occur in the form of joy. "On s'amuse mieux à deux," Levinas claims, yet the English translation of this as "two is better than one" does not do justice to the sense of the French verb *s'amuser,* which means "to have fun, to have a good time, to enjoy oneself." The expression in fact means that "two have a better, more fun, more enjoyable time"—one could even say that there must be *two* to have time, in the genuine sense. That is, pluralism, society, relations, encounters—briefly, what Levinas names "ethics"—are the way out of boredom and its repetitive temporality that is no time whatsoever. The overcoming of boredom is not brought about by the self's own search for enjoyment, but rather by the joyful enjoyment that passes through, and is produced by, the presence of the Other.

THE WONDER OF PHILOSOPHY

Whereas the Platonic philosopher enjoys being alone (like Socrates at the end of the *Symposium*), and other thinkers enjoy themselves at home and within a family made of similar individuals (Descartes's *cogito* in the solitude of his own room until the thought of a rational God comes to rescue him from solipsism; Heidegger with the Greek and German traditions with which he is so familiar and from which a brief conversation with a Japanese visitor does not distract him), the Levinasian philosopher enjoys being with the Other in his or her radical diversity, as Levinas does by maintaining a conversation between the Greek and the Jewish, the Jewish and the Christian, the philosophical and the religious, and the ethical and the ontological-epistemological traditions. It may very well be that in this age of globalization and multiculturalism, the only nonboring chances for a philosophy inspired by *Totality and Infinity* lie in crossing the borders of traditional Western philosophy in its ontological and epistemological aspirations. "The true life is absent," writes Levinas at the opening of *Totality and Infinity* (*TI* 33). Wonder comes from where "true life" is—not from where the I is, but where the alterity of the other is: in the figures, themes, and concepts that Western philosophy has marginalized, in nonphilosophical disciplines such as the arts, politics, the sciences, or economics, and even in non-Western ways of thinking. When such a wonder is avoided, neglected, or dismissed, boredom ensues, as the concluding statement of *Totality and Infinity* warns.

Where there is no Other, there is no good time but only the time of the self and its self-entertainment, masturbation, and, in the end, boredom. In Plato's *Symposium*, the most exciting, adventurous, and titillating of all topics, *eros,* does not prevent those in attendance from falling asleep during the conversation. At the very end of the dialogue, only Socrates remains awake—Socrates, the man who claims for himself a traditionally womanly profession (midwifery); the man who attributes his only knowledge, namely, his erotic expertise, to a womanly priest (Diotima); the man who perhaps is not a man but rather a hermaphrodite, thereby displaying a totalizing attitude in his very way of being; the man who in the end is left alone precisely when arguing for a philosophy of identity formulated in terms of the fact that "a skillful tragic dramatist should also be a comic poet."[23] By this time, the other symposiasts have either left or given in — to wine, not to boredom, it must be said. But their love of wine (and sleep) over philosophical inquiry signals that the philosophical project conducted in a Platonic mode may not be exciting and enjoyable enough for anyone except the philosopher — "ad se ipsum", as Kierkegaard's inscription reads. In other words, Plato's wonder, born out of the self and its epistemic abilities, contains in itself the germs of boredom and inefficacy, and therefore is not truly wondrous.

Levinas's different conception of wonder, inspired by the Other and the exteriority of being, keeps philosophy from turning into boredom. In the end, philosophy itself is not inspired by the self, or its being, but the absolutely Other in his or her exteriority. This move toward the Other as the anarchic origin of wonder legitimizes a new definition of the philosophical project. "Philosophy is never a wisdom, for the interlocutor whom it has just encompassed has already escaped it (*TI* 295);" nor (and for similar reasons) can philosophy be the "love of wisdom," as suggested by its etymology. Rather, Levinas redefines philosophy as the "wisdom of love";[24] this formulation situates the origin of philosophy in the amorous act (a "love without concupiscence" [*EN* 103]) that invokes and maintains the Other in the wondrous separation of his or her existence without possibility of recuperation. Only the wonder of the Other's existence can lead philosophy to wonder genuinely, and thus escape the grip of recurring boredom. The wonder of the Other — the wonder that the Other is — originates philosophy and makes it wonder even more.

In this context in which the sleep of boredom is interrupted by the approach of the Other, who awakens the self, in this traumatism of the awakening, philosophy reconfigures itself not as determination of the true map of reality, not as progression toward the highest and most transparent levels of knowledge, not as uncovering and retrieval of the forgotten modalities of being (here Heidegger too would appear as a renewed maieutic teacher trying to retrieve, from the oblivion of metaphysics, the truth of the ancient visions), not as creativity, inventiveness, and fabrication (as, for example, in Nietzsche or Deleuze), but as break and rupture. The task of philosophy as a wondrous activity becomes that of welcoming the other and accepting the confusion, puzzlements, and unsettlements brought about by the other's presence; of unsaying the said, that is, of being the source of continuous, destabilizing, and traumatic shocks to the tendency of thought to rest in its being, rather than in the otherwise than being. Philosophy becomes the site of constant renegotiations and reformulations so that if there is creativity, it is *shared* creativity. In this sense, philosophy becomes eccentric as well as excessive — eccentric, because its center, its balance, its *raison d'être* is outside of itself, in the Other who inspires it and makes it wonder beyond itself; excessive, because its task becomes that of always exceeding the boundaries to which the limitation of the speculating self necessarily constrains it, and of wondering about the surplus that the Other is. In both of these aspects, philosophy reveals its utopian aspirations — it is wonder and marvel at that which is not nowhere but elsewhere.

Such an eccentric, excessive, traumatic, and ultimately utopian configuration of philosophy may not be very far from Plato's understanding of it, were one to recall that according to Plato too, in the *Symposium*, the self-giving of the forms to the loving soul occurs *ekphanes*, that is, suddenly, as a shock or surprise for which the self or soul cannot account.[25] Or that, as Levinas himself remarks, "against a thought that proceeds from him who 'has his own head to himself,' [Plato] affirms the value of the delirium that comes from God, 'winged thought'" (*TI* 49). It is in these moments of discontinuity, interruption, seeming madness and laceration that wonder emerges as the traumatism that leads to wonder. Philosophy develops as the attempt to bear testimony to what has been ruptured and moreover, to the one who has brought about this rupture. In this sense, as an essay on exteriority, that is, on a being (the Other) that by definition, in a reformulation of the ontological argument, has exteriority "inscribed in its essence" (196), *Totality and Infinity* is a powerful testimony to the wonder of exteriority—truly a wondrous and wonderful work, that is, a work full of wonder.

Unspoken Unity
I, Who Enjoy and Desire

Stacy Bautista and Adriaan Peperzak

This book is presented...as a defense of subjectivity...as founded in the idea of the infinite.
— Levinas, *Totality and Infinity*

In Levinas's phenomenology, the face is one term involved in the metaphysical relationship moving between the face of the other and the subjectivity of the same. His analysis of the face is often seen as his fundamental contribution to phenomenology. The relationship with the face is the basis for a wide-ranging analysis that seeks the refoundation of philosophy as such.[1] *Totality and Infinity* places the metaphysical relationship between the subject and the other at center stage. Much scholarly attention has gone to the revelation of the Other, which is the key moment of the facing relationship, but we wish to take the epigraph above as our investigative warrant (cf. *TI* 26). *Totality and Infinity* is a *defense* of one term in particular within the metaphysical relationship, namely, the subject, more specifically the subject insofar as subjectivity is founded in the idea of the infinite.[2] What can this mean? What, or how, is this subjectivity founded in the relation to the infinite? What is this idea of the infinite that the subject has?

To begin to answer such questions, we must first note that Levinas's use of the term "infinite" occurs only in the metaphysical relationship between a subject and an other, who is either the other person or God, or (obscurely) both at once.[3] He never suggests that the term "infinite" has a meaning outside of such a relationship.[4] The *idea* of the infinite arises also within this relationship and will be seen to describe the subject's response to the other—a response that is revelatory of the other. The idea of the infinite is then our access to the subject's foundation in the infinite, and one part of our essay will be dedicated to fleshing out Levinas's analysis of subjectivity so founded.

However, Levinas's way of articulating the sense of the term "infinite" results in a subject whose unity is problematically unspoken. It seems clear that Levinas presupposes that the subject is a unique person, a unified being who both desires and enjoys; yet he never addresses the unifying moment of the subject, and in general, his analyses do not lend themselves to an investigation of this moment. Rather, they tend to articulate different aspects of the subject, in its relation to the infinite other, in such a way that the subject is split between desire and enjoyment. In fact, were we to consider that a subject always both desires and enjoys, and that the other in relation to whom the subject is founded also both desires and enjoys (presumably, though Levinas does not say this), we would find that of the four affects that could enter into relation with each other—namely, my enjoyment, my desire, the other's enjoyment, and the other's desire—only my enjoyment in relation to the other's need is directly discussed, and the interrelations between enjoyment and desire are limited to the way in which my desire for the other exceeds my enjoyment and so my being. The difference between my enjoyment and my desire delineates the sphere of sameness (the sphere of my being) as absolutely other than the sphere of relationships I can sustain with the other. But even allowing for this disarticulation of enjoyment and desire, the other's desire is not discussed, and my desire in relation to the other's desire is not discussed, leaving problematic silences in Levinas's text. The fact that *Totality and Infinity* does not say anything about the subject's own dignity, for example, is one consequence of the failure to address the subject's unity.

Why is Levinas silent concerning the subject's unity, and why does he seem hardly able to address such concerns that arise from his silence? The problem lies in Levinas's way of articulating the meaning of the term "infinite," which passes through a hard distinction between interiority (or ipseity) and exteriority (the other), but which is supposed to describe *both* a human other *and* the other who is God (or both at once, somehow).

Our essay, then, will proceed as follows, with an eye to the above points: To establish that the subject's unity is at issue, we will review Levinas's analysis of the subject in its enjoyment or *ipseity*, and the subject in its desiring aspect. This will lead to a critical section, which reveals that the thrust of these analyses splits the subject between enjoyment and desire. Our demonstration will hinge on showing several gaps in Levinas's description of the subject, namely, his silence concerning not only the dignity of the subject, but also concerning the face as having any aspect but a commanding one. We will try to furnish phenomenological analyses that show that an adequate description of certain paradigmatic interpersonal relationships—love and violation—requires attention to the dignity of the subject and to the noncommanding aspects of the face, and that attention to these aspects requires us to give up the hard distinction between interiority and exteriority that had done so much to govern the sense of the term "infinite" and of the subject founded in it.

In the final section, we argue that the infinite which founds subjectivity must be differently construed in order to overcome the silences in Levinas's text: Levinas's own claim that the infinite other is both the other person *and* God may indeed suggest a way forward, even if in a direction other than the one he himself later took.

Ipseity: The Enjoying Subject

The term "ipseity" is first introduced as a synonym for "separation," and is described as the product of enjoyment:[5]

> We will show further how separation or ipseity is produced primordially in the enjoyment of happiness, how in this enjoyment the separated being affirms an independence that owes nothing, neither dialectically nor logically, to the Other [*l'Autre*] which remains transcendent to it. This absolute independence, which does not posit itself by opposing itself [qui ne se pose pas en s'opposant], and which we have called atheism, does not exhaust its essence in the formalism of abstract thought. It is accomplished in all the plenitude of economic existence. (*TI* 60; translation modified)[6]

From this passage we glean that ipseity belongs to the constellation of terms that describe the subject [*le moi*] as an independent, economic entity, whose existence and being are irreducible to a logical or dialectical relationship to some other, to which the subject would, by *op*posing itself to the other, posit or identify itself. Here, Levinas argues against conceiving the ipseity of the subject in Hegelian or dialectical fashion, as an identity arising through its opposition to some other identity or being. For, if identity is a function of opposition, then the identity of terms that oppose each other, because *different* from each other, must be referred to a broader context or *totality*, which constitutes the identity of the subject as one of its moments over against the alterity of the opposing term. Levinas's refusal to say that separation or ipseity posits itself by *opposing* alterity, or even by opposing the totality it ruptures, comes from his Hegelian reading of the term "opposition." Thus, ipseity does not owe its identity to its opposition within any totality, but neither is it *opposed* to totality, lest ipseity recapitulate a totality at a higher level.[7]

Then to what does ipseity owe its being, its independence? Levinas claims, and attempts to show in his phenomenology of the relation of ipseity with the elements, that ipseity arises and is constituted in the *enjoyment of happiness*. Enjoyment is a self-affirming response to what is in my environment, an appreciation of qualities or *elements* that happen to be present (or that I attempt to make present through labor). The relation between myself and something other than myself here is like the relation of a bather and bath water: I am immersed in sensations, which testify to the presence of other elements around me, but also and essentially to *me*. For I sense and, in the same moment, react to them as pleasant or loathsome. I am identified with elemental alterity, and identify myself in it by my enjoyment: I and the element, as sensible other, are differentiated in my feeling united with it. Hence in enjoyment I possess what I enjoy to the degree that it possesses me, and vice versa.[8] I am dependent upon what I am immersed in, and react by welcoming or by rejecting that to which I am delivered.

Three points seem relevant here. First, this reaction to elemental alterity is not the same as the response to the infinite other; it promotes my identity as self-same and as at home. Why does enjoyment function this way? This question leads to the second point, namely, that we must understand that happiness is not an ideal or objective sum of pleasure for Levinas, but an original *agreement* with that on which the subject lives: "The relationship of the I with the non-I, produced as happiness which promotes the I consists neither in assuming nor in refusing the non-I. . . . The acceptance or refusal of what we live from implies a prior *agreement*. . . the agreement of happiness. . . . [T]o live does not alienate the I but maintains it, constitutes its *being at home with itself* [*chez soi*]" (*TI* 143). The subject as separated is founded in the agreement with what it lives on. The agreement of happiness is the living of my life: all impersonal otherness that the subject enjoys (or refuses because it is *not* enjoyable) is enjoyed (or rejected) as a modulation of my living life, which is always my life. The agreement between myself and the entirety of elemental being occupies my life prior to my having chosen to interact with the elements just because there is no "before my life" from which *I* could approach them. The elements are there—my being agrees with them as a whole, integrating them into my life (living on them) in an initial *yes* that presupposes neither that their existence comes from my constituting or producing them, nor that I first assume them out of an initial absolute independence (living is spontaneous *reaction*).

Third, this implies that the subject's ipseity—its very self-hood, or existing as this unique individual being separate from all other beings and from their totality—testifies to an irreducible and always initially unassumed, but specifically qualified, relationship with a *nonpersonal* alterity.[9] Happiness—agreement or enjoyment—shows that this original relationship with non-personal beings, which is necessary for there to be a subject at all, is not an alienated relationship, although it is not a relationship assumed or chosen out of an original freedom. Agreement simply means that the subject exists originally as living, which is not mere survival but "love of life" (*TI* 144). Thus, the subject is embroiled in relationships out of an existential situation it did not choose, but which nevertheless affirms and uplifts it. Happiness as agreement or enjoyment, and not free noumenal reason or the free self-knowledge of an absolute spirit, establishes the "absolute independence" of the subject. Enjoyment—and even rejection of some being as unenjoyable—testifies to this original, affirmative, and irreducible dependency of myself on impersonal alterities on which I live.

Therefore, absolute independence, although not illusory, is nevertheless other than what (modern) philosophy has most often understood it to be. My initial self-sensing (the "*gnosis of the sensible*" [*TI* 145]) is an emphatic affirmation of my being at home in the elements on which I live. I am "promoted," lifted up, "exalted" as myself (144). Levinas writes, "The personality of the person, the ipseity of the I, which is more than the particularity of the atom and of the individual, is the particularity of the happiness of enjoyment" (115). Only in living on other beings do I acquire my identity, which is produced as enjoying (or loathing) the different beings that happen into my life; but for them to happen into my life at all, I must have affirmed already, in the very act of enjoyment, my relational and dependent existence.

Before examining Levinas's description of desire, one more term Levinas uses to describe ipseity must be addressed, namely, egoism. "Egoism" is regularly used as a synonym for the subject's ipseity—for the whole realm of its interiority as a response to impersonal alterity, that is, enjoyment.[10] Such usage might seem unwarranted, since "ipseity," translated literally, just means "selfhood." However, a careful examination of the text shows that the term "ipseity" is throughout used to describe the identifying principle of the subject and nothing else.[11] It is *not* used to describe the subject in its desiring aspect, or to refer to the whole of the subject. What Levinas designates with this term is, properly speaking, a component of the subject, or rather, selfhood is made into a (substantial) component of the subject. Levinas alerts us to this restriction by making ipseity equivalent to identity, and identity equivalent to egoism.

In short, for Levinas the ipseity of the subject refers to enjoying egocentric identity, understood as egoism. Nevertheless, it must be said that the use of the term "egoism" as an equivalent to ipseity and its related terms is unfortunate, since it assimilates an *abstract* analysis of the subject (as isolated from all infinity—an impossibility, as Levinas says) to an *evaluation* of the subject's selfhood that can only signify the presence of another person. Such assimilation obscures the need to delineate between (1) the pejorative evaluation of the subject's overly egocentric enjoyment (egoism proper), which reduces the alterity of others to elements of my world (thereby degrading and/or injuring the others), and (2) the ineliminable egocentrism of enjoyment that we cannot do without, lest we cease to be. Although most of the time, Levinas does not mean for ipseity-as-egoism to refer to egoism in a moral sense (egoism proper), the fact that he later argues that the subject finds itself, in the face of the other, to have always already been unjust in its egoism-ipseity seems to undermine his own attempts to present the egoism of the subject in amoral terms. This equivocation on the sense of egoism raises the question of the relationship between the enjoying ipseity and the subject to whom we will turn in the next section, the subject who desires: for, if desire is always present, because the infinite other has always already faced me, then is it worthwhile or even possible to distinguish an *amoral* egoism, or must we admit that our enjoyment is always already implicated in ethical relations?

I, Who Am Called to Goodness: The Desiring Subject

Despite (or rather because of) the identification of my personality with ipseity-as-enjoyment, and of my ipseity with egoism, ipseity does not exhaust subjectivity. The precise relationship that the absolutely independent subject, subsisting through enjoyment, bears to the other's face remains, despite all the scholarship produced on this topic, extremely difficult to articulate.[12] Yet we can say Levinas asserts categorically, "The conversion of the soul to exteriority, to the absolutely other [*autre*], to Infinity, is not deducible from the very identity of the soul, for it is not commensurate with the soul" (*TI* 61). This means that although enjoyment and ipseity are irreducible *in me*, I am not reducible to my enjoyment and ipseity. What is left out of account in the analysis of ipseity is the metaphysical movement of the subject.

Levinas says that this metaphysical movement in the subject is desire.[13] What exceeds my capacity to enjoy and the ego that emerges in enjoyment is my desire for the infinite (*TI* 33–35, 50). It is important here to be very clear about the claim we are making: the *intentum* of desire—the other, who is both God and the other person—is infinite because it transcends the subject absolutely. Levinas does not find it necessary to say that desire is infinite (although its essential insatiability may tempt us to call it so [34, 50]), but even so, his description requires that desire exceed my ipseity. It is irreducible to the structure and movement of interiority or egoism, which is why Levinas's analysis of the subject breaks into two segments. Ipseity and desire describe radically different movements and orientations that are not products of each other, but which nevertheless are found in a single subject. *How* they relate to each other, and how they together constitute the *unity* of the subject that moves (or, rather, is moved) in two directions, remains to be seen. For the moment, we will concentrate on Levinas's account of how the infinite reveals itself, of what infinite means, and of the nature of desire and its implications.

The earliest, most formal sections of *Totality and Infinity* tell us that metaphysics designates a relationship in which I aspire to an *intentum* that exceeds my ipseity *absolutely*, and so cannot be integrated into my world or my person: the absolutely excessive or *exterior* is that which does not become a moment of my ipseity (which is interior). But what exceeds my ipseity absolutely is not any world: for Levinas, "world" names the situation of the subject in its enjoyment, as being at home in its situation among other impersonal beings that it enjoys and manipulates. But if not the world, then what absolutely exceeds my enjoyment, and so myself? Appealing to Descartes, Levinas answers: the infinite, which is not a *what* but a *who: autrui*, the personal other, "and the Most High."[14] Such a claim confronts us with a question that the philosophical tradition has never before asked; even more remarkably, Levinas does not ask it either, though he in a sense begs it: how can one say that "the infinite" is *both* God and the finite, other person?

Evidently, we need at least some explanation of the term "infinite," insofar as it describes the term of our desire. First, for Levinas, the infinity of the infinite is not a given—it is not present *for me* as a being that could satisfy me in some way by feeding enjoyment. Levinas writes that the relationship of the other to me is a relation in which *infinition* (*TI* 25, 26) occurs or "shows up." The French verb that we translate as "shows

up" is *se produire,* which Levinas calls "ambiguous": the meaning stands between the fact of an occurrence and its *process of
revealing.*[15] Both senses of *se produire* are at work in Levinas's
use of this term to describe infinition, or the way in which the
infinite "shows up." The appropriate question to pose is therefore: in what sense is the infinite revealed *in* or *through* the
occurrence of "an idea" in me?

Levinas appropriates Descartes's "idea of the infinite" to
describe the formal structure of infinition as a revelation of
absolute exteriority: that there is in me an idea of the infinite is
a unique event, unlike the advent of any other idea of any finite
being. For, the idea of the infinite is the sole idea that occurs
as a moment of the other's relationship to me, rather than as
a product of my own interiority, that is, of the self-identifying
enjoyment of ipseity.[16] Moreover, although the idea is an idea
of the infinite, I do not grasp or comprehend the infinite that
provokes the idea in me: the radical incommensurability of the
idea to its *ideatum* marks the exteriority of the *ideatum.*

But what is this idea? From the formal analysis, it appears
that the idea directs me to the other person and God—how
though? What sort of direction does it provide? Levinas answers
that the idea shows up in me as desire for the other and God,
who are superlatively incommensurable to me: "The infinite
in the finite, the more in the less, which is accomplished by
the idea of Infinity, shows up [*se produit*] as Desire" (*TI* 50;
translation modified). In other words, the idea of the infinite is
not a representation or a concept—it is a unique (and uniquely
provocative) intentional affect that relates my living my life,
as always interior to what I enjoy, to a radical exteriority. By
measuring my absolute inadequacy to reduce the other to me,
desire thereby reveals the other to be infinite in the sense of
absolutely transcending my ipseity and all of its possibilities.
The infinity of the other, because it transcends my life as lived
within the elemental world and the movements of enjoyment
and loathing appropriate to it, is then designated as essentially
exterior to my essential interiority.

Yet the fact that the feeling that reveals the other as infinite is desire implies that "infinite" does not mean simple excess: to desire is to affirm dignity, and for Levinas, dignity differs from the kind of worth involved in needing or wanting to use and enjoy impersonal beings. The excess is an excess of significance or of worthiness, beyond what an impersonal being can sustain. The dignity that desire affirms is expressed in the fact that the other speaks to me or invokes me, which no other being does; and in speaking, the other *moves* me to attend and value the absolute difference between the other and a comestible (or any other being simply used and enjoyed).[17] My desire for the other reveals that the infinity of the other is different from me, *and* that this difference transcends all values, including moral values, without thereby being neutral, for this difference establishes all values. The sense of the transcendence of the infinite is therefore measured neither by enjoyment nor by moral excellence; desire itself measures the difference and the height, distance or separation between enjoyment and the other as infinite, between my ipseity and you.

For Levinas, enjoyment is subordinate to desire, because the worth of enjoyment's *intentum* is subordinate to the dignity of the *intentum* of desire. But how does he concretely show the subordination of my ipseity to the infinition of the other and God?[18] Levinas's analyses of the facing relationship are clear: in relation to the infinite, my enjoyment is not *lacking* (that is, the other does not nullify or eliminate my enjoyment), but it is *unjust*—not inherently, but in the sense of "as yet unrectified." What is involved in its rectification? Levinas focuses attention almost exclusively on economic generosity (*TI* 34, 83) or hospitality (205, 216), in which I make available the world of my enjoyment, with all its resources—and in the most extreme cases, my very life that is "my power of powers" [mon pouvoir de pouvoir]—to the other (198; translation modified).[19] For, the other whose face reveals his or her dignity does not reveal riches; rather, the other's face, exterior to my world of joys and revulsions, confronts me with his or her vulnerability and neediness.

It is not as my equal that the other approaches me but as both more destitute (in terms of ipseity) than me and as higher than my ipseity (because desirable, rather than needed).[20]

From this, it becomes clear that the essential inadequation between the subject and the other, which desire "measures," signifies not only the failure of my power to reduce the other to a moment of my ipseity: it signifies an ethical asymmetry. In the facing relationship, my own needs and enjoyment are shown to be less worthy than those of the other because they are not dignified. This is not to say that they are dispensable: my needs and enjoyment—my ipseity—are presupposed by, but subordinated to, the other's call or facing. They are presupposed because I must be identifiable as a unique being situated in the midst of a world of resources in order to answer the obligations the Other's face reveals to me. The desire the face provokes moves me to approach the other in his or her neediness and vulnerability "with full hands" as the only way to respect his or her dignity (*TI* 205). Henceforth, it becomes possible to argue that, thanks to the asymmetric character of the desiring relationship, and thanks to the inéliminable economic dimension of the other's facing, I can make my life itself an offering to the other.

Although more detail might be amassed, at this point we have sufficient understanding of Levinas's account of the subject in its ipseity and desire to make six main observations:

1. The individual personality of the subject—its ipseity and interiority—is absolutely dependent in its very egocentric selfhood and independence, upon enjoyment (*TI* 115). Enjoyment is necessary for there to be a subject, and since ipseity is produced in enjoyment, there is no subject that lacks ipseity.

2. Because, however, ipseity is only a necessary condition of the subject, and the subject is essentially related *at all times* to the infinite (both God and the other person), the fact that ipseity and enjoyment are characterized as egocentric ("owing nothing" [*TI* 60] to the other) leads Levinas to characterize the

ipseity of the subject as ego*ism*. The other's infinition awakens me to the dimension of dignity beyond my enjoyment. Because my ipseity is identified absolutely with enjoyment, it gives no ground for experiencing myself as just or dignified. In the face of the other, I find that I am (and have been) unjust and undignified because so thoroughly identified with my unrectified enjoyment. This judgment is always implicitly present in Levinas's writing about the subject and is signaled by his calling the ipseity of the subject egoism.[21]

3. Correlatively, there is no argument in *Totality and Infinity* that I ever face myself in the same (or even a relevantly similar) way that the other faces me.[22] Because I am absolutely dependent upon the other's facing me even to accede to the dimension of dignity, I am incapable of experiencing myself as an (ethically obligating or dignified) other *for myself*. Levinas gives no analysis that suggests that I obligate myself, whether or not I have been faced by the other person. My being, or my ipseity, is enjoyable, yet it is not in itself dignified, for it can only constitute itself as the same, never as an other in the relevant sense of an absolutely exterior alterity.[23]

4. What, though, of my desiring self, which is always in relation to the other person? Is not my unchosen desire a source of obligation with respect to me, which affects me in a way comparable to the facing of the other, just because the subject of such unchosen desire *is* the sort of subject that desires goodness? Levinas does not pursue this question. By construing the ethical subject only as a desiring self, in the tradition of the Platonic meditation on *eros*, he seems to have assimilated the lover/beloved dichotomy in a certain way: ethically, the subject is a desiring subject but not a *desired* or *desirable* subject. Conversely, the other is a desired or desirable subject, but is never said to be a desiring subject. Correlatively, the face is only a commanding face; the desire of the other and other modes of facing than as ethical height are not described.

5. The third and fourth points together imply that Levinas's account of certain, paradigmatically ethical situations is limited:

if I do not experience my ipseity as dignified, but *only* as enjoyable, then it seems impossible for me to respect my *own* being unless I refer to the fact that the other's dignity commands me to maintain myself in a certain fashion. Such "self-respect," however, has a distinctly instrumental flavor that is at odds with the notion of finding myself to be dignified.

6. Because dignity is strictly associated with exteriority, and exteriority is strictly and absolutely separated from interiority (it is the "foreign country...whither we can never transport ourselves" [cf. *TI* 34]), the unity of the subject who both enjoys and desires becomes an urgent but unaddressed question.

Levinas's silence on the unity of the subject, which shows up in the hard distinction between the subject who enjoys and the subject who desires, and in the consequent failure to speak of the dignity of the subject who is faced, seems to originate in his campaign against the notion of autonomy and its attendant self-sufficiency. At every stage of his analysis of the subject, as we have seen, Levinas emphasizes the dependency of the subject on alterity of various kinds. Were the subject self-obligating, then the specter of self-sufficient autonomy and the elimination of alterity might seem to rear up once more and threaten to return the subject to its position of absolute sovereignty. The hard distinction between the interiority of the subject and the exteriority of the other, which helps articulate the sense of the term "infinite," seems to be a response (perhaps unconscious) to that threat.

Such fears are unwarranted by examining two paradigmatic ethical phenomena, both of which are suggested by analyses that Levinas has himself undertaken: the phenomenon of parental love and the phenomenon of being-violated. Both of these phenomena, though not analyzed by Levinas, challenge the hard separation between interiority and exteriority, while maintaining the priority of the other's facing me, and consequently point to both a more unified subject and a more richly expressive face.

THE CHILD TO ITS PARENTS: "WHY HAVE YOU LOVED AND CARED FOR ME?"

Levinas's analyses of paternity and the relationship of the father to his son have provoked many readings of the gendering of ethical relationships in Levinas's work. Without denying the usefulness and necessity of such analyses, we wish to ask whether, as a part of his genealogy of ipseity, Levinas should have analyzed the child's perspective in relation to its parents, since, although not everyone will be a father or a mother, *everyone* has been someone's child.[24] That this is so allows us to ask a question: if I am here today only because some unique and namable other—whether my birth parents or foster parents or persons who are father*ly* or mother*ly*, whether one parent or two or even more—has loved and cared for me, what can explain this extraordinary dedication to my often burdensome existence?

Levinas invites this question, not only thanks to his analysis of the father-son relationship, but because earlier he had argued that the ipseity of the subject includes the moment of dwelling (*TI* 38). Dwelling does not involve an impersonal shelter: rather, the dwelling's sheltering character is constituted essentially by a relationship between me and another person, who welcomes me into a world made human already for me (154–55).[25] The humanity of this world is the gentleness and warmth that are the very stuff of worldly familiarity, insofar as the world is welcoming. But the welcoming familiarity of the world is not "chemically" or "magically" generated by a simple structure or set of projective references that articulate my existence (153): it is "an *intimacy with someone*" (155), who renders the environment such as makes possible a home, as living intimately somewhere particular. It requires a fully human personality to accomplish dwelling in a home, a personality that speaks in dwelling in a mode other than the commanding or teaching mode of language usually emphasized in Levinas's work (155).[26] It is not teaching, however, that is immediately responsible for the creation of a home: although Levinas does not use the term, love creates a home. That the loving other is fully other, despite the fact that the loving other's speech does not teach, means that there is no sharp distinction between exteriority and interiority in this case. We feel at home while being-with such an other, who is not a thing or an element, but a person who maintains a lovingly shared atmosphere.

Although the relationship of the welcoming other to me is never fixed with a name, we would like to suggest that since enjoyment *is* my ipseity, without which I would not be, then if the other in the dwelling facilitates my enjoyment from the first, the familiar relationship Levinas describes is that of a parent who makes a home for her child. Levinas's account of dwelling is essentially an account of the way my relationship with being depends upon the orientation of a parental other toward me. This account affirms the full humanity and ethical character of the parent who makes a home for me, but does not ask or answer the question: why should parents love and deploy their economic resources for the sake of their child? Two possible answers might be considered: that it arises out of egoist enjoyment or that it arises in being faced by the child.

Parental care might be for the sake of the parents' own egoist enjoyment.[27] Pleasure of the egoist sort may partly explain such solicitous concern, but it seems difficult to say that such pleasure completely explains the loving parental face. For, a child is not always a source of enjoyment. A child is relatively helpless, heedless, self-centered, a burden on its caretakers, yet the majority of human beings are moved actually to care for children rather than to destroy or neglect them, despite the trials that children pose. Why, then, do my parents love me?

If pleasure is an inadequate motivation for parental love, and no positive quality or imagined potential in my ipseity, considered strictly as egoism, is adequate to explain their years of service to me,[28] especially when I was patently ungrateful to and heedless of their own irreducible dignity, must I not finally conclude that I have called my parents to goodness—faced them—unwittingly, unintentionally, without knowing that I did? Must I not conclude that there is *something* in me, some unwilled, yet appealing or desirable aspect of myself that is lovable because it is oriented toward (and so invites) goodness, or enjoys some enigmatic proximity to goodness, which my parents recognized before I did? If it is true that there is some aspect of myself that commands or solicits goodness from the other, then is it not also true to say that, since I have always been in relation to others, that which, in me, calls others to goodness, also calls me to rectify myself, so that I do not, in pursuit of my ipseity, degrade that aspect of me that has already faced others, and which responds to the facing of others?

If these points have merit, then they require us to develop the description of how economic generosity, inspired by the other's response to *my* face, manifests itself as also (rightly) enjoyed. This phenomenology must show the ambiguity of parental response, which enables me to overlook its ethical character and often to fail to see the commanding face of my parents because their face shows as caring for me. We should ask ourselves: do not my parents' faces, when they care for me, show that the face is not only commanding? Smiling, welcoming, caring, and consoling faces introduce me to another face (or another aspect of the face), one that lessens the distance between the face and my inner life without the former becoming a mere moment of the latter.

Do these considerations not suggest a need to rethink the relation of my desire (and the other's desire) to my ipseity (and the other's ipseity)? My ipseity would not come to be (or long survive), save that I desire and face my first others—my parents or my parent*al* others. My parents' response to me shows that somehow, I have dignity. Yet at the same time, their response does not seem to be premised on any single talent, quality, or ability that I may have: thus my dignity is not reducible to an order of pure enjoyment, *nor* to one of pure desire. If indeed my dignity lies somehow in my desiring and facing *as* a needy being, then I am dependent on the other's presence and response for the experience of dwelling and caring that point toward my own dignity precisely as a bodily and needy subject.

BEING VIOLATED

One of the major gaps in Levinas's account, and one that presupposes that the subject both has dignity and knows that it has it, is the phenomenon of me-being-violated-by-you.[29] Levinas's analyses of violence include my violence toward the other and systematic violence toward *some*one, but the concrete experience of violation of oneself is almost completely absent.[30] The words "violate" and "violation" *do* occur in a handful of places.[31] One place where Levinas uses these terms is in the phenomenology of eros (*TI* 256–66), where I (the lover) violate the beloved in the attempt to uncover her (or him), and expose the secret of the other. The attempt fails because the other, in her (or his) secrecy, refuses herself (or himself) to erotic unveiling, but violation remains at the heart of the profanation that is an ineliminable, distinctive moment of eros as between two people (258–66). In the analysis of eros, I violate "the secret" of the other (259–60), which shows as secret in its being refused to my grasp or to the attempt to bring it to light in love.

Otherwise, "violate" and "violation" occur mainly where Levinas is concerned to speak of the subject as a will, or an active being. To act requires freedom on a number of levels, which can be undone by seduction (which Levinas says is equivalent to violation [*TI* 171]) or by force. On such occasions, when the subject fails to overcome seduction or force and preserve its own willed orientation and course of action, then "it reveals itself as exposed to influences, to be a force of nature, absolutely tractable" (237). To succumb to an influence reduces one to the rank of a force of nature, which is subject to manipulation not contingently, but by its very nature. In these instances, the subject is "violated" in its self-consciousness. "Its 'freedom of thought' is extinguished" (237).

For the purposes of this argument, the use of "violation" in the phenomenology of eros is unhelpful. First, it is written from the perspective of the violator. As in the analysis of violence and the face, the phenomenology of eros gives an account of how I violate the other in her (or his) essential "secrecy"; it does not give a description of what is involved in the experience of *being violated*. Moreover, Levinas writes of the beloved that she (or he) is "wanton" in the relationship where she (or he) is violated as "secret"—the other in a sense participates willfully in this violation (*TI* 261). The passages on erotic nudity are concerned with a violation that is eminently *playful*, in which the other is not offended or outraged but involved in fostering the erotic relationship; this raises questions about how justified the use of the term "violation" is in this context. To demonstrate that seduction between lovers is essentially a violation outside of the bounds of just response requires more argument than Levinas gives, and in any case, is not the meaning of violation with which we are concerned here.

The discussions of violation of freedom in relations with the state come much closer to focusing on the phenomenon of violation, but these are rather brief. Violation as such is not described so much as attributed to the relationship between the subject as active will and the economic world, which is articulated among actors and given a more permanent structure in the institutions of the state (*TI* 175–77, 226–32). The economic system does not "engage the interiority from whom the work proceeded";[32] nor does the state, which gives the economic world its stability. Rather, the state, which realizes its very essence as an impersonal system of works, makes visible my necessary absence from these works and from the system of exchange: this is the "tyranny of the state" (176). The failure of the economic world and of the state to engage my interiority offends my liberty. How, though? Levinas says nothing more, but the concern that Levinas conceives here about the "tyranny of the State" and the alienation I suffer with respect to my work, which participates in the anonymity of the market and state institutions, is resolved already through the relationship of commerce between you and me in a later pair of sections (226–36). These later analyses do not contain the word "violate," and their overall focus is not given to the phenomenon of violation, which is presupposed rather than elucidated.[33]

Even where one might most expect elucidation—namely in the description, from the perspective of the victim, of hatred and torture (*TI* 238–40)—one finds that Levinas again most often takes the perspective of the violator, and remains mostly silent about the concrete intentional stance of the victim. What we find in these descriptions, which seem as though they should provide the culminating analysis of the way in which the subject is disposed when violated by the most severe forms of violence, is that Levinas's concern is ultimately to combat the notion that existence is finally absurd—a concern that is derived not from his own philosophy, but almost certainly from prominent existentialist thinkers, for whom, if freedom were extinguished, existence would be meaningless. His goal is to show that these philosophies generate a false problem. Its falsity is shown up by his own analysis of the facing relationship as the originary locus of meaning, which is not dependent upon an originally free subjectivity. This explains his peculiar handling of one of the most graphic and memorable passages of *Totality and Infinity*, to which we now turn.

The fear that existence is absurd appears in "Time and the Will: Patience" (*TI* 236–40). After giving his analysis of suffering as the self's experience of itself as thing-like in its unfreedom with respect to physical suffering (238), Levinas claims, "The supreme ordeal of freedom is not death but suffering" (239); then, he proceeds to explain that hatred has a privileged understanding of this point:

> Hatred wills this passivity [the passivity of suffering that makes a person thing-like and that gives suffering its acuity] in the eminently active being that is to bear witness to it. Hatred does not always desire the death of the Other, or at least it desires the death of the Other only in inflicting this death only as a supreme suffering. The one who hates seeks to be the cause of a suffering to which the despised being must be witness. To inflict suffering is not to reduce the Other to the rank of object, but on the contrary is to maintain him superbly in his

subjectivity. In suffering the subject must know his reification, but in order to do so he must precisely remain a subject. Hatred wills both things.... Therein resides the logical absurdity of hatred. (*TI* 239)

Hatred is logically absurd for desiring two contradictory states of affairs: that the other be a thing *and* that he or she know his or her thinghood, and so testify to it and to the hateful one as the *cause* of suffering. This is impossible, however, since the other cannot be a thing, and no thing can be a witness. Yet hatred does not thereby fail to exist, nor does it fail to achieve its end: namely, that the other experience his or her passivity as an agony that degrades and humiliates. The hateful one accomplishes this end by making the other experience the passivity of helplessness. The victim of a hatred that inflicts suffering and death—the tortured subject—experiences this contradiction as an *absurdity*, as the collapse of a meaningful world into a meaningless nonworld. Yet a total collapse of meaning into meaninglessness or absurdity is a fantasy scenario:

> The supreme ordeal of the will is not death, but suffering. In patience, at the limit of its abdication, the will does not founder [*sombre*] in absurdity, for—over and beyond the nothingness that would reduce the space of time that flows [*s'écoule*] from birth to death to the purely subjective, the interior, the illusory, the meaningless—the violence the will supports [*supporte*] comes from the other as a tyranny. But for this very reason it is produced as an absurdity that is detached from signification [*qui se détache sur la signification*]. Violence does not stop Discourse; all is not inexorable. Thus alone does violence remain supportable [*supportable*] in patience. It is produced only in a world where I can die *as a result of someone* and *for someone*. This situates death in a new context and modifies its conception, voided by the pathetic [*vidé du pathétique*] that comes to it from the fact of being my death. In other words, in patience, the will breaks the crust of its egoism and...[wills] as Desire and Goodness limited by nothing. (*TI* 239; translation modified)

The fact that the will is being tortured *by* someone places suffering (and the death that the torturer wills as the infliction of supreme suffering) within the realm of meaning.[34] The absurdity of suffering is not what is originary. Instead, it occurs only in my relationship with you, a speaking that has already revealed us as meaningfully involved with each other. Absurdity is therefore a defect of meaning, not the priority of meaninglessness out of which meaning would somehow have to arise.

Although it may be necessary to demonstrate that the capacity of people to torture and so to eradicate another's freedom does not indicate that meaningless absurdity is original or that evil has priority over goodness, we would ask: in the concrete, horrific situation of suffering torture, is Levinas's concern the concern of the one being tortured?[35] Does not the one being tortured have other concerns at that very moment? A saint or an extremely dedicated person may fear for his or her friends and compatriots in the midst of torture: records of such concern do exist.[36] Yet, not all those who suffer are saints or extremely dedicated, and in any case, as Levinas has been at pains to demonstrate, "the human will is not heroic" (*TI* 229). What does the nonheroic will under torture tell us?

Surely the first thing it tells us is: "STOP!" If indeed, as Levinas wishes to point out, we are dealing with an interpersonal (and so irreducibly ethical) situation, this "STOP!" does not only testify to that interpersonal element. It also orients this interpersonal relationship in a very concrete and specific fashion: it makes a demand on the other. What is the ethical or significant content of this demand that the victim makes upon his or her torturer? Is it not that in touching in so heinous a fashion the ipseity of the person, the torturer violates the dignity of the victim? If *I* am the victim (and every victim is an I), then when I say "STOP!" I am not testifying simply to the interpersonal relationship of being faced (although I am faced, as Levinas shows, even by the hateful one, which is in part why I can still desire goodness or to respond in a right fashion to him or her). I am testifying to my own dignity in desire, which is inextricably linked (somehow) to my ipseity. It is this same link between my ipseity and my own dignity that should be understood to give substantial content to the idea that I can will "Desire and Goodness that nothing limits." What could this mean for me, or for anyone subjected to torture but that I (or anyone subjected to torture), in protesting or being outraged, act well by *teaching* the other that he or she does wrong? This teaching may take many forms: from a 'simple' "STOP!" to questions posed to the torturer about why he or she acts this way, to reprimand or anger on my own behalf and on behalf of other victims, and even to pity for the torturer. To teach *well*, in such circumstances, may indeed require a long and sophisticated education that involves the institutions of society, as Levinas says (*TI* 241). But such a teaching, if it teaches the hateful other that he or she wrongs *me*, must reveal, concretely, in and through the experience of such suffering, that I who suffer have a face, am dignified in my vulnerability and neediness, am *inviolate* despite the violation. Insult and violation are experiences that teach me not only that I am faced, but that in being faced, I, too, "*fais face*" and know that I do. If, phenomenologically speaking, I do not *see* that I face the other, then I must feel, hear, will, and produce my face (in the sense of "showing myself"), and so know in these moments that I, like you and from out of the experience of myself as violated by you, have dignity that is inextricably bound to my ipseity, whose suffering you wield as an offensive weapon.

The Problem of the Unity of the Self

Levinas persistently characterizes the relationship with the face as one that is articulated through a hard separation between interiority and exteriority. The asymmetry of the facing relationship is presented as exclusively the experience of your face revealing a height that my ipseity, with which I am identified, essentially lacks. I never experience asymmetry from the perspective of height, which implies that I cannot be an other for myself. The height or dignity involved in the asymmetry of facing relationships is a height I cannot experience as my own. Consequently, my enjoyment and my desire remain sharply distinguished, and seem often to be isolated from each other, just as I and the other are both absolutely separate from each other as interiority and exteriority, respectively. Levinas's fear seems to be that if I could experience myself as infinite and obliging myself, then I would be *entirely* self-sufficient and autonomous. Likewise, if the other and I were not so strictly separated, he seems to fear that we could become confused with each other, and that I could then, by participating in the other, experience myself as self-sufficient and autonomous, because the opposite of separation is confusion, blending, merging into a self-same identity in which only I remain.

Such fears, however, do not seem warranted. The moment of self-perception and self-recognition need not mean that I am an ethically self-sufficient being: as the above analyses of violation and parental love tried to show, it is only in relation to the other person, who cannot be confused with me, that I am capable of recognizing myself as dignified and as facing both others and myself. That this is so argues for a *double asymmetry*, in which both parties experience themselves as faced and as facing, as enjoying and as desiring. We experience double asymmetry as a consequence of our being in relationship, and as a second moment or movement of the significational sweep of your facing me. That you face me reveals that I also face, and even that I face you (and always have, though sometimes unwittingly).[37] The experience of parental love presents us likewise with a relational structure in which interiority and exteriority are not maintained as strictly as Levinas would have them be, and yet it need not be the case that this blurring of bounds *necessarily* leads only to confusion: although love creates a shared, intimate warmth, as well as requiring the sharing or even sacrifice of goods, this intimate warmth reveals a facing situation that persists despite our participation in this humanizing warmth—really, a sort of atmosphere—that accomplishes dwelling.

But if we are correct to say this, then it seems necessary to revisit the question of the unity of the subject who desires and the subject who enjoys: how is this subject, which is not only its ipseity, but whose desiring and dignified aspect is inextricably bound to this ipseity, such that to touch that ipseity in a violent fashion is to wrong the person? Who is the subject who can participate in the warmth of human intimacy, which is both economic and ethical, without attention to any strict separation between the subject and the other? *That* there is a link between desire and enjoyment is clear from Levinas's work, yet its precise nature remains mysterious.

Levinas has shown that in being faced, my ipseity is subordinated to the ethical height of the other, and the imperative that this height delivers to me. Enjoyment is rectified (justified) in the moment of its subordination to the desire to answer the other. This initial rectification of enjoyment lends itself to analyzing the culpability of unrectified enjoyment on the one hand, and the character of responsibility, which offers *economic* succor because the other's needs are sacred (whereas mine are not), on the other. Economic responsibility tends, however, to emphasize giving objects, which can be shared only limitedly. This limitation seems to exclude any rectification other than rectification as self-sacrifice. Consequently, the hard distinction between infinite exteriority and totalizing interiority tends to limit the self to its interiority and the other to exteriority. The experience of myself as dignified and vulnerable to unjust violation is then almost entirely occluded, as we have seen from previous analyses. At the same time, the status of my own desire, which goes beyond me, is problematically both mine and yet not able to be said to be "myself." Subordination of my ipseity to the other's height and vulnerability can therefore be only one aspect of the justification of enjoyment. Describing justified ipseity—that is, enjoyment in a nonegoistic way, as having been shot through with (and so fundamentally converted or transformed by) desire for the other(s)—remains an outstanding and extremely difficult task. But this task would, we think, be necessary to show the unity of the subject who both desires and enjoys, in order to support an analysis of a greater range of relationships with the other. It seems likely, were we to raise the question of the other's enjoyment and desire, that the unity of the subject would begin to be revealed.

Overall, we find that there *is* a limit—that between enjoyment and desire, between interior and exterior—at work in Levinas's analyses, despite his attempts to avoid conceiving the subject in relation to the other in terms of limit. If we are correct, then this limit is especially problematic given that the Levinasian subject is founded in the desire for the infinite, which should not so much transgress as transcend limitation as such. This spurs us to ask: does the opposition of exteriority to interiority and of desire to enjoyment not compromise the infinity of the other, by circumscribing it within a limit?

In fact, we cannot understand the meaning of "infinite" in Levinas's work without referring to the mutual limitation of enjoyment and desire, of interiority and exteriority: the infinite shows up through infinition of the other. Infinition is the very way in which I and the other are in relation with each other, that is, I must be *only* interior, which requires the other to appear as *only* exterior. This strict separation subsequently restricts certain terms (desire, ipseity, infinite, goodness, egoism, dignity, worth, etc.) to being used of only one party to the metaphysical relation. While this limitation may facilitate an appropriate description of many *but not all* of our relations with human others, whose infinity means absolute exteriority that can *never* become interior (a limited infinite, in other words), if Levinas wishes to found the unified subject *also* in its desire for the infinity of God, then a description that relies so heavily upon a limit becomes untenable. God's way of being infinite cannot be captured by ascribing an isolated or separated exteriority to God: traditionally, divine infinity has been expressed as God's transcendence of all limitation. This transcendence cannot result in the confusion of God with finite beings, but neither can it admit of a separation or a failure to be present (somehow!) "in all beings." The term "infinite," if it is to be said of both God and the other person, cannot have one and the same meaning. If Levinas is sincere (and we have no reason to think he is not) in saying that the infinite other is both God and the other person, then it becomes necessary to rethink how the subject can be founded in desire for an infinite that signifies differently *as soon as it is said or thought.* For, it is not the case that one is only alternately in relation to God and to the other person: one is *always* founded in desire for both.

Because the foundation of the subject in desire for the infinite is driven by a limitation that affects how one conceives and experiences the infinite, the unity of the Levinasian subject must remain largely undiscussed, for want of conceptual resources. Despite Levinas's efforts to bypass the traditional ways of examining this unity as a unity of a material body and a spiritual soul, he cannot show the subject's unity as *both* desiring *and* enjoying. It is true that for Levinas, the subject is always a corporeal self, a spiritual body whose elements are inseparable and refuse any sharp distinction. Arguably, however, the problem of a dual unity, which usually plagues analyses that examine the subject in terms of body/soul, reappears in Levinas under the relationship of desire to enjoyment, and of exteriority to interiority. It is one thing to say that desire desires to enjoy justly; it is another to show how desire and enjoyment are related as moments of one self, who both desires *and enjoys* the Other—the Other whose face, especially in its hospitable and caring expressions, summons and informs me of my own, unchosen respectability, and who shows up as more than commanding and strictly separate from me.

THREE

"All that Is Holy Is Profaned"

Levinas and Marx on the Social Relation

Asher Horowitz

The presence of a deep affinity between Marx and Levinas, especially in *Totality and Infinity,* is a subject that, though occasionally broached, largely has been overlooked.[1] An essential level at which to explore this affinity—without which certain tensions would also not exist—is in what may be called their respective social ontologies.[2] I will proceed by first drawing attention to what seems to be an all-but-unnoticed ambiguity in Marx's social ontology by way of a brief analysis of the concept and provenance of species-being. Marx, in his concept of species-being, both approaches and withdraws from an understanding of the social relation as something eerily like Levinas's sense of the ethical as an imperative obligation directly binding me to the other in an asymmetrical and thereby radically plural fashion. There is an ambiguity or equivocation about this which traverses Marx's career, beginning from the early "Excerpt Notes on James Mill," and it never goes away. It is this double understanding of what it means to be a social-historical being that, as much as anything else, allows for the quarrels between "humanistic" and "structural" readings of Marx.

Totality and Infinity is a book that also contains a social ontology; it can and should be read as a phenomenologically inspired answer to the question of what it means to be a social-historical being. The social historicity of the human is a theme that is already crucial to Levinas in his first book on Husserl, recurs in "Reflections on the Philosophy of Hitlerism," and remains present in his subsequent works.[3] Yet in *Totality and Infinity* he both approaches and withdraws from the question of the ethical relation's own social historicity. The historical future is not approached as a potential field for the realization of the ethical relation on the societal plane. The ultimate meaning of being human is in a fecundity that enshrines goodness as good deeds, but not, one might say, as good works.[4] The concept of fecundity, as a result, is not extended or linked up to the institution of a good society.

After tracing the ambiguity in Marx surrounding the relation between what could be called the ethical bond and positive subjective freedom, along with a few of its implications, the analysis will turn to the ways in which *Totality and Infinity* resolves it. But while resolving it, Levinas will also unnecessarily introduce an important equivocation concerning the necessary extent of alienation into his own social ontology, an equivocation that he does not clearly see as already, in principle, resolved by Marx. Finally, I would like to go on very briefly to suggest that this mutual correction points not so much toward a synthesis, but to an alignment in which these thinkers supplement and enrich each other. In filling out and actually strengthening the concept of species-being, *Totality and Infinity* can immeasurably enrich future conceptions of socialism. By introducing a clear distinction between alienation and objectification, Marx can lead Levinasian ethics in the direction of its realization on the planes of the societal and the political.

▌▌▌▌▌

Underlying Marx's critical theories of class societies and their past and potential transformations, there is a social ontology of the human, an interpretation of what being human means. To be human for Marx means to be social, as the sixth Thesis on Feuerbach so forcefully announces. Humanity is not "an essence inhering in each single individual. In its actuality it is the ensemble of social relations." Moreover, as the eighth Thesis asserts, "All social life is essentially practical."[5] It is not simply theoretical, but involved and expressed in the active life of the senses. These propositions are not simply asserted as facts, they are referred back, in the *Economic and Philosophical Manuscripts,* to what is perhaps the most ambiguous and opaque, but also most central and foundational concept in his work, the notion of the human as a "species-being," a being that, because its life activity expresses both "universality" and "freedom," is capable of, if not impelled to, making its own history and thereby itself. Species-being cannot be simply taken as a constant. It refers both to actuality, to the past and present, and to a potentiality; species-being is not whole and complete at the beginning of the process, but is also to be realized in future. Species-being functions not only as something like a transcendental condition of possibility for human life as social and historical, but also as something like the orientation for a goal inherent in a process already long underway and irreversible. The realization of species-being would imply the realization of an ensemble of social relations radically unlike all the ensembles that have obtained up to this point; yet, it would be a realization of and by the same species as well as a social relation inasmuch as its realization would mean the undoing of the practical contradictions between the life of the species and the lives of its individuals. Real community and true individuality would become conditions of each other. The separation of the individual, its freedom, would be expressed and fulfilled in sensuous-practical, or, objective forms that also directly enhance and vivify the lives of other individuals.

Thus, central to the concept of species-being or, alternatively, understandable as something that follows from it, is the notion that humanity creates itself, forms and reforms itself, expands and develops its own capabilities and potentialities even as it blocks and distorts these same potentialities and capacities. Humanity has a history essential to its being, but it is one that need not take place with a conscious purpose or agreement. The concept of species-being, however, has two sides to it, two sides that, in Marx's writings, are, at best in a rather tenuous relation to each other and, at worst, potentially contradictory. On the one side, species-being comprises what we might call the human-to-human relation, something social in the sense of the relation of inward intentions to other beings with other inward intentions. Despite being taken as an enemy of inwardness, Marx has a strong almost commonsensical, all-but-unphilosophical appreciation for it (which may be a relative strength, compared to the philosophical tradition). Yet it would be impossible to be human—in the second sense of species-being as a positive subjective freedom—without the inwardness Marx includes in the first, and that Levinas will call interiority. Marx's quarrel is with any view that reduces freedom to inwardness, or that holds that inward freedom suffices as freedom. On the other side, the side more familiar inasmuch as it also lends itself better to the sociological and political-economic analyses of feudalism and capitalism, species-being refers to the freedom and universality without which human labor in all its historically institutional forms would be not much different from that of bees or beavers. Let us examine each of these sides briefly before turning to their relation with each other and its implications.

** | | | | |**

The human-to-human facet of the concept of species-being shows itself most clearly when Marx is criticizing the experiential-social world of political economy, private property, exchange and money. Marx writes, "The division of labor and exchange are the two phenomena on whose account the political economist brags about the social nature of his science, while in the same breath he unconsciously expresses the contradiction which underlies his science — the establishment of society through unsocial, particular interests."[6] The human-to-human here is announced negatively, as the inversion of the relation of instrumental reciprocity that political economy projects into the being of the social. In this world money "is for me the other person" (*EPM* 375), "the bond of all bonds" (377), the "universal inversion of individualities" (387). It converts the social bond of the human-to-human into the asocial and antisocial bondage of individuals to each other, of the worker to capital, and of each to the whole. The human-to-human, reduced to an exchange of objects mediated by money and driven by the needs of the particulars of the social whole degrades, stupefies, and literally demoralizes social beings in their sociality. The laws of political economy have no moral judgments to make about almost any inhuman acts (362), and the stupefaction that the imposition of instrumental exchange imposes on individuals reaches down into the senses themselves (352–54). The human senses are shrunken into the sense of having, such that "all senses and all passions are lost in greed," to the point that "you must be chary of participating in affairs of general interest, showing sympathy and trust, etc. . . . if you want to avoid being ruined by illusion" (361).

In the less-visited and underrated "Excerpt Notes of 1844," Marx is, if anything, more direct and more commonsensical about the human-to-human. Examining, for example, the claims made by the St. Simonians about the credit system as tending toward a gradual overcoming of social alienation (because it rests on trust in the debtor to repay his debt), Marx discovers there the most "odious" alienation insofar as it involves "moral and social existence, the very inwardness of the human heart." In credit, the social virtue of trustworthiness in the debtor represents nothing more than the "reimbursement of . . . capital with the usual interest."[7] In general, in the world which political economy represents, "exchange or barter . . . is

the social, genuine act, the common essence, the social intercourse and integration of man within private property...hence
it is likewise the opposite of the social relationship" (ExN 47).
Political economy thus "establishes an alienated form of social
intercourse as the essential, original and definitive human
form" (46). Exchange, presupposing private property, turns
the human-to-human relation into a relation of equivalent to
equivalent (48), and this, in turn, makes possible not only wage
labor but the depersonalization of production and productive relations, which allows for "transforming him [the agent
of exchange] into a spiritual and physical monster" (48–49).
Here, "human nature is not the bond of our production for
each other" (50). In the world of political economy the other
is always a means to my self-satisfaction; even providing for his
satisfaction is a means to my own. Production "for each other"
could not have this structure.

Marx's interpretation of the human-to-human facet of species-being is, however, not entirely negative. Positive indications
are present as well in, for example, his discussion of sensuous
appropriation under communism, where the sense of having,
possession, and consumption gives way to active senses open
to the unique qualities of the object.[8] This involves a vision
of production for others in which "need or enjoyment have
lost their egoistic nature, and nature has lost its mere utility"
and where activity in direct association with others becomes
an integral facet of my own life expression (EPM 352). The
return from the inverted world of money, "as the existing and
active concept of value," to a world in which there is a human
relation to the other, or to nature, would mean that "love
could be exchanged only for love, trust for trust and so on"
(379). The human-to-human is thus not reducible to a fun-
gible third term. It is directly, frankly, categorically, and concretely the self for-the-other without being against itself. There
is no stronger assertion of the human-to-human relation than
that which occurs in the last two pages of the "Excerpt Notes
of 1844." There, Marx first alludes to what he calls a "human

language," human because not ensnared in the mutually decep-
tion-inducing mediations of the exchange relation. In exchange
"our objects [the objects we produce for exchange] in their
relation to one another [as expressions of equivalent abstract
value] constitute the only intelligible language we use with one
another. We would not understand a human language, and it
would remain without effect." A human language would be
open to a direct expression of need on the part of another, to be
answered directly in its satisfaction by my activity. In the condition of alienated species-being, this call would be considered
an affront and an indignity, an affront to the one receiving the
demand, an indignity on the part of the one in need: "We are
so much alienated from human nature that the direct language
of this nature is an injury to human dignity for us." Marx contrasts production "as human beings" with production mediated
by what will be called later the law of value, where "our mutual
value is the value of our mutual objects for us. Man himself,
therefore, is mutually valueless for us" (ExN 52). As for the
meaning of production as human beings, the passage requires
nearly full quotation:

> In his production each would have twice affirmed himself and the
> other. (1) In my production I would have objectified my individual-
> ity and its particularity and in the course of the activity I would have
> enjoyed an individual life.... (2) In your satisfaction and your use of
> my product I would have had the direct and conscious satisfaction that
> my work satisfied a human need.... (3) I would have been the media-
> tor between you and the species and you would have experienced me
> as...a necessary part of yourself; I would have been affirmed in your
> thought as well as your love. (4) In my individual life I would have
> directly created your life...I would have confirmed and realized my
> true human and social nature. (ExN 52–53)

From within the inverted world of commodity production this
will, of course, seem like a romantic fantasy or a bad bargain.
If it is ever realized, however, the world of commodity production will seem in retrospect to have been a nightmarish prison
only realizable by a malignant genius with Kafka's imagination.

But my concern here is not with the pragmatics of production as humans, but with the meaning of species-being.

▌▌▌▌▌

If the human-to-human relation is one axis of the concept of species-being, its other axis is the relation of the human to itself. According to Marx, humans are species-beings inasmuch as they "look upon" themselves as "universal and therefore free" beings (*EPM* 327)—not immediately this now, but also something and someone before and beyond this now. Universality presupposes difference and distance from, and at the same time relation to, this or that particular quality, attribute, sensation, situation, instant, etc. It thereby turns the relation into a relation of subject to object. Because of this universality a human will also "make the species…his object," that is, she will grasp the universal in or out of the particulars, including making of the human species an object as well. A human will *therefore* grasp herself as both separate and distinct from other humans and, *at the same time,* a member of the species. And because of that grasp of the species, of the general aspect of objects, the human being has the capacity to imagine and infer, but also to recognize and project possibilities only latent in being, invisible, unheard-of potentialities. The effectuation of species-being as universality, moreover, will take place not only in the realm of thought, but in and through all of the vital activities of the human. Human labor and production, the realm in which human capacities and powers unfold and develop, because they are objectified, are therefore immediately different from those of other animals. An animal "is not distinct" from its life activity, "it *is* that activity. Man makes his life activity itself an object of his will and consciousness" (328). Other animals will repeat themselves as they are; only humans will continuously produce themselves differently in their production and reproduction of different social formations. As with other living beings, labor is the correlate of need and distress; but unlike other living beings, human labor also affirms its freedom and universality in its objects.

Inasmuch as human labor objectively realizes human universality and freedom, humans have a different individuality from other animals. Each and every human can take up a stance separate from the activity they find themselves engaged in; and by the same token, each and every activity becomes an expression to other humans of the (potential) individuality of each unique human being. The reach of an individual human's human-individual free self-realization is also thereby a function of social history, and vice-versa as well. The more developed are the social capacities, the more developed are those of individuals as well, at least potentially. The level and type of self-realization becomes dependent upon the level of the development of the powers developed over time within a society with a division of labor.[9] However, because universality and therefore freedom are only made real in the course of objectification, and because products in the broadest sense (including the sense in which relations of production are historical products) may break loose from the intention, foresight, and knowledge of their producers, there is what Marcuse rightly sees as "a conflict in the human essence—that it is in itself objective is the root of the fact that it can become alienation and that externalization can become reification."[10] With the realization on Marx's part that the alienation of human life activity has its necessary basis in objectification, the task of thought is moved from philosophy as social ontology to the special theories, to historical materialism, the critique of political economy, and the theory of revolution, including their anticipations of human freedom in socialism.[11] These, however, would not be possible if abstracted from the general theory expressed in Marx's social ontology. The social ontology of the general theory, however, contains a serious ambiguity and a related philosophical lacuna. Levinas, particularly in *Totality and Infinity*, may supply a resolution for the ambiguity and a bridge for the gap. If this turns out to be the case, the prospect of refounding a socialism clearer about its essential ethical substance will emerge as a result.

▮▮▮▮▮

The ambiguity surrounding and the gap between the two axes of species-being are related. In question is the nature of the relation between species-being as objectification and species-being as the human-to-human. Is one the condition of the other? Does objectification either characterize or give rise to the specifically human-to-human, or does the human-to-human play a constitutive role in the possibility of freedom and universality? Even if they are conceived to arise together, Marx does not, and arguably cannot, give an account of how this might come about or what their respective roles might be.[12] And to this extent, his social ontology remains incomplete and equivocal. The theoretical and practical consequences of this equivocation at so fundamental a level will also have further ramifications for his thought at other levels. Is it conceivable that the power and the promise of objectification somehow follow from the human-to-human relation? Or is the human-to-human subordinate to the framework and structure of objectification? In the first case, the logic of the analysis leads in the direction of the subordination of human powers, individual and collective, to the relation of the gift, to the "human language" he mentions in the "Excerpt Notes of 1844." In the second case, the logic of the analysis leads to the very instrumentalization of the gift itself. Thus, in the *Grundrisse,* Marx announces that the working out of creative potentialities and the development of all human powers is the end-in-itself.[13] This is a noble goal, to be sure, and one that does not *eo ipso* undermine the human-to-human. But, as Terry Eagleton has pointed out, as an ethic, this has its quandaries and limitations.

Something needs to be decided about which powers and capacities are to be fully developed, and the developmental imperative itself is not a sufficient criterion of itself.[14] Under the developmental imperative, the human-to-human relationship is conceived as simply another power of the human subject, a power that has been alienated via objective conditions of social domination. The recovery of the human-to-human becomes a reassertion of the power of somehow-now-social individuals over their collective, but externalized and alienated power. The power of the (illusory) other is defeated and recovered by the (real) power of the same. But in the course of this recovery, organized by the logic of objectification, the human-to-human relation verges on being, if it has not already become, a mere region of objectification. In Marx's discussion of real human production above, it is hard to say that the other is affirmed unequivocally; it sometimes appears as though the affirmation of the other occurs for the sake of my self-affirmation, my reality, and my power. It is because of the universality of the human that it recognizes itself as separate and member of a species, both the particular and the universal. This is the logic of totalization.[15]

I am not arguing that Marx moves away from the human-to-human to a developmental imperative pure and simple, but that both are present in different profiles and degrees throughout his work. Both the human-to-human and the developmental imperative are present, for instance, in Marx's analysis of commodity fetishism in the first volume of *Capital*. But the relation between them is not an issue for Marx; he does not see a (potential) problem. There is not enough, however, in Feuerbach's introduction of passive sensibility into the essence of the subject to move Marx's materialism sufficiently beyond Hegelian idealism. In that idealism freedom is the development of the freedom of the same, where identity achieves its unity in the richer and more articulated form of dialectically recovered particularities in a concrete universal. As Marcuse observes, having appropriated Feuerbach's insistence on passivity, need, and sensuousness, Marx does not simply adopt Hegelian method but also goes back to Hegel's root problems and thinks them through to a further stage.[16] Marcuse writes, "Marx's theory has its roots in the centre of Hegel's philosophical problematic."[17] Under the sign of species-being, one of Marx's great Hegelian (rather than Feuerbachian) discoveries is that labor is objectification and thus the potentially disalienable development of freedom. But this also means that the *subject* is essentially objectification, and that objectification is conceived essentially in idealist terms, as a relation in which subject and object meet and are unified through a third term: the "species" or the universal. The object in objectification is not simply something detachable from its makers; it is, as object, grasped as the universal. In labor I make it my own through the grasp of what is universal in it.

The relation with the other human, the social relation, when it is conceived in terms of objectification, thus hovers on the razor's edge of a contradiction: is the other, and are others collectively, the (potential) means to the self-realization of *my* powers? Or is the retrieval and return of the alienated social power a medium within which each affirms each and every other in the unconditional obligation Marx indicates in his notion of a human language responding to the other's need?[18] Is the egoism of the exchange relation—which is raised by several levels of magnitude under the commodity fetish—actually transcended? Or are the egoisms now mutually reinforced in a higher rational unity? It seems that this equivocation is imported into the ontological level of Marx's materialism primarily through his reappropriation of the Hegelian subject.[19] To the extent that the subject is once again seen through the lens of objectification, a gap opens between the human-to-human relation and the relation of the human to itself. Not seeing this problem (perhaps other problems are more pressing), Marx does not seek to determine the priority of the one over the other.

▌▌▌▌▌

Levinas, however, will see that need and, in *Totality and Infinity,* not only assigns priority to the human-to-human over the human-to-itself, but provides a complex and subtle argument for its priority. *Totality and Infinity* is not simply a metaethics; it also unfolds metaethics as a social ontology. Levinas understands the ethical relation as, or as a function of the social relation, even as the ensemble of social relations. The instances in which Levinas refers to the ethical relation as the social relation, and vice-versa, are in *Totality and Infinity* so frequent as to not even bear enumeration. But the social relation itself is not understood as primarily or primordially a relation of objectifying subjects to each other. Neither is it understood as the social fact, as a prior or alienated totality within which individual lives gain their existence and their meaning. Instead, the possibility of objectification is itself dependent on a relation prior to objectification: the human-to-human. The relation of the human-to-itself, which is essentially mediated through the process of objectification, has, as its condition of possibility, the human-to-human relation. Given this priority, the unconditional ethical bond may be seen to be the heart of species-being, and more than ever, Marx's vision of socialism can be grasped in its transcendence of the dichotomy of the individual and the communal.

Thus Levinas, like Marx, also goes back into the Hegelian problematic, and *Totality and Infinity* is meant, among other things, to supply an alternative understanding of the meaning of the realization of freedom that takes its concept beyond both the ethical State and Absolute Spirit. But unlike Marx, it might be said that Levinas goes back *beneath* Hegel, in order to transcend the Hegelian problematic. Unlike Hegel or Marx, he does not begin with a spontaneous subject in relation to an object, even if, as in the *Phenomenology*'s discussion of sense-certainty, that object is the merest "this" and that spontaneity is the most bare and abstract, untried and inexperienced form of objectifying consciousness. Thus, in a key formula, Levinas will say that "the sovereignty of thought is posterior to the world of which it is anterior" (*TI* 170). In this way, the material social relation always already precedes the sovereign ego apotheosized in idealism.

Both Marx and Levinas take issue with the abstractness of Hegelian idealism and orient their corrections of it by way of a search for the concrete or the "material" (*TI* 36). And to that end they both reintroduce sensuousness into the heart and essence of the life of the subject. But—and this is key to my argument—whereas Marx tends to assimilate sensible life to the process of objectification in labor, Levinas maintains their distinction. Sensibility, and with it separation, have a form and a meaning of their own, insofar as "living from" and enjoyment are not relations with an object. They are preobjective, prereflective and nonthematizing, even when they are practical. Labor is thus not the primary or the primordial form in which sensuous life takes place. For Levinas, those primordial forms will be enjoyment and eros. And, in the end, this reconfiguration of the sensuous is what allows him to construe the human-to-human, the ethical, as the Desire that transcends egoism.

Like Marx, Levinas will also see the subject as essentially wrapped up in a history of alienation. But phenomenology unfortunately does not lend itself to the historical analysis of the possible succession of structures in which alienation might produce the conditions for its own abolition. As a result, Levinas will generate an ambiguity and equivocation of his own, which will call for a certain Marxian correction, an ambiguity about the relation between the "primary alienation" and what we might call the alienation of social domination. It is not clear whether Levinas conflates the primary alienation with social domination or whether, given the centrality he assigns to eros and fecundity, he is simply not as troubled by it as Marx is. In either case, his treatment calls for revision.

IIIII

The ambiguity in Marx's concept of species-being lead one of its facets, universality and the freedom it brings with it, to be understood all too easily as primary. For Levinas, this freedom is insufficient as a starting point, as is Heidegger's starting point in doing and care (*TI* 109). Although it is necessary to begin with a concrete relation between the I and the world (36), this world in which the I finds itself is already embedded in a world of language, thought, society, perceptions, horizons, and so on (139–40). The social relation is effected before the existent who expresses himself in it (109). In *Totality and Infinity* the equivalent or analog to the universality in Marx's species-being is to be found in the freedom gained through the power of representation in thematizing cognition. Although the power of representation is necessary for action and labor, thematizing cognition is itself dependent; it leads back, according to Levinas, to the relation with the Other (89). The relation of the human-to-itself will thus depend on the human-to-human, conceived outside or beyond the processes of objectification, which it precedes.

For Levinas, the concrete relation between the I and a world is essentially always also one of enjoyment, and is therefore sensual in a way that frees sensuality, "the very pulsation of the I" from its subordination to thematizing cognition (*TI* 113). Intentionality itself is different in enjoyment, in comparison with representation (127). Both Marx and Levinas conceive sensual existence as "active," but "living from" is not referred back to to a system of inferential-practical relations (130) and has no relation to mastery (123). One of the things that essentially differentiates enjoyment from need is that enjoyment is a refusal of distance, whereas need and its satisfaction always involves a distance between the human and the world upon which it depends (116).

At the level of enjoyment in the sensuous, the subject is radically separate from others. This is certainly an instance of egoism, although innocent; but it is also a separation that is absolute, such that a number of such egoisms cannot be related to each other through any exchange of equivalencies; among them, there is no possibility of a neutral third term. Interiority as a function of enjoyment, utterly unlike interiority as a will or a reason conceived as spontaneous, although dependent on the world it lives from, is therefore also beyond all forms of totalization. Sensuous enjoyment is not to be conflated or confused with need, nor can it be inserted into the possibility of what Hegel calls the system of needs. This absolute separation and interiority only transcends its own egoism in what Levinas calls

Desire. But the separation in sensuous enjoyment is also, by itself, abstract. And concrete subjectivity is considerably, intricately more complex.

For Levinas, need is something essential to concrete subjectivity, even though the latter, individually or socially, is not exhausted simply in its responsiveness to need. Need is discovered in the possible perfidiousness of the elemental, which is itself *not* an object but "content without form" (*TI* 131); and, if need is to be overcome in labor, this will presuppose the achievement of distance, both of the subject from itself and from what it must, if it is to engage in labor (and, by extension, exchange), constitute as a world of objects. In other words, labor presupposes the possibility of representation (150). If Marx and Levinas differ (without yet or necessarily "diverging"), it is not only through the different ways in which sensuousness appears on the scene, but also in that Marx, a good Hegelian in this respect, will assume that the power of representation is simply "there." By begging the question of the power of representation and undialectically taking it as an ontological given, Marx will also tend toward reducing the human-to-human relation to the relation of the human-to-itself.

The question, then, would be about how it is that the distance of the human from itself might appear on the scene? Is such a distance further reducible in a phenomenology of the social relation? What type or degree of distance might be required in order to make representation, hence labor, hence works and the whole miserable story of human history possible? Broadly speaking, Levinas has a twofold response to these questions, both of which place the social relation, the human-to-human relation prior to the presumed anteriority of thematizing cognition. One aspect of the human-to-human preceding representation has to do with the prior reception of the human into an already human habitation—the dwelling; the other aspect has to do with the moral summons of the other. Both are at once ethical and social. Only both together—the dwelling and the moral summons of the face—would be sufficient to elicit the power of the subject of representation *together with* its limitation and transubstantiation in Desire.

The interruption of enjoyment by need is, according to Levinas, not a sufficient basis for representation. Thus "dwelling," properly so called, is not yet situated in an objective world, but is its precondition (*TI* 153). The objects of objectification are themselves predicated on the possibility of a recollection that suspends the immediacy of the reactions that the world of enjoyment and need solicits, allowing a greater attention (154), a narrowing and reiteration, as it were, in the field of intentionality that enables the disclosure of a world with objects. The element, "fixed" and "calmed" within the space of the home, appears there as a thing (158). Labor is impossible for a being with no dwelling (159). And the reception of the subject (to be) within a human habitation requires the presence, but presence in the form of a discrete absence, of the other human presenting itself as familiarity, intimacy, gentleness and affection (155). The distance of the subject, ambiguously a removal and a connection, grounds the possibility of a look that can dominate, the look of Gyges, who sees but is not seen in turn (156). But this distance of the subject from its objects in the look of Gyges is also not yet sufficient to fully establish the separation or distance required for representation (170) and therefore not yet sufficient for what Marx intends by the universality of a free being within the concept of species-being. It has gained distance from the object of labor, but not yet simultaneously a distance from itself.

▌▌▌▌▌

The simultaneous distance of the subject from an object and from itself—which even allows the subject to take itself and its relations as themselves objects—which gives it the new energy, says Levinas, to "swim upstream, against the current" (*TI* 169), is gained only in its interpellation by the face of the absolutely other. The subject needs a "new event…in order that I be able to free myself from the very possession that the Home establishes, in order that I be able to…represent,…refuse both enjoyment and possession I must know how to give what I possess. Only thus could I situate myself absolutely above my engagement in the non-I. But for this I must encounter the discrete face of the Other that calls me into question" (171). Whereas labor, in the final analysis for Levinas, cannot be called violence, because it applies to what is faceless (160), my exclusive possession, my "self-possession" as it were, can be. And this violence of mine can be called into question by the face of the Other, by the approach of a neighbor in speech, whose speaking to me is the direct language of the moral summons: thou shalt not murder. The subject in this new event "discovers itself as a violence, but thereby enters into a new dimension" (171).

The new dimension into which the subject enters is at once both the human-to-human relation and the relation of the human-to-itself sufficient to establish its universality and freedom. Representation, according to Levinas, gets its freedom from the relationship that is essentially moral. Thus, "Morality is not added to the pre-occupations of the I, so as to order them or have them judged; it calls in question, and puts at a distance from itself, the I itself. Representation began not in the presence of a thing exposed to my violence but empirically escaping my powers, but in my possibility of calling this violence into question, in a possibility produced by the commerce with infinity, by society" (*TI* 172). This "commerce with infinity, society" is hardly the commerce—or society—of the separated subjects in the exchange relation. The structure of speech in the face-to-face is an invitation to a relationship "incommensurate with a power exercised" (198), even when the power exercised is a (putative) exchange of equivalents. Rather than being an instrumental reciprocity in which the separation of the agents is effected and maintained through a mutual transfer of equivalents, in other words, already within the commodity form, the commerce with infinity is effectuated as my responsibility for the other who is not a "theoretical idea of another myself" (84), but whose "distance is inflected into height" (291), and who "counts for more than myself" (247).

In Levinas's phenomenology, sensuousness pertains to that subject throughout the levels of enjoyment, interiority and separation, need, labor, responsibility, eros, and fecundity. But, otherwise than with Marx, who also insists on the essentiality of sensuous life in the specifically human, sensuousness is not primarily modeled on the role it might play in the epistemic relation. Marx sees the activity of the senses as already a form of objectification and thus as a privative form of knowledge, a crude but essential grasp of the universal among the particulars. Levinas, on the other hand, understands sensuousness as refusal of distance, as attachment, to the point where, in pure enjoyment, there obtains the nonexistence of exteriority. At its most primordial level, then, my subjectivity is beyond any subject-object relation. It has a different intentionality than thematizing cognition. And because the Other is not an object but exteriority *par excellence,* my relation to the other as absolutely Other will be responsibility in the medium of Desire, a sensuous relation to exteriority that cannot be brought within the orbit of the Same, even as another, equal and equivalent Same.

Desire, *metaphysical* Desire, goodness, properly understood as a movement in the subject going beyond the Same, is not an intellectual achievement over and against sense. Being sense, Desire still refuses distance while pursuing infinite exteriority, that is, Desire desires. Its object—and it has an object because the subject is also representation as well as sensuousness—does not fulfill it, but deepens it." It becomes "nourished by its hunger," a "desire without satisfaction which precisely understands, the remoteness, the alterity, the exteriority of the other" (*TI* 34). Desire and representation occur together when the sensuousness of enjoyment is disrupted and the Other introduces an infinite distance between itself and the Same, and within the Same as well.

▍▍▍▍▍

By tracing back the human-to-itself to the human-to-human, Levinas supplies the grounds for a resolution of the all-but-unnoticed equivocation in Marx's founding conception of species-being. At the level of social ontology, Marx's notion of species-being can be nested inside Levinas's prioritization of the social relation, the human-to-human, over the power of objectification, the human-to-itself. But the reverse does not obtain. Marx would be unable to derive the human-to-human exclusively from the human-to-itself (mediated by objects). Despite his critique of crude communism, he does not articulate the philosophical resources needed to derive the human-to-human from the human as the universal being, except in the—shall we say it—bourgeois form of mutual recognition.

Here Marx would have nothing to lose, however, but a world to gain—a world in which a "human language" of appeal and response incommensurate with exchange finally and decisively trumps the alienation of the human-to-human relation, an alienation that perhaps returns too easily in the concept of socialism as cooperation in the control over the mode of production essentially for the sake of expanding the creative capacities of individuals. Desire is not a power alienated from the subject, or a self-abnegation, but an un-power. The social ontology of *Totality and Infinity* would push the Marxian critique of Hegelian idealism to the point where that critique categorically sheds all residues of idealist abstraction and intellectualism. Along with that divestment of Hegel there might ensue a reorientation and renewal of the socialist idea in which the realization of the social relation is conceived in terms of radical plurality rather than unity in association, in asymmetrical responsibility rather than mutual recognition, and in a development of individuality that does not lead back to the ontological priority of the individual.

It would be inaccurate to think of Levinas as having raised the ethical bar for critical materialism. Instead, in a materialistic way, he has shown how it must reconceive itself, if it is ever to be a true vehicle of social transformation and liberation. But the fact that Levinas's social ontology cannot be nested inside that of Marx in no way means that Levinas negates, trumps, or supersedes Marx. And the two cannot be simply added together, either. To bring them together, instead, means to take each of them in directions they themselves did not pursue. There is also a crucial ambiguity in Levinas that issues perhaps from his Rosenzweigian aversion to Hegelian history.

For Levinas as well as Marx, humanity has and must have a social history. Levinas insists that the works of labor suffer a primary alienation (*TI* 226–27), but he does not pursue the ways in which the historical forms of alienation that appear in various forms of social domination could be abolished. As a result, he cannot open up the possibility of fecundity taking the form of works, including works in the broadest sense — cultures, social and political institutions. For Marx also, as Marcuse pointed out, objectification is the precondition of alienation. According to Levinas, however, it is because there is "an abyss" between works and expression (229) that works come into the world detachable from the will; works, up to and including the exchange relation (which is itself a work), can and do thus mediate the exploitation of the other human. This is, he says, a "part of the eternal truth that materialism involves... that the human will can be laid hold of in its works" (228). As a result, wills can and do come to systematically oppose each other and, in the process, the human-to-human relation acquires a history that is an economic history, a history of unintended consequences — reified social structures enforcing alienation — that he recognizes opens an "unlimited field of investigation" for sociological theory (228). Yet Levinas also insists that the face-to-face relation is not enacted outside the world, but amounts to a certain form of economic life, that there is no human relation outside of economy (172). The gift is not a fine and exalted feeling, or a heroic act of self-abnegation in which the subject asserts its overcoming of need. The surpassing of inward existence is an offering to the Other of one's own being (183).

Levinas, although he goes back behind Hegel to a subject not conceived primordially as the subject-object relation, remains within the Hegelian problematic by not decisively separating alienation from objectification. Here he exhibits the obverse of

Marx's entanglement in the Hegelian totality. Such a separation in principle, and worked out in the theory of historical materialism as possible in practice, is arguably Marx's most important and fundamental departure from Hegel. But Levinas, not being an absolute idealist—far from it—does not simply conflate alienation and objectification. Sometimes Levinas appears to think that the difference between alienation and objectification does not amount to much. His turn toward eros and fecundity in the later sections of *Totality and Infinity,* as ways of recovering the freedom the subject loses in history, is the main indication of that; or he will seem to think that works come into the world already "destined" to take on the "anonymity of merchandise" (*TI* 226–27). But he also indicates that the will has possibilities beyond becoming the "servile soul" that will "not only sell its products but... sell itself" (229). For "in the possible betrayal that threatens it in the course of its very exercise, the will becomes aware of this betrayal and thereby keeps itself at a distance from it. Thus... it... escapes its own history, and renews itself" (231). The face-to-face or human-to-human relation thus cannot attain its full meaning or possibility without that which Marx puts at the center of human species-being, the human-to-itself, even if it might be second on the scene. So, in allowing clearly for the differentiation between alienation and objectification, Levinas's human would also having nothing to lose, but a world to renew.

FOUR

Emmanuel Levinas as a Philosopher of the Ordinary

Michael L. Morgan

CAVELL, LEVINAS, AND ORDINARY LIFE

From early in his career Stanley Cavell has sought to show how ordinary language and our ordinary, everyday lives ought to be the primary locus of philosophical interest and concern. In this regard he has drawn first and foremost on philosophical forerunners, preeminently Wittgenstein, Austin, and Heidegger.[1] Like those three, and others as well, Cavell has argued that the presuppositions of traditional philosophy—epistemology, metaphysics, ethics, and philosophy of language—direct attention away from the nuanced, complex, conflicted, and rich character of everyday experience in which the most significant human projects are carried out and in which we human beings come to understand ourselves and our relationships with others.[2] His writings and his philosophical examinations have focused, then, on how to diagnose traditional philosophical biases and distortions in order to treat them, to set us on the way of clarifying and enriching for ourselves our ordinary social and personal lives.

Cavell's project is about our ordinary lives, and it is also about philosophy. In his voluminous writings one finds a great deal of disclosure, clarification, and illumination; reading Cavell one can learn a good deal about our relationships with others and the implications of such relationships for self-understanding. At the same time, one can come to a very nontraditional or at least nonorthodox view about what philosophical thinking is, both by following his critique of it and by observing Cavell's own philosophy of the ordinary at work. It is in this sense that Cavell's philosophical inquiries are modernist; they are inquiries into the very nature of philosophy and what it means to philosophize, at the same time that they are examples of philosophy.[3]

In this essay, I will preliminarily show why I think Emmanuel Levinas should be understood as a philosopher of the ordinary in roughly this sense, that is, in the sense that Cavell, following Wittgenstein and Heidegger, is a philosopher of the ordinary. To be sure, Levinas and Cavell do not see eye to eye on everything, but on their attitudes toward the tradition of Western philosophy and their attentiveness to our ordinary lives as the primary locale for our ethical lives to be worked out, they do agree. I say this even though many readers of Levinas may find this proposal surprising and perhaps simply wrong. Especially in his early writings, *Totality and Infinity* preeminent among them, Levinas presents himself often as a critic of totality, of ideologies and institutions. He also presents himself as an opponent of traditional humanism or of the traditional primacy of the subject or self. On occasion he calls his philosophy a form of Platonism, and Platonism certainly seems to be antiempirical and hence a corrective and even a radical corrective to the distortions and deficiencies of the ordinary and the everyday. On the face of it, then, Levinas might seem to be a poor candidate for a philosopher of the ordinary and the everyday. However, a careful and deep reading of Levinas and especially

Totality and Infinity will show such a judgment to be false and itself a distortion.

In order to explore the way in which Levinas is a philosopher of the ordinary, I want to juxtapose Levinas specifically with Cavell's use of some claims that Peter Brooks, in his important book *The Melodramatic Imagination,* makes about melodrama. By considering Cavell on melodrama and the way in which it figures in his film criticism and his philosophical disclosure of the everyday, we can come to understand how Levinas might be said to have developed a melodramatic philosophy, a philosophical disclosure of the meaningfulness of our ordinary social lives that employs the tactics of the melodramatic imagination and exposes in that way the ethical character of our ordinary lives.

BROOKS ON MELODRAMA

Cavell cites Brooks primarily in the introductory chapter of his book on the "melodramas of the unknown woman," *Contesting Tears.*[4] The chapter introduces the themes, which his subsequent reading of four Hollywood films is intended to explore. These themes include the relationship between the comedies of remarriage and the melodramas of the unknown woman; the sense in which both concern that aspect of moral choice that involves the self being true to itself or what Cavell calls "moral perfectionism" or "Emersonian perfectionism"; the role of excess or exaggeration in melodrama; the way melodrama focuses on the ordinary while at the same time calling attention to the "moral occult," to use Brooks's expression; the figure of marriage as a metaphor for all human sociality; and the sense in which the protagonist of the Hollywood melodramas is "unknown." Several of these themes are involved in Cavell's reading of Brooks. Especially pertinent are the claim that melodrama seeks to expose a domain that accounts for the moral character of everyday life (Brooks's "moral occult"), and attention to the ordinary that carries with it the commitment to seeking in it forms of relationship in which one seeks to be true to oneself or to care for oneself.[5]

In the course of acknowledging his debt to Brooks's book, Cavell cites five passages from the beginning and the end of *The Melodramatic Imagination*.[6] Let me summarize the gist of these quotations by reorganizing passages from them and knitting them together to expose their central message. Melodrama, as Brooks characterizes it, focuses attention by means of exaggeration and excess on an "underlying Manichaeism" or "conflict between good and evil" that lies under "the surface of things." "The surface of reality" manifests and yet masks this "domain of spiritual values" that Brooks calls "the moral occult." Melodrama seeks to make us aware of this domain, "from which man feels himself cut off" and "yet he feels to have a real existence somewhere behind the façade of reality." Human existence, however, is in itself "secular," and hence "the moral occult...stands as an abyss or gulf whose depths must, cautiously and with risk, be founded." The moral occult, therefore, is not precisely or exactly a sacred or divine realm or a "metaphysical system." Rather it contains "the fragmentary and desacralized remnants of sacred myth." It is "the spiritual in a world voided of its traditional Sacred." Brooks calls these remains "a sort of *deus absconditus* which must be sought for, postulated, brought into man's existence through the play of the spiritualist imagination." Hence, melodrama is part of a movement to respond to the thirst for the sacred in a world where it has been lost, and its role is to call attention to the normativity of the ethical without drawing on that traditional notion of the sacred. Cavell summarizes these citations as Brooks's "idea of the mode of the melodramatic as a response to what I gather is understood as a historical event, the loss of conviction in a transcendent basis for the distinction between good and evil." Nonetheless, Cavell is cautious about how much of Brooks's account he can recover, "since [his remarks] seem to invoke so many of the modern fates or echoes of the, let's say, beyond" (*CT* 40–41).

Brooks's own comments elsewhere in *The Melodramatic Imagination* sharpen what he here seems to be saying about melodrama, the ordinary or surface of reality, and the moral occult that melodrama seeks to disclose. One of the heroes of Brooks's story about the melodramatic imagination is Balzac, and the first point he makes about him is that he puts pressure on the surface of reality to reveal what lies behind it. In Balzac, he says,

> We have in fact been witnesses to the creation of drama—an exciting, excessive, parabolic story—from the banal stuff of reality. States of being beyond the immediate context of the narrative, and in excess of it, have been brought to bear on it, to charge it with intenser significances. The narrative voice, with its grandiose questions and hypotheses, leads us in a movement through and beyond the surface of things to what lies behind, to the spiritual reality which is the true scene of the highly colored drama to be played out in the novel....The novel is constantly tensed to catch this essential drama, to go beyond the surface of the real to the truer, hidden reality, to open up the world of the spirit. (*MI* 2)

And what applies to things also applies, Brooks points out, to Balzac's treatment of human encounters and human relationships. There too the "façade of manners" is shown to "reveal the essential conflicts at work—moments of symbolic confrontation which fully articulate the terms of the drama" (*MI* 3). Balzac, that is, "push[es] *through* manners to deeper sources of being" and in so doing, as Brooks notes, melodrama shows no fear or hesitation about saying everything; "nothing is left unsaid" (4). And this is what gives rise to melodrama's inflated style, its level of hyperbole and exaggeration, its heightened expressivity. Hence, the Manicheism, the struggle between good and evil that works itself out below the surface of things and human encounters is expressed explicitly in the narrative. Brooks concludes that the "hidden relationships and masked personages and occult powers in Balzac" point to his "true subject [that] is hidden and masked. [It is] the site of his drama, the ontology of his true subject [that] is not easily established" and toward which his narrative only points and requires a special kind of reading to expose or disclose. It is at this point that Brooks introduces for this "site" the expression the moral occult. It designates the domain or landscape in which the struggle between good and evil takes place. He calls it a "domain of operative spiritual values which is both indicated within and masked by the surface of reality" and a "realm of meaning and value." It is a kind of moral ontology.[7]

Reflecting on Balzac, then, provides Brooks with some crucial elements of the melodramatic imagination: the attention to the everyday, the exaggerated accounts of what lies behind it, and the suggestion of a moral ontology that is what gives everyday life its meaning. The exaggeration is executed, he elaborates, by "using the things and gestures of the real world, of social life, as kinds of metaphors that refer us to the realm of spiritual reality and latent moral meanings. The key term here is "metaphor." Things and gestures, for Balzac and for someone like Henry James, perform acts of transportation; they "are made to release occult meanings, to transfer significance into another context" (*MI* 9). But the transporting of attention, the transference, is distinctive, for the domain to be disclosed is itself "ineffable." The metaphor points to what cannot be said, and it is here, as we recall from Cavell's quotation, that Brooks introduces the idea that the moral ontology in question is obscure; it is "the spiritual in a world voided of its traditional Sacred," a hidden God that requires reimagining in a new key, that somehow speaks to the secularity of a world in need of a surrogate for the divine.

Brooks turns to the world into which melodrama speaks and the world out of which it emerges. This will help us to understand the peculiar character of the moral ontology he takes melodrama to call to mind and its role. First, by recalling the roots of melodrama, Brooks notes that someone like Diderot already "proposes serious attention to the *drama* of the *ordinary*" and the "clarification of the cosmic moral sense of everyday gestures," and this attention to what is interesting and provocative about everyday life brings us "near the beginnings of a modern aesthetic in which Balzac and James fully participate: the effort to make the real and the ordinary and the private life interesting through heightened dramatic utterance and gesture that lay bare the true stakes" (*MI* 13–14). Brooks's point here is two-fold, that melodrama arises out of an interest in ordinary life and yet that its interest is to show what the "true stakes" of ordinary life really are. As he goes on to show, melodrama fully formed remains true to this commitment to everyday life and also to the intuition that what gives ordinary life its special character is something behind it or beyond it in some sense or other.

In the book's conclusion, Brooks returns to the contrast between the commitments and the hopes of melodrama and the resignation or even irony of deconstruction and naturalism. He compares Balzac and James with Flaubert, but what he says of Flaubert could have been said of Derrida. There is at least some hope in the former pair; they care about ordinary life but they refuse to see in it less than meets the eye. There is in ordinary life both suffering and the demand for reducing it. "Balzac and James remain convinced that the surface of the world... [harbors] indices pointing to hidden forces and truths." Flaubert, on the other hand, is "preoccupied with representation itself as a textual system." The effort to overcome the gap between signs and signification can be found in the former pair, but not in Flaubert. There is a difference here akin to that, say, between Levinas and Derrida, as we might put it. For Levinas there is something on which the everyday is grounded; for Derrida all there is is the everyday as a textual system. It is no wonder, Brooks argues, that melodrama is so much a feature of popular culture today; it offers us heightened theatricality, "heroic confrontation, purgation, purification, recognition" that show us "we do not live in a world completely drained of transcendence and significance." Rather "we live on the brink of the abyss, the domain of occult forces which...infuse an intenser meaning into the life we lead in everyday reality." Unlike tragedy, melodrama cannot offer reconciliation under the banner of a new Sacred mantle, as Brooks calls it, for as "a form for secularized times, it offers the nearest *approach* to sacred and cosmic values in a world where they no longer have any certain ontology or epistemology" (*MI* 205).

We might call this the "melodramatic predicament." Commentators from Nietzsche to Anscombe, MacIntyre, and beyond have drawn attention to this situation. Brooks is distinguished by his framing of the modern condition in terms that feature the literary expression of it. The literature he focuses on refuses to abandon everyday life to naturalism. It refuses to abandon the moral sensibility. Nor does it fall back into old, traditional truisms. It shows how inflation, hyperbole, and excess can be tooled to signal our moral needs while showing how corrupted they have become. These terms are worth appropriating. In a sense, Cavell does so. If the comedies of remarriage that he examines in *Pursuits of Happiness* portray a critical moment in the fragility of marriage and thus for ordinary human relationships, then the melodramas of the unknown woman are one response to that critical moment, a response in which marriage is rejected in favor of some kind of transcendent hope. In order to show *how* Cavell appropriates from Brooks, however, I need to say something about how he reads him, and this brings us back to the Introduction to *Contesting Tears*.

CAVELL ON BROOKS ON MELODRAMA

It is not easy to clarify how Cavell responds to Brooks. To begin, Cavell does agree with Brooks that the melodramatic mode contrasts sharply with deconstruction, which he takes to be hostile both to metaphysics and to the ordinary. Philosophy, as Cavell puts it, is in "chronic flight from the ordinary or everyday," and he associates such a flight with logical positivism as well. But, if I am right, the primary impulse to such flight we should associate with Platonism or Gnosticism. It is the denigration of the everyday world, the world of the senses, and taking refuge in a transcendent domain that is safe from the world's ambiguities, fragility, and instability. Cavell points to many figures or images for that flight, including paradigmatically Plato's cave, Rousseau's chains, Emerson's jail, and Nietzsche's crowd. And he takes it to be Wittgenstein's primary opponent in the *Philosophical Investigations*—"metaphysics as a kind of melodramatic answer [viz., a "superorder of superconcepts"] to a melodramatic discovery [viz., Descartes's "presentation of skepticism"]." Cavell takes Wittgenstein to see in metaphysics, philosophy, and skepticism—they are companions in the Platonic canon—the locus of excess or exaggeration, emptiness, and madness ("an inability to get our meaning across") and to point us to "understanding ourselves despite our inexpressiveness" by returning us to ordinary life (*CT* 39–40).

This is a moment when Cavell returns to Brooks. He cites the texts I have already discussed as evidence for Brooks's claims about melodrama and the attention to a "moral occult." He puts it this way:

> My philosophical placement of the melodramatic as the hyperbolic effort to recuperate or to call back a hyperbolic reliance on the familiarity or banality of the world bears relation—clear and perhaps not so clear—with Brooks's idea of the mode of the melodramatic as a response to what I gather is understood as a historical event, the loss of conviction in a transcendent basis for the distinction between good and evil. This loss has, on Brooks's account, led to an intuition of the "moral occult," a region or source of lost order the melodramatic attests to and is meant to reach. (*CT* 40–41)

Earlier, Cavell had basically called Platonism or metaphysics a melodramatic answer to skepticism, which is a melodramatic question, about the certainty of our knowledge of the world's existence (but could include a question about our knowledge of other minds as well). Presumably there is hyperbole in all this and in Wittgenstein's techniques for exposing all this hyperbole. Hence, in this summary, the hyperbole that is employed to call attention to Platonism and hence to recuperate the everyday is the good works of Wittgenstein's writing or what we might call "good philosophy" or, after Franz Rosenzweig, "new thinking."[8] Elsewhere Cavell speaks of it as modernist, after Michael Fried, and now we might call it "melodramatic philosophy."

Cavell's next move in this passage is to suggest—albeit tentatively ("clear and perhaps not so clear")—that this account of Wittgenstein and others as melodramatic recuperations of the ordinary "bears relation" to two claims that Brooks makes in the texts I discussed above. One is that melodrama in the nineteenth century is a response to the loss of commitment in God or the transcendent as a moral source, to use Charles Taylor's expression, that is, as a source of authority for moral values. I have always taken Kant's refutations of traditional natural theology and the arguments for God's existence and with them the rejection of a divine command theory of moral obligation, along with the reductionisms of Feuerbach, Marx, and later Freud, as the clearest intellectual indications of such a loss. The most famous literary expression of it is in fact quoted by Cavell a few short pages after this passage; it is Nietzsche's parable of the madman who cries out in the city square that God is dead. Brooks's second claim, as Cavell understands it, is that in some way the melodramatic response to this event is to acknowledge and seek to reach a kind of moral ontology, as I have called it, which expresses or underpins the "lost order."

Having associated himself with Brooks, however, Cavell does show some caution. After citing the several passages from *The Melodramatic Imagination,* he adds, referring to Brooks's claims about the mode of the melodramatic: "Valuable as these thoughts assuredly are, it is hard to take them up clearly since they seem to invoke so many of the modern fates or echoes of the, let's say, beyond" (*CT* 41). For all that is to be learned from Brooks, Cavell is worried—but about what?—about the lingering suspicion that Brooks's moral occult is too much like the lost transcendent. Brooks may be right that the proper focus of our attention, and of philosophy's attention, ought to be the everyday lives we live and that these lives do have moral character, an ethical cast to them. But the notion of a moral occult may itself be hyperbolic and excessive. Why think that there is a "façade of reality" and a "real existence of [ethical forces] behind or beyond" them? Is the response to the loss of transcendence to seek to recover what has been lost? And hence, why think that there is some event to which melodrama is the response, Cavell asks. Perhaps melodrama itself is the event and what is to be learned is to respond melodramatically to that melodramatic moment?

But what event? Cavell is suggesting that melodrama marks a moment that wonders whether the secularism of our human relationships, of our social lives together, can survive. That is, Brooks says that "the desire to express all seems a fundamental characteristic of the melodramatic mode." One way of reading this claim is that melodrama respects no limits to what it wants to say. But Cavell's point is that in response to the loss of a transcendent ground for our moral values, we are struck with the "terror of absolute inexpressiveness, which at the same time reveals itself as a terror of absolute expressiveness, unconditional exposure; they are the extreme states of voicelessness." Moreover, this crisis of expressiveness is also a way of characterizing solipsism and hence it is a "characterization of what has become of human exchange as such" (*CT* 43). Here is the moment when melodrama comes on the scene, with the fear of having lost all capacity to speak and yet a desire to say all. In a sense, the outcome of losing a transcendent ground might be to seek it personally but to find it only in a way beyond thought and language, which would make the moral occult a sort of hidden God, as Brooks puts it. Hyperbole points to silence. But this melodramatic moment may not be the end; it may prepare for another moment, when, Cavell asks us to suppose, "the secularity of remarriage comedy shows that its moral perfectionism really can survive, can retain itself within, the unknown woman melodrama and its Manichean, demonic lights" (45). What Cavell means is that the ordinary character of our interpersonal relationships may be sufficient to provide us with the means to find ourselves and to be true to ourselves, to live out the ethical character of our days in the wake of utter chaos and loss.

LEVINAS, ETHICS, AND THE ORDINARY

I want to treat this engagement between Cavell and Brooks as the vehicle for returning to the focus on the ordinary in Levinas, but first, let me summarize the point of the conversation. Can we isolate what Cavell and Brooks share and where they differ? Surely there are subtleties, but we can risk ignoring many of them and focus on the following issues. First, for both, melodrama's characteristic features tell us something about our world and our lives, as well as something about literary and intellectual figures and styles. Second, melodrama involves an exaggerated or excessive treatment of ordinary life and in particular ordinary social relationships and interactions. Third, melodrama is about the moral character of everyday life; it reflects something important about that moral character; it reveals what is persistent and valuable about our interaction with one another, what is necessary for it, and what is crucial for its current career. Finally, both Cavell and Brooks care about the once-generally-accepted commitment to a transcendent ground or source for the moral order that characterizes our everyday lives. But it is here, most of all, where the two diverge. There is a lingering sense one might have, reading Brooks, that melodrama is pointing to a replacement for the ground that has been lost and that it hence has a tendency toward the behind or beyond, toward the transcendent, in order to locate that ground, to secure the moral order, to remain convinced that the order is still in place. The expression Brooks uses, the moral occult, suggests something along these lines. Cavell, on the other hand, takes the secularism of our ordinary human exchanges and relationships to be confirmed and accepts the fact that the rejection of these relationships is not final. Something about these relationships, the way they are lived, negotiated, recuperated, endured, and cultivated enables us to find ourselves within them, and this occurs without any return to the old thinking and to the old securities, anchors, grounds, or indeed to anything akin to them.

The very first, famous line of *Totality and Infinity* signals how central these themes of the engagement between Cavell and Brooks were for Levinas: "Everyone will readily agree that it is of the highest importance to know whether we are not duped by morality" (*TI* 21). "Everyone" includes all of us in our everyday lives, and "duped" means fooled. Are we in our daily lives somehow being tricked into taking morality seriously, taking it to be preeminent and primary? Levinas seems to be speaking within a world shaped in part by a crisis about morality that is marked by Nietzsche's criticisms of it and also by the ways in which political power has shown itself to be capable of horrific acts that take advantage of how human beings can be manipulated and immobilized. After Marx, Nietzsche, and Freud, we ought to be suspicious about what is being demanded of us by traditional authorities and elites and what we are told rationality and true freedom require of us. It may be that morality is a trick, a scam, a "noble lie." At least one way of looking at Levinas's great early work is to see it as an attempt to show how our ordinary lives, which must be subject to categorical articulation, to organization by institutions and practices, and to conceptual schemes or frameworks, are nonetheless always grounded in the ethical character of our very existence. Hence, ethics or morality is not bogus; it is no device for manipulating or cheating us. It is deeply ingrained in our social existence itself. But if so, it is not ingrained in something deeper. If Levinas is concerned to redeem the ordinary, it is without a return to a traditional transcendent. But the ground of the ethical is nonetheless transcendent in a sense. What we need to understand is this joint attention to everyday life and to its transcendently grounded ethical character.

Totality and Infinity is a large, complex book, but its structure is simple. First, it explores how human existence involves the self situated in the world; Levinas calls this economy: "It is necessary to begin with the concrete relationship between an I and a world.... [T]he true and primordial relation between them, and that in which the I is revealed precisely as pre-eminently the same, is produced as a *sojourn* in the world. The *way* of the I against the 'other' of the world consists in *sojourning,* in *identifying oneself* by existing here *at home with oneself*" (*TI* 37; cf. 109–83). Second, it shows how within that situated existence, each subject is related to that which is absolutely other than it, other persons. Levinas calls this relationship the encounter with the face of the other; he also calls it "conversation," "goodness," and "Desire" (38–52). That social relationship is the locus of the ethical; the other puts the subject into question, makes demands of it, and yet does so from a position of vulnerability or weakness, nudity or nakedness, what we might call "need."[9] Levinas writes, "The transcendence of the Other, which is his eminence, his height, his lordship, in its concrete meaning includes his destitution, his exile, and his rights as a stranger" (76–77). This is the point where goodness enters human existence, alongside our natural appropriation and enjoyment of the world, which nourishes and sustains us.

In a sense, then, Levinas's account places social existence within worldly, situated existence. He "describe[s], within the unfolding of terrestrial existence, of economic existence, a relationship with the other that does not result in a divine or human totality.... Such a relationship is metaphysics itself" (*TI* 52). This bond, which is shown to exist between the self and the other person, that does not form a totality but rather an ethical bond, is also called "religion" (40). Levinas then goes on to show how ethics is fundamentally determinative of that existence; ethics precedes ontology. The ethical claims on us are always already present at each and every moment of our lives, and such claims do not derive from anything more fundamental or basic than they are.

This "primary sociality" that brings the ethical to our situated existence is not a form of worldly solitude to be sought outside of human arrangements, society, and the state.[10] Ethics is not an aspiration for isolated moments of unique, human intimacy. Rather it is what motivates and orients all of our lives. It is the way the subject has access to universality; the way to universality is through plurality, so to speak. Or, alternatively, totality and infinity are two sides of ordinary social existence, what Cavell calls our human arrangements or marriage and what opposes them. For Levinas, we are never alone in a fundamental sense. From the particular point of view of our situated existence, each of us is related to the very being of each and every other person. That fundamental relatedness is what Levinas calls the "face" of the other person; it is the other's separateness from us that is also her relatedness to us. It is one mode of utter difference or alterity; Levinas also calls it the "infinite" or the "transcendent." Recognizing that there are others to whom we are related and yet who are utterly different from us indicates that all of our experience is not shaped and homogenized by ourselves, by our concepts, principles, frameworks, and more. Much of our world, embedded in it as we are, is subject to our framings, but there is something—the face of the other person as our way of understanding its relatedness to us—that is a rupture in our conceptual space, as it were, a presence from the outside or a transcendent that engages us. Other persons are not the only such different beings, but they are the primary ones.

Levinas characterizes our engagement or encounter with the brute being of other persons as a kind of reception or passivity. But it is not the passivity of sensory perception, of receiving a visual or tactile impact. It is the passivity of the mother whose infant child depends utterly upon her and hence makes a claim on her attention, her love, her care, her time, and her energy. Hence, this passivity is ethical in character. Levinas uses various terms to clarify, explore, and elaborate this passive relationship, a relationship that is deeper and more determinative than every ordinary relationship, whether active or passive. But the terms are not systematic. They are terms like "Desire" and "goodness," "revelation" and "epiphany," "glorious humility," "responsibility," and "sacrifice."[11] They are terms often associated in ordinary discourse with religion and the sacred, drawn from biblical vocabulary and motifs, and yet by Levinas they are associated in their most original sense with the face-to-face encounter of a subject with a particular other person and hence with the dependence and majesty or authority of that other person who calls me into question, appeals to me for acceptance and more, and commands my acknowledgment.

As we saw earlier, Cavell seems to agree with Brooks that the melodramatic imagination exaggerates its everyday dialogue and descriptions in order to expose something that has been in decline or been occluded, but Brooks gives the impression that this lost character of the ethical involves a recovery of something beyond or behind. Cavell, however, takes the ethical resonance of ordinary engagements and arrangements to lie solely within them as opportunities for each of us to find ourselves and to be true to ourselves. If we look carefully in *Totality and Infinity*, we shall, I think, discover Levinas attending to this same tension, between transcendence and the everyday, and finding in his grasp of the face-to-face as the locus of the ethical in our everyday lives a complexity and depth that does not lose its grip of either. He puts it this way: "To reach the Other through the social is to reach him through the religious" (*TI* 68). What exactly does Levinas mean by this unity of the social and the religious?

If the face-to-face is that dimension of all particular interpersonal relations in terms of which ordinary life takes on its meaning, that is, its ethical character and aspiration to justice, and if the other person, as an absolute Other, is transcendent, the infinite, then does it not follow that the other person is divine, is indeed God? Levinas, in a section entitled "The Metaphysical and the Human," poses and responds to just this question, and he denies its conclusion. There is, to be sure, a relationship between ordinary discourse about God and the divine, on the one hand, and the fact of sociality, on the other.

To begin, we must realize that the primary relationship with transcendence in our lives is ethical and not epistemic: "to hear the divine word does not amount to knowing an object." The transcendent is not the God of myths and theology. The face-to-face, "the idea of infinity" or "the metaphysical relation is the dawn of a humanity without myths" (*TI* 77). Levinas continues, "our relation with the Metaphysical is an ethical behavior and not theology, not a thematization, be it a knowledge by analogy, of the attributes of God" (78). As we have seen, for Levinas, the relation of the subject with the transcendent is a structural feature of all interpersonal encounters or engagements—an "irreducible structure upon which all other structures rest" (79). The transcendent is not the object of mystical experience or a kind of intellectual intuition. It is the absolute otherness of the other person with whom I speak, to whom I relate. Hence, Levinas will say that "to posit the transcendent as stranger and poor one is to prohibit the metaphysical relation with God from being accomplished in the ignorance of men and things" and "the dimension of the divine opens forth from the human face." Everyday and even theological expressions of our relationship with God, that is, express our responsiveness to the other person's vulnerability and need. The meaning of an expression such as "God reveals his will to us" rests on its being an expression for our awareness of what others demand and need from us: "the Transcendent, infinitely other, solicits and appeals to us. The proximity of the Other, the proximity of the neighbor, is in being an ineluctable moment of the revelation of an absolute presence, which expresses itself" (78). Levinas's elliptical expression for this situation is that God is accessible only in justice: "Ethics is the spiritual optics" (78; cf. 23).[12]

Hence, "there can be no 'knowledge' of God separated from relations with persons. The Other [person] is the very locus of metaphysical truth, and is indispensable for my relation with God" (*TI* 78). Furthermore, one should not be confused into thinking that somehow the other person is the bridge between the divine and the human; the other person is no "mediator."

Nor is the other person the "incarnation" of God. Rather the other person "precisely by his face... is the manifestation of the height in which God is revealed" (79). That is, the other person is not divine or God; she or he is not the incarnation of God or the mediator between individuals and God. God is manifest in the height, that is, the normative authority, of the face of the other person. But even this use of the word "God" and its claim about God are metaphorical; the word "God" and discourse about God express, at the everyday level, what at the structural level is experienced as the normative necessity of the other person's relation to me. The other person's vulnerability and nakedness define the needs the other has of me, and it motivates me; the other person's height or authority makes a claim upon me to acknowledge those needs and to satisfy them.[13] The priority and force of such claims enter into ordinary life as ethics, morality, and such; positive religions, their mythology and practices, are one way in which the seriousness of such claims and needs are expressed in our lives and are acknowledged publicly, ritualized, revered, and elevated.

Levinas's vocabulary, his rhetorical elevation, the extremity and drama of his authorship, all seek to call attention to the sociality of our lives as the locale in which we realize our subjectivity and the demands placed upon it. He admitted regularly that he was enamored of hyperbole and exaggeration, and in this regard one might read him as Cavell reads Wittgenstein and the Hollywood cinema he called the "melodramas of the unknown woman." Unlike Brooks, Levinas is careful to explain how ordinary life does not point to a moral occult in any traditional sense. But unlike Cavell, he does believe that ordinary experience reveals a structure common to all human existence that is implicated in the moral character of our lives, determinative and orienting. He calls it transcendent, but he distinguishes it from traditional conceptions of the divine and the theological discourse that is regularly invoked in everyday life. Levinas does not shy away from the use of traditional vocabulary—terms such as "prophetic eschatology," "revelation," "epiphany," "religion," and later "prophecy," "holiness" and "glory." In his nonphilosophical writings, he uses the word "God" regularly and the biblical or rabbinic discourse in which it is employed. But the meaning of such expressions applies only metaphorically to the face-to-face; they are carried over from the ordinary domain and theological discourse in order to illuminate what the ethical and the religious share, even while they are marked by the subtleties of their application.

TOTALITY AND INFINITY: SOCIAL-ETHICAL EXISTENCE

I have been trying to show how Levinas might be thought to engage in a melodramatic philosophical exploration of our everyday lives in order to expose the ethical character of our interpersonal conduct and relationships. The terms I have employed to frame his endeavor are taken from Richard Brooks's account of the melodramatic imagination and Stanley Cavell's appropriation of it and engagement with it. On the one hand, to have engaged in such an inquiry, Levinas must be concerned to illuminate what our ordinary lives are about and what it means to redeem those lives; on the other hand, to have been engaged in such a project along the lines of Cavell's reading of Brooks requires Levinas to disclose as the "ineluctable structure" of everyday life a transcendence that is not a recovery of a traditional notion of the sacred or divine. I have tried to show that this is precisely what he does or takes himself to be doing. But is it so clear that Levinas has a primary interest in ordinary, everyday life? Is Levinas a philosopher of the ordinary or a philosopher opposed to the ordinary? Is his critique of totality and totalization not a form of Platonism or Gnosticism? Is he not recommending the rejection or disposal of the everyday in favor of something else, something that ruptures the everyday and is radical, or, as he calls it, "anarchic"?

It is a mistake to read Levinas as criticizing all conceptual schemes or institutional frameworks. To be sure, there are times when Levinas appears to be engaging in such a wholesale rejection, but this is hyperbole and must be read in context. He writes in the preface to *Totality and Infinity*, that the face-to-face, when understood as our aspiration for "messianic peace," is not purely negative. It may be that this "eschatological vision breaks with the totality of wars and empires," and it "does not envisage the end of history within being understood as a totality, but institutes a relation with the infinity of being which exceeds the totality." It is a "breach of totality." Still, this encounter with exteriority, with the face, what is "beyond" everyday, objective experience "is reflected *within* the totality and history, *within* experience" (*TI* 23). The face-to-face is a structural relation between particular persons that occurs within everyday life; it is an aspect of each and every interpersonal relationship. Moreover, it calls each of us to "full responsibility" and gives history and our lives the meaning they have. And that meaning is not found in an escape from the world, from everyday life; rather it is realized within it. But if so, what is the relationship between totality and infinity, between the world and our lives, on the hand, and the fact of sociality, on the other?

In *Totality and Infinity* Levinas refers to this relationship more than once as one of conditionality or presupposition. That is, the face-to-face is a "situation that conditions the totality itself," and the philosophical method that exposes it or brings it to our attention is "phenomenological" and "transcendental" (*TI* 25, 28–29). Hence, Levinas's philosophical method is intellectual and rational, but its object is to reveal the fundamentally social character of all human existence, and that social character is normative. It motivates and obligates and hence directs human conduct toward acts of acceptance, assistance, humanity, and such. He writes, "The relationship with the Other...commands...the comprehension of Being in general. I cannot disentangle myself from society with the Other, even when I consider the Being of the existent he is." The relationship with the other person as interlocutor, the face-to-face, is the "ultimate relation in Being. Ontology presupposes metaphysics" (47–48).[14] It "presupposes" the reality of the ethical as a structural and coordinate dimension.

It works this way: I may notice that you are taller than I am, have brown hair, are smiling, and are sitting with your legs crossed, and my observations and my attentive posture treat you as an object to be noticed and described, at least in my inner sense. Nonetheless, at the same time, and unavoidably, your presence in relation to me appeals me to acknowledge you, to notice you, and perhaps to do more—to say hello, to extend a greeting, to offer a ride, to arrange lunch together, and more. All of this, the ordinary life of our interpersonal being and the normative claims you make upon me and I upon you, occurs together, at once. It is one event with many aspects, one of which, Levinas wants us to take seriously, is normative, burdensome, obligating, petitionary, and thereby determinative or what he calls "primordial."

Furthermore, the normative character of the face-to-face, its call to responsibility, brings with it a critical role. Everyday life with its conduct, social institutions, and political arrangements is subject to critique precisely insofar as it realizes or fails to realize, to varying degrees, the claims of responsibility that bear on it. Levinas writes, "The relationship with the Other is not produced outside of the world, but puts in question the world possessed" (*TI* 173). That is, the subject is put in question because the other person depends upon the subject for acknowledgement and aid; the other person needs me, most radically not to kill her, which means to share the world with her, a world that nourishes me and I enjoy. The other person needs my attention, my help, and my stuff. Or, as Levinas puts it, sociality means that the "center of gravity" of my life is the other person's being. My responsibility is always an already-obligated. Hence, "the surpassing of phenomenal or inward existence does not consist in receiving the recognition from the Other, but in offering him one's being. To be oneself is to express oneself, that is, already to serve the Other. The ground

of expression is Goodness. To be *kath' auto* is to be good"
(183). To be oneself is to respond to the other person who
needs me, calls out to me, depends upon me.

Hence, the face-to-face is a kind of internal, social standard for my being just and hence for my being true to myself.
In a subsection of part one of *Totality and Infinity,* entitled
"Metaphysics Precedes Ontology," Levinas describes how theory or knowledge in its most comprehensive sense, ontology,
"reduces the other to the same" and "promotes freedom" by
not allowing the other to alienate the self. That is, ontology
promotes freedom by taking the other to be assimilated to the
same, to the self, by means of ideas or reason or form or matter
or whatever. "Western philosophy," Levinas says, "has most
often been an ontology: a reduction of the other to the same
by interposition of a middle and neutral term that ensures the
comprehension of being." But ontology is not only comprehensive; it is also critical. Although ontology is dogmatic and
a form of imperialism, it is also critical of itself, of its "dogmatism" and the "naïve arbitrariness of its spontaneity." It "calls
into question the freedom of the exercise of ontology." That
is, it turns back on itself and criticizes its own expansive and
arbitrary freedom. But there is a risk here of an infinite regress,
of ontology reasserting its dogmatic comprehensiveness each
time it recoils in critique, unless a form of critique emerges that
points beyond ontology altogether, to a recognition of an other
that could not be comprehended. In Levinas's words, here is a
form of critique in which "a calling into question of the same
[viz. the self or subject]—which cannot occur within the egoist spontaneity of the same—is brought about by the other
[person]. We name this calling into question of my spontaneity
by the presence of the Other ethics.... Metaphysics, transcendence, the welcoming of the other by the same, of the Other
by me, is concretely produced as the calling into question of
the same by the other, that is, as the ethics that accomplishes
the critical essence of knowledge" (*TI* 43). Critical reflection
about who we are, how we act, how we arrange our lives, the

institutions we organize, and the roles we play—all this, to avoid regress, must be grounded in what lies outside our everyday lives and yet at the same time what is presupposed by them as a normative, ethical directiveness. This normativity is an irreducible feature of our social relationships, in all their concrete reality. The critical role of the face-to-face, then, shows that for Levinas, the burden of its normative force applies to how we live in everyday life.

CONCLUSION

Writing about Ibsen in a book that is indebted to Cavell's reading of Ibsen, Toril Moi has argued that Ibsen should be understood not as a representational realist but rather as a modernist attentive to the primacy of ordinary life for our understanding of the project of self-enrichment. Moi argues that Ibsen and many nineteenth century authors wrote in a context shaped by idealism in literature and philosophy, and she distinguishes different ways in which various forms of realism might have responded to that idealism. At one point, Moi clarifies these different forms of realism in terms of how an author might treat the ordinary, and she uses Balzac and Flaubert as examples alongside Ibsen. She is much less generous to Balzac than is Brooks, but nonetheless her classification helps us to clarify three ways a realist might approach the ordinary, everyday world:

> Balzac is highly critical of the ordinary, which he tends to exaggerate, make grotesque, and infuse with melodrama. Flaubert, on the other hand, finds the ordinary indescribably dull, a place where no values, no thrills, no excitement can possibly be found. Ibsen, for his part, turns to the ordinary and the everyday, not as something that has to be overcome, exaggerated, or idealized, but as a sphere where we have to take on the task of building meaningful human relationships. If we fail at this task, the everyday becomes unbearable; if we succeed, it becomes a source of human values.[15]

For Moi, if idealism dispenses with the ordinary altogether, Balzac and Flaubert represent attentiveness to it that finds little of value in it. Ibsen is another story. Moi's book makes a very compelling case for this thesis about Ibsen's realism of the ordinary, the view that everyday life is the domain in which we work out human relationships that become a source for human values and also, that becomes the venue in which we come to understand and express ourselves in varied and enriched ways. Cavell reads Shakespeare this way; he interprets various classic Hollywood films similarly; and he reads a host of other authors and philosophers in this light.[16]

As I have pointed out, however, he does not take melodrama's treatment of the everyday to be utterly dismissive; nor does he treat Balzac that way. My contention is that Levinas too takes our ordinary, everyday lives to be a "sphere where we have to take on the task of building meaningful human relationships," but I would then say that his judgment is that if we do succeed, then our lives will express the values that make our lives human — responsibility, concern, justice, and freedom. In this sense, Levinas respects the everyday but locates within it and beyond it a standard of relationship and responsibility that it regularly fails to meet. Levinas stands somewhere between Cavell's reluctance to recover such a standard (a mode of transcendence) and Brooks's tendency to identify it (his moral occult,) with an old beyond.[17] For Levinas, our ordinary lives are the settings for interpersonal relationships, human conduct, and arrangements in which the fundamentally ethical character of our lives is worked out, manifest, occluded, and expressed. It is the venue of ethical realization, and in this sense it is the locale for our self-fulfillment insofar as we achieve it. It is not exactly Cavell's self-fulfillment—his being true to oneself or care of the self, which as in Brooks is about autonomy and authenticity, but it is a kind of subjectivity, albeit one grounded in the claim of the other, our ethical sociality. If there is something Platonic about Levinas, it does not register in the dismissal or transcendence of the everyday but rather in its redemption.

Levinas, then, cultivates in his own way a form of the "melodramatic imagination." He uses hyperbole and exaggeration to point beyond the prosaic in order to call attention to something fundamental about it. He uses metaphor as a device to carry our intellectual imagination and our understanding beyond our often self-interested and egoistic concerns to appreciate what is fundamental and determinative about our lives with others. In a way even more dramatic and serious than Cavell, he takes our interpersonal relationships to be the venue in which our selfhood is worked out, for he claims that social existence itself is what makes us responsive to others, accountable to them, and obligates us to acknowledge and to aid them. All of this places Levinas as a philosopher who has a commitment to our ordinary lives as the locale within which our social and ethical lives are conducted and can better be served by our concern for others. Moreover, Levinas follows Husserl, Heidegger, and Rosenzweig in taking philosophy to be the articulation of what it is for a human being to exist in the world, an articulation conducted from the situated agent's point of view as a participant in life and not as an observer of it. It is this kind of philosophical thinking that can under certain conditions clarify what it is to live in the world.

But if human existence is ethical through and through, then in what sense is philosophical inquiry, even when properly conducted, an ethical act? Is philosophy a way of seeing more clearly what is often occluded or obscured by traditional philosophy and other modes of experience, or is it that and more? Is it also an act of responding to and helping others? In *Totality and Infinity* even the fraternal community that brings us together is a network of particular relations, each of which is ethical. Each is a dialectic of claim and response, of a petitionary and command face and a reaching-out that responds to it. Hence, even philosophical thinking occurs as a network of dialogical encounters with others. In later writings—in particular in an essay on the Holocaust, entitled "Useless Suffering"—Levinas goes beyond such a general point. He indicates that the extremity of horrors and atrocities in our day have brought us to a time we might call the "end of theodicy." At least part of what this expression means is that we live at a time when we ought to realize that the time for taking refuge in thinking, in explanations and theories, is past; we ought to respond to suffering not by thinking more about it but rather by acting to reduce it. That is, the horrors of the twentieth century ought to mark the end of our dependence upon and the temptations of theodicy, of explanatory theorizing. But more to the point, we ought to realize that even when we do turn to thinking, our thinking is itself a response to all those others who need our help and our support. At a time when the needs of others confront us powerfully and urgently, the real end or function of theodicy, of thinking, shows itself as a mode of acknowledgment, education, and more. If this is so, then there is a sense in which Levinas himself has understood something about philosophical thinking in our day, that the greater awareness it yields is also an ethical act. In this respect, one might say that Levinas's philosophy is both melodramatic and ethical. It constitutes not only a contribution to a philosophy of the ordinary; it is also a philosophical reflection about a philosophy of the ordinary.

FIVE

The Fundamental Idea of Emmanuel Levinas's Philosophy

Georg W. Bertram
Translated by Diane Perpich and Nathan Ross

According to a standard way of thinking, philosophy is occupied with a diverse set of questions. It deals with questions of knowledge, action, art, and still others. For the most part, philosophers understand their task in such a way that their purpose is to answer these questions — one after the other, more or less. And it is rare for philosophy not to start from one or another of these questions. That this is so can be found in philosophy's being concerned with the unfolding of an idea. Philosophers who are concerned with an idea in this sense frequently write works that are hard to distinguish from one another. Their project is ongoing; it is the unfolding of their idea. They modify, correct, and often bring a single thought, in ever new forms, to expression. Their works read like layered and interlinear versions of a single text. The philosophy of Emmanuel Levinas is of just this type. His essays as well as his main works, *Totality and Infinity* (1961) and *Otherwise than Being* (1974), stand before the reader as a series of variations on a single problem: how is alterity, the otherness of the other, to be thought?[1]

The peculiar construction of Levinas's thought is one of the reasons for the fascination it exercises on the reader, but also one of the reasons for its inaccessibility. It is crucial that interpretations be made that put Levinas's fundamental idea in connection with other philosophical questions. Most interpretations of Levinas's philosophy commit themselves to the slogan "ethics as first philosophy" (see *TI* 304). They take up the idea that access to the other is of a fundamentally ethical nature. An autonomous individual submits to a demand from the other. This demand is understood to be something that cannot be anticipated or comprehended. The other is thus presented as an entity that continually withdraws itself. Levinas makes clear how much effort and attention of thought is needed to think this. Such a reception of Levinas's philosophy assigns it to a specific area of philosophy: to practical philosophy, that is, to philosophical reflections on ethics and morality.

In general, one can distinguish two different ways in which Levinas's idea has been taken up as a perspective within practical philosophy: on the one hand, it has been understood as the *completion* of ethical thought and, on the other hand, as the *founding* of ethical thought. Someone who completes practical philosophy by way of Levinas considers the experience of an absolutely irreducible other as a relevant part of a picture that otherwise consists of different experiences and concepts.[2] Someone who founds all ethical thinking on this experience considers it the original scene of the ethical.[3] In the one case, the other is viewed as an extraordinary object, in the other case, as a challenge to construct a practical philosophy. No matter which side one takes, the reception is guided by the phrase "ethics as first philosophy."

In my view, these ways of reading Levinas miss a certain radicality in his thinking. The radicality lies in calling for a fundamental expansion of philosophy's perspective. Levinas formulated this

expansion in terms of the conceptual alternative between totality and infinity. He begins from the fact that in most philosophies concepts of totality predominate. Concepts of infinity,
however, are not available. In what follows, my concern is not
to figure out whether Levinas's diagnosis is on the mark or not.
I am much more concerned with the expansion of philosophy
Levinas claims by means of the concept of infinity. My thesis is that Levinas is concerned with the intersubjective bonds
that irreducibly determine our entire way of being in the world.
He correspondingly claims that these bonds cannot be reconstructed with the concepts through which we grasp the rest of
our dealings with the world. For this, we require concepts of
infinity rather than concepts of totality.

In my view, there is far too much consensus around the idea
that Levinas's philosophy is rightly classified in the realm of
ethics.[4] If there is a rubric that makes sense for this philosophy
at all, it is that of the theory of normativity.[5] Levinas explicates
what it means to be bound—a being-bound that plays a role
just as much in the moral orientation to action, for example,
as in the use of words. Levinas begins from the notion that in
our dealings with the world, we do not arrive at the concepts
we need if we want to grasp our essential being-bound. In his
view, this requires concepts of alterity. Only with these concepts can we gain an understanding of normativity. Such an
understanding of normativity concerns all domains of practical
and theoretical philosophy to the same extent. The ambition of
Levinas's philosophy is thus far reaching.

The following remarks will sound out the fundamental idea
of Levinas's philosophy along the lines of the foregoing sketch.
It will be a matter of clarifying why Levinas came to speak of
questions of normativity; in what, for him, the particularity of
normative relationships are grounded; and which special features his explication of normativity exhibits. I will go about
this task in a manner that is more programmatic than encyclo-
pedic. In the first part, I start out from Husserl's concept of
intentionality, in order, in the second part, to comprehend why

alterity according to Levinas cannot be grasped in a Husserlian framework. The third part goes one step further again to demonstrate that with the concept of alterity a certain homogenous conception of consciousness is foreclosed. In light of this foreclosure, it becomes clear that an explication of normativity is won through the concept of alterity. I will extend this explication in the fourth part by asking how normative relations are to be understood according to Levinas. I will close my considerations with some further perspectives.

Consciousness as Fulfilled Correlation

Levinas gives shape to his concept of alterity above all through a confrontation with Edmund Husserl's phenomenology. He begins from the conception of consciousness as intentionality, whose incarnation can be found in Husserl's *Ideas* at the latest. Levinas's critique of this conception sounds very simple at first: Husserl is criticized for the fact that his understanding of consciousness does not include all kinds of consciousness. The consciousness that has otherness (others, not something other) as its object, eludes this Husserlian understanding, according to Levinas. He speaks about the fact that a completely different form of consciousness develops in this case, which he calls among other things "moral consciousness."[6]

The specificity of this form of consciousness, which Levinas writes about in ever new ways, is best explained in contrast to Husserl's concept of consciousness. The latter is primarily connected with the idea that consciousness is always shaped by the duality of *cogitum* (object of consciousness, for example the representation of a glove) and *cogitatio* (the act of consciousness, the seeing of a glove).[7] Husserl time and again varies the formulations of this duality, but he is concerned with a basic correlation in all intentionality: an intended object (noema) always correlates to an intending act (noesis). For Husserl, this determination fulfills the demand to think an object always in terms of "how it is given."[8] I designate this type of consciousness as *correlation-consciousness*. The basic correlation has three aspects that, in Levinas's view, make it impossible to grasp alterity by means of the concepts of intentionality.

1. Harmony

The most tangible moment of Husserl's definition is the idea that in an occurrence of intentionality one thing fits with another. Along with Husserl, I have used the notion of correlation. One could, however, just as easily say that the act "fits with" or "belongs to" the object. Both moments, the interplay of which makes up consciousness, stand in a relation of fit to one another. Consciousness is thus understood as attunement (harmony) between act and object.

2. Activity and Passivity

Husserl's definition of consciousness as a correlation of intended object and intending act stems from a certainty about the answer to the question of which things are to be thought of as active and which passive, and of what it means for something to be thought of as active or passive. Even if Husserl leaves behind classical subject-object dualism, even if he does not understand objects as independent entities, toward which subjects may or may not direct themselves, he is still certain that the object occupies the passive side. Husserl thus conceptually inherits Kant's dichotomy between spontaneity and receptivity. He actualizes this dichotomy in the framework of a correlation between act and object, thus moving beyond mere subjective capacity. The act corresponds to the spontaneous side; the object to the receptive side. Husserl does insist that both sides belong together, hence that there is not first a potential to act, which then seeks out objects in order to join itself to them. Nevertheless, the two sides in the correlation are held apart by the dichotomy. The spontaneous capacity survives in the concept of the intending act, which is sovereign in joining itself with the object.

3. *Feasibility*

The last characteristic I consider relevant might sound a bit peculiar at first. I will formulate it as follows: the correlation of act and object can always be produced; it is always feasible. The correlation is understood in such a way that there is always space for new act-object formations. The correlation thus implies an open horizon for the productivity of act and object. In this sense the world is thought of as open, as something that shapes itself into ever new figures of consciousness. Consciousness is open to disclosing ever new objects in the world. In this sense, consciousness is always something that is feasible, that can be produced.

THE SPECIFICITY OF MORAL CONSCIOUSNESS

The characteristics I have explicated thus far seem suitable for explaining the reservations that Levinas brings forward against the idea that this understanding of consciousness encompasses everything that deserves to be called consciousness. All of Levinas's reservations assert that there are moments of consciousness that cannot be subsumed under the type of correlation just described. Speaking in a much abbreviated manner, one could say that for Levinas the cases Husserl cannot take account of are those in which consciousness is consciousness of the other (*genitivus objectivus*).[9] Levinas also speaks of the "face of the other," but what is meant here are not actual facial features, as for example, the object studied by the physiognomist. Rather the face is a metaphor for everything in the face of the other that expresses otherness. One can perhaps say more comprehensibly, that when the object of consciousness is a persistent demand [*bestehender Anspruch*] that comes to me from the other, it points to those moments of consciousness that Levinas has in mind.[10] The important thing is that we are dealing here with a persistent demand, a demand that is not called forth by my presence, though possibly I am a participant in its genesis. The consciousness of such a demand points to three characteristics (I am going in reverse order through the characteristics that I have taken from Husserl's concept of intentionality):

1. Nonfeasibility

When I am overcome by a demand, then I am confronted with an object that is not constitutively in connection with an act of consciousness on my part. Quite the opposite: it is a demand precisely when the object precedes the act of consciousness to a certain extent. The act of consciousness, in this case, points to a certain belatedness. This has the consequence that the correlation between object and act cannot be simply produced as such. The correlation is not feasible [*ist nicht machbar*]—when it becomes apparent, it has always already been made [*gemacht*]. Levinas develops a variety of descriptions of this basic state of affairs. He speaks of consciousness as being the "welcome" of the demand (*TI* 86, 89). Behind this concept of welcome is hidden the idea that the demand does not appear as an object within a feasible correlation. It can only be received as an object that leads consciousness. Levinas later sharpened his description of this and spoke of it in terms of consciousness as hostage to the demand. This sharpened formulation makes it clear that here consciousness is, as it were, made by its object, that the correlation is already made. Consciousness is trapped by its being made in the object; in this sense, it is hostage or, to use an equally severe concept, "obsessed" (*OB* 83). The idea occurs in yet another formulation when Levinas puts it the following way: "It is a matter of the putting into question of consciousness, and not of a consciousness of being put into question."[11] If consciousness implies feasibility, then the insistent demand surpasses the structure of consciousness itself. It intervenes in the structure; it is a placing in question of the structure of consciousness, in that it substantially alters it.

2. Absolute Passivity

A persistent demand equally affects the distribution of activity and passivity in the correlation. As an object, the persistent demand is not a passive object (an object that will be experienced). Rather it is an object that makes its own being-experienced. But it does not make it in the sense of an activity. It is never active as such. This means precisely that it persists, that it must be thought in terms of its persistence. But if the object is not active, then the act side of the correlation cannot be understood as passive. The designations active and passive cannot simply be switched between the object and the act. Perhaps it can be described in the following way: consciousness does not suffer [*erleidet*] the demand. It has always already suffered it as a persistent demand. The demand withdraws itself from consciousness and, as it were, forms an activity that is not active. It is precisely this moment of the object that shapes consciousness, according to Levinas. It is a passivity that correlates to an activity, which again is not active in its own right. For this reason, Levinas speaks of a passivity that is "more passive than all passivity," of a "total passivity of obsession" (*OB* 110). The self-withdrawing activity of the persistent demand evokes an absolute passivity from the side of consciousness. This passivity—attempting another formulation—is not limited by an activity that corresponds to it. It is a passivity whose boundaries have been dissolved, this is what makes up its absolute character. Levinas must be read on this point as saying two different things about the type of consciousness under consideration. On the one hand, it must be described in terms of activity and passivity; these concepts do not lose their relevance here. On the other hand, activity and passivity lose their boundaries in the case of a persistent demand. It amounts to more than a simple switch between the two sides of consciousness.

3. *Asymmetry*

But how can there be an intending of (an intentional directing-oneself-at) an insistent demand? To say that something is a persistent demand means that it goes beyond its being grasped. For this reason an intending of this demand always remains insufficient. It is always such that it does not do justice to the demand. The correlation between act and object in this case is thus not harmonious. The act lags behind the object. Levinas mostly speaks here of an asymmetry. Behind this term is the idea that the object in this case exceeds the consciousness of it, that consciousness is not in a position to fulfill the demands of the object. Thus, asymmetry means that there is always a remainder, an excess of the object over and above its being grasped. This remainder is irreducible. It cannot be worked off by approximation. The consequence of this asymmetry is that object and act can never be brought into agreement.

The three characteristics of nonfeasibility, absolute passivity, and the asymmetry of act and object outline in a general way the extent to which Levinas conceives the demand of the other as something that defies intentional correlation. He conceives of such a demand as a type of consciousness that is not taken account of by Husserl's reconstruction of intentionality. But this does not explain Levinas's entire motivation for moving alterity to the center. He is also of the opinion that the phenomena of consciousness he explicates are fundamental. Levinas already suggests in an early text that "the face of the other" is "the starting point of philosophy."[12] With this, the critique of Husserl is expanded: the reproach is not just that the correlating type of consciousness does not cover all of consciousness, but also that this type of consciousness does not represent the fundamental type. Levinas holds the view that all intentionality derives from the nonfulfilling consciousness that begins from the demand of the other. He is also to be understood in this way when he writes, "The manifestation of the face is the first discourse."[13] The first discourse is however not simply an instance of discourse, an instance of comprehensible speech. Levinas understands discourse as address and demand (always an affliction), and from this address he derives all the talk that fills everyday communication, from sermons to talk shows.

ALTERITY AS NORMATIVITY

My reconstruction of Levinasian philosophy to this point can be summed up with two theses: (1) Moral consciousness[14] can be reconstructed in such a way that its object is a persistent demand; (2) Moral consciousness represents a special kind of consciousness that cannot be grasped in terms of correlation; (3) The claim that this latter kind of consciousness is fundamental has yet to be commented upon. Of course, the reconstruction cannot rest with these theses. These considerations will be driven further by the tension between (1) and (2). If moral consciousness, as (2) says, is not correlation-consciousness, then it is unclear to what extent one can even speak of an object of such a consciousness. Only for a correlation-consciousness does one know what it means to say that it has an object. This talk of a possible object of moral consciousness must ultimately be revised. I will demonstrate that thesis (1) cannot be maintained. But this also affects thesis (2): it is not certain that one can speak of consciousness in general without some kind of object. I will propose that thesis (2) must also be given up. It is against this background, I argue, that the extent to which the demand of the other must be conceived as fundamental first becomes intelligible. Only by giving up theses (1) and (2) will thesis (3) become plausible. The demand of the other is a relationship that is in play in all forms of consciousness, without being a special type of consciousness. I will try to retrace how one can understand this change in perspective, from the reconstruction of a special kind of consciousness to the reconstruction of a relationship that does not make up an independent kind of consciousness.

Levinas elucidates the peculiar nature of moral consciousness, among other ways, through the question: What results from the demand of the other? How is the demand of the other reflected in someone who is overcome by it? Levinas answers these questions with the concepts desiring and responsibility (a number of other concepts that could be read as answers to these questions are also found in Levinas's texts). The concept of responsibility is of special importance. One can grasp the change in perspective that Levinas suggests in the following way: the constitution of consciousness as consciousness of responsibility [*als eines Verantwortungs-Bewusstseins*] corresponds to the nonfulfillment of the persistent demand as an object of consciousness. However, consciousness of responsibility is not constituted in the same way, for example, as consciousness of a table. Responsibility is not an object of consciousness. Instead of this, one might speak of the directionality, the sense of direction, of consciousness. Someone who is responsible is not relating to an object, but is directed in a certain way toward others or directed from others. Levinas grasped this sense of direction of consciousness in such a way that its nonobjective aspect clearly expresses itself. He speaks of a "movement without return."[15] Responsibility is one form of such a movement, desiring is another. Levinas has also spoken of goodness or works (œuvres) as such a movement.

One can understand Levinas in such a way that the concept of movement without return characterizes the sense of direction of a consciousness of the demand. This characterization brings two aspects to the fore: first, in this case the how of correlation, rather than an object correlated to an act, stands at the center of consciousness. Second, it is characteristic of this that it does not consist in a reciprocal occurrence, but rather in a peculiarly interlacing occurrence. Because of the condition of being without return, one might be tempted to speak of a one-sided movement that exhausts itself in pursuit of an unreached object. But it is not merely a one-sided movement. The movement without turning back is certainly to be understood as a response to the demand of the other. It begins from the impetus [*Bewegung*] of the demand. Two movements thus converge in the consciousness of the demand in such a way that no closed circle results, no fulfilled correlation comes about. The interlacing in question can be grasped by a term already mentioned: "welcome" (*accueil*) (*TI* 89). Consciousness welcomes from the other to be directed toward this other, but without reaching it. Consciousness welcomes, is a movement without return. The concept of welcoming expresses the absolute passivity of consciousness. On this basis, it can be understood why Levinas speaks of an infinite responsibility: the responsibility that is welcomed in this way cannot in any way be exhausted, since it has no objective moment.

From these considerations it is clear how thesis (1) will be revised. Moral consciousness must be reconstructed in such a way that it is shaped by this particular how of the correlation — and thus not by a particular kind of object (the persistent demand). We can speak of a particular nonobjectivity of moral consciousness.[16] In positive terms, this nonobjectivity corresponds to the special directedness of moral consciousness. But is this talk of such a directedness reconcilable with the thesis of a special type of consciousness? Must one not also give up thesis (2)?

This newly developed revision to the conclusions of the previous section represents a puzzle, as it were. A good solution to the puzzle appears to me to be possible on the basis of thesis (3). Levinas characterizes moral consciousness as fundamental. This fundamental role of consciousness has to be introduced into the puzzle as it has been formulated thus far: How can a type of consciousness be fundamental, when it cannot even be said for sure that we are dealing with a type of consciousness? The solution to the puzzle can be found by understanding the concept of the fundamental in a different way; in this sense, I propose explaining this fundamentality as irreducibility. What is fundamental is not a certain type of consciousness, but a structure at work in all consciousness. Thesis (3) is thus compatible with this if we no longer begin from the assumption of a particular type of consciousness. In my view, the solution to the puzzle must take exactly this path. The fundamental role of moral consciousness must be understood in such a way that it enters into all other forms of consciousness. A particular directedness lies in all consciousness as such. By interpreting the role of moral consciousness in this way, one can make its fundamental position understandable. But with this, one lets go of thesis (2): the consciousness on which Levinas focuses is not to be conceived of as a special mode of consciousness, but as a structure that is irreducibly at play in all consciousness.

Levinas gives us an image of how the consciousness of a demand shapes other forms of consciousness. This image orients itself—like many explications from Levinas—by way of language, the linguistic articulation of world. He writes, "The word that designates things attests their being shared [*partage*] between me and the others.... The thing becomes a theme. To thematize is to offer the world to the other in speech" (*TI* 209, translation modified). With this description, Levinas points to a connection between thing and other. He conceives of words as witnesses of this connection. If indeed things are "shared between me and the other," then in every thing that comes to consciousness there is a relation to the others. But it is just this relation that Levinas conceives of as the structure of being related: being-related-to-an-other-from-an-other. From this one can also posit a further condition for things and for the words that refer to them: things only exist insofar as they are shared with an other. In each thing that comes to consciousness there resides a relation to others. Levinas's explications can be varied in this sense, to gain a consciousness of something means to offer the world to another through (one's own) consciousness. Every object, as an object of consciousness, becomes in this way a theme between me and others.

Setting aside the specific picture and understanding of language that Levinas employs, then one can put it another way: alterity and the relation to objects hang together irreducibly.

Every relation to an object is connected with the fact that one is related to others. The particular nature of this relationship is the focal point of Levinas's philosophy. But this does not mean that it amounts to an independent type of consciousness. This special manner of being related to others comes to bear on our relation to the world of objects. One can speak of two dimensions that shape all of consciousness: objectivity and alterity. The two dimensions cohere irreducibly. For all objectivity this means: it only comes to be on the basis of a being-related to others that is welcomed as coming from them. Being related to others means, as demonstrated, responsibility—it means that those who stand under this responsibility must do justice to the others. Every consciousness of an object is connected with this demand of responsibility and justice.

Insofar as one ties the concept of consciousness, as Husserl does, to objectivity, only one dimension of this irreducible coherence will be marked as consciousness. Alterity then seems to be a structure that stands outside of consciousness. The fundamental idea of Levinas's philosophy, it has seemed to me, stands in opposition to this, suggesting that alterity participates in the coming to be of objectivity. One can only speak of consciousness when the world comes into view in a way that is bound up with others. That means, however, that consciousness is not only connected with objectivity. Alterity is also always in play. But again, Levinas insists that alterity cannot be grasped through concepts of objectivity. It is a matter of a nonobjective being-related, into which those who share a world experience themselves as being placed. The dimension of alterity is thus to be conceived of as the binding of objectivity to others, according to Levinas. It is not a matter of distinctive forms of relation or consciousness, but rather an explanation of the normativity in all forms of relation or consciousness. In this way, we come from the reconstruction of a particular form of consciousness that motivates Levinas to questions of normativity. Alterity must be understood according to Levinas as the foundational concept of all normative contexts.

This reconstruction makes good on the aim stated above: alterity explains the being bound that shapes moral actions, for example, just as much as the use of words. The demand of the other is the nonobjective manner in which every position in the world is normatively bound. This normative being-bound does not stand on its own. In just this sense, in the foregoing paragraphs, has the talk of a particular form of consciousness been amended. Alterity does not represent some special form of consciousness. It is rather an irreducible dimension of all — objective — consciousness. As noted, it is helpful to explain the fundamental character of the demand of the other by means of the concept of irreducibility. This explanation makes it possible to avoid a false alternative between the objective and the nonobjective: even the objective dimension of consciousness is irreducible. Thus alterity is part of the interplay between different dimensions, which are interdependent.[17]

NORMATIVE FORCE ACCORDING TO LEVINAS

In order to sharpen the understanding of normativity that has been sketched to this point, one can take a look at decidedly normative relations.[18] Such normative relations can be grasped as a special case of the more generally normative nature of consciousness. How does alterity come into play in places where rules or norms or laws are predominant? I will take as an example the rule follower Regula. Regula holds herself to the rule, "When eating in society you shouldn't make any noises that are too loud." That she holds herself to the rule as a rule means for Levinas that her action demonstrates the dimension of alterity. In her action (the following of rules), she relates herself to others. In the rule that is the object of her behavior, she is related to others. She welcomes this relation coming from the other. Being receptive in such a way, she is responsible to others, she must do justice to others. This is just what gives the rule normative force. Regula is to a certain degree placed by others in the position of following the rule — even when she does not follow the rule and smacks away. She thus does not set her own following of the rule (even if it might sometimes seem like it). Rule-following has been imposed on her by others. She is only following rules insofar as this imposition exists.

According to Levinas, normative force may be explained through the concept of alterity. But how does it stand with the content of the rule? The content of the rule can be understood by recourse to what others do. Others therefore impose a rule in that they themselves behave in a certain way. Their actions are decisive for Regula being able to connect up with them. It is always a case of concrete others, whose actions are decisive. Let us take two rule followers, Peter and Paul. In their actions they hold themselves to the rule, "When eating in society, you shouldn't make any noises that are too loud." Now Regula follows this rule as well, when her action is related to that of Peter and Paul (welcoming the relation coming from Peter and Paul). The action of others is the rule to which Regula must do justice. She follows the rule when her action implies the demand to do justice to this action.

Every action is thus to be understood in Levinas's sense as a particular action—as individual action. Peter for example works as a waiter, Paul as a consultant, Regula is an etiquette teacher. The circumstances in which they follow rules are always different. One person tests the flavor of a food, another sits with business partners at a table, yet others hectically grab a breakfast on the go. If Regula receives her rule from action that is in each case individual, then she is confronted with the individual action as the demand that she follows. She does not receive a universal, but rather varying action from others. For this reason she is responsible not to a universal content, but to variable action. In following rules she must do justice to an act that is in each case individual. Here we see once again the aforementioned infinity of the demand of which Levinas constantly speaks. This responsibility can never be exhausted or offset. The following of rules is constitutively an infinite concern.

The point of this explication of Levinas's thought is as follows: a rule is always binding plus regular. In the concepts of the previous section, this means that a rule is alterity plus objectivity. The side of objectivity (that is, acting in relation to an object) plays no great role in Levinas's considerations. It would have to be made more definite through a concept of public action. However, through these considerations Levinas suggests that normative force is to be explained as a particular dimension that cannot by grasped through a normative content. Normative force is accordingly the infinite responsibility that I receive from others and whose action I relate to through my own action. Normative force is to be related to someone who puts me in a relationship. The decisive accent of this suggestion consists in the idea that normative force is to be found neither in the rule that Regula follows, nor in her relation to the rule. Normative force is a matter of intersubjectively initiated demands, which always commence from individual others. Normative force results out of particular relationships, which so direct my action that it is imposed on me. This reconstruction, according to Levinas, requires a conceptualization of alterity. In particular, it requires us to take into account that relationships display a peculiar interlacing. This interlacing is of such a kind that an action, standing in such a relationship, is received as coming from the action of another. A demand initiates the fact that a relationship is turned toward him, without his ever being able to do justice to it. Normative force only comes into being insofar as living beings develop an action that is bound by such relationships.

This scenario of following rules now serves more generally as a model for structures of consciousness. All intentionality is, according to Levinas, shaped by alterity. To put it another way, it is thoroughly impregnated by normativity. Objective consciousness always comes into being on the basis of responsibility. This responsibility rests on the demand to do justice to the other, from which all objectivities are received. The relation to others reaches into all corners of consciousness. In working out his main idea, Levinas's whole effort aims at this insight. Nevertheless, it is crucial to pay attention to the separation, as well as the interplay of dimensions that, for Levinas, are constitutive of consciousness. An objective side must also always be in play. Alterity without objectivity is like having a rule be binding, without having regularity. Being related to others would have nothing to be responsible for if it did not have a world. Shared contents are required; from them arises the necessity of doing justice to others, being infinitely responsible with respect to others. Alterity emerges in interplay with the intentional structures in which objects and states of affairs of the world and of social life have their places. Alterity endows structures that make objects and states of affairs binding.

Normativity, as Levinas understands it, has a completely different style than other relationships. It is not a case of intentionality, not a case of being directed toward objects. It is far more a dimension of the activities of many individuals, who each take each other's activities as a demand and, in this sense, receive that to which they try to do justice. To see oneself as under a demand that comes in various ways from various others — this is the primal scene of normativity. Levinas repeatedly formulated this primal scene referring to language: every speaking implies seeing in the speaking of others a demand directed to oneself, with respect to which the sense of having to do justice emerges. This insight can be varied for a general concept of normativity in which every norm-directed activity implies seeing a demand directed at oneself, in regard to which the need to do justice emerges. Norm-directed activity means standing under a demand from many others, which is always particular and yet not singular.

Further Perspectives

I would like to add a two-part perspective to the reconstructions of the previous sections. On one side, I am concerned to contextualize the fundamental idea that Levinas's philosophy gives shape to. On the other side, out of this contextualization, the question emerges as to what can be learned from Levinas's philosophy for a theory of normativity.

It seems to me that Levinas's enduring work on alterity must be grasped as paving the way for an understanding of the particular constitution of normativity. It makes clear that no conceptual path leads from the intraworldly and common activities of living beings, which understand normative relationships.[19] What is rather required is recourse to relationships with others—relationships in which I see myself placed before I can place myself in them. Levinas thus insists implicitly on the irreducibility of normative relations. Irreducibility also means that no translation into nonnormative concepts is available. The normative brings with it a very particular structuring for which, according to Levinas, one can use the concept of alterity. My reading sets itself over against the interpretation of Levinas's work on the other according to which he aims to demonstrate the incomparable and incompatible position of the other. According to this latter interpretation, outlined above, the other is regarded as an extraordinary object in two senses: first, it is a matter of an object that is not an object (in phenomenological terms, a nonconstitutable phenomenon).[20] Secondly, it is a matter of an object that can only be grasped by someone who sets up his theory in an exceptional manner. According to this view, what is needed is another way of speaking, which makes itself into a vessel for the demand of the other.[21] On both levels, such an interpretation orients itself around the category of the extraordinary (*Ausserordentlichen*). By contrast, the reading suggested here makes clear that Levinas's thinking is not captured by the category of the extraordinary. In fact, it reconstructs the structures of an order (*Ordnung*). However, the focus of Levinas is not directed at the order of things, but rather at the order of norms, which we impose on ourselves in a reciprocity achieved by individuality. Thus, Levinas's thinking is oriented around the notion of the extraordinary only in the sense that it counts on there being more kinds of order than the order of things. The intuition by which Levinas is guided may be understood as follows: there is a heterogeneity of orders that make up consciousness. Over and above the order of objectivity, at least one other order must be factored in; it is this other order whose concepts Levinas's philosophy seeks to explain.

With a glance at Levinas's critique of Husserl, I have held fast to two main thrusts: first, alterity is not to be reduced conceptually to objectivity; second, alterity shapes every coming into being of objects for consciousness. Taken together, these thrusts lead to the thesis of a strong conceptual as well as factual irreducibility of the normative. Such an interpretation of Levinas's philosophy, however, raises the question: Why should one have to learn once again from Levinas what one knows already from Sellars and Brandom (and perhaps even from Kant and Hegel)?[22] To confirm the irreducibility of the normative from a French thinker, rooted in the Jewish tradition, might create agreement, but no new knowledge.[23]

If one, however, takes the sum total of Levinas's thinking in this way, one stops too short. The core of the idea that it pursues does not rest in the thesis of the irreducibility of the normative. Rather, it rests in two other points: first, in a reconstruction of normativity that illustrates its interdependence with objective content; second, in the conceptuality developed in the course of this reconstruction. Normativity is based on alterity and does not constitute an independent dimension of the coming to be of objectivity—this formula summarizes Levinas's idea. Over and above this formulation, one can characterize the stimulus to this idea as follows: normativity comes to be from intangible [*unverfügbaren*] relationships; it is—as Levinas often emphasizes—structured asymmetrically. The demand that places one under a responsibility, which allows one's action be related to the action of others, is intangible. Levinas thus makes the suggestion that norm-guided action be grasped as action in the irrecusable. Normativity is not constituted or, as Brandom says, instituted by (symmetrical) action. It lies in being related to demands.

With the concept of the irreducible, Levinas denies the idea that normativity comes to be in a tangible way. Normativity thus does not allow itself to be explained as a particular communally based activity, but must instead be understood as a particular orientation to individuality in the framework of activity. It is not our shared activity that grounds normativity, but instead it is the extracommunal aspect of our actions that binds us. The space of the normative is thus that of the demand, to which I experience myself being related. The founding concept of the normative is thus not that of entitlement or of obligation (that in my activity I respectively attain or enter into). The founding concept is that of responsibility or justice (which my activity respectively stands under or is demanded to produce). In this way, Levinas opens up a new perspective on norms and their basis. He sketches an image of the intangible foundation of norms that bind us and that always also bind us to each other. To work out this image will mean following the fundamental idea of the philosophy of Emmanuel Levinas.

Six

Don't Try This at Home

Levinas and Applied Ethics

Diane Perpich

As Levinas's thought has become more familiar in disciplines as diverse as sociology, nursing, psychology, education, and law, the question of the import of his work in practical and applied fields needs to be addressed. Can Levinas's philosophy serve as support for the claim that nurses or other health care workers are infinitely responsible for patients? Can the face-to-face relation set out in *Totality and Infinity* serve as a model for doctor-patient care, for the psychotherapeutic encounter between therapist and client, or for the relation between teacher and pupil? Can his writings on the face-to-face relationship help us deliver better online education or a richer appreciation of the transformative possibilities of music and music education? Can his claims about the infinite alterity of the Other be assimilated to the idea that we can never fully know the other who is our student, our patient, our client, or the defendant who stands before a judge? And, perhaps most significantly, does Levinas's thought show us that this failure of knowledge must be the occasion for renewed moral consideration or ethical respect? All of these have been claimed, but we need to ask directly, is there a way to *apply* Levinas's thought? Can notions like the alterity of the Other, the face, or infinite responsibility be transported usefully into applied ethical contexts?

As a first stab at this question, the present essay looks at the way Levinas's thought has been taken up in two applied fields, nursing and psychology. Theorists in both areas have seen in Levinas's work the possibility of infusing their discipline with an ethical dimension that is otherwise thought to be missing or to have been construed too narrowly. Care and care-giving are central to the theoretical understanding of both disciplines as well as to their professional practice; moreover, Levinas's thought has increasingly been appealed to in both fields by theorists interested in conceiving care in a directly ethical manner. But is it possible to interpret Levinas's thought as an ethics of care or would these disciplines be better served by turning more straightforwardly to feminist care ethics or to a virtue ethics that emphasizes empathy or compassion? After elucidating some of the reasons theorists in these fields have understandably turned to Levinas, I argue that they cannot find in his work what they most often hope to find there. Specifically, I argue: that Levinas's notion of "the face of the other" is misinterpreted where it is invoked as a direct source or origin of ethical responsibility; correspondingly, that his writings are misunderstood if they are read as a constructivist ethics that offers ethical norms that can be put to work in care-giving professions; and finally, that his work is not a defense of our inherently ethical nature nor a guarantee of our ethical responsibility. But rather than concluding that Levinas therefore has nothing to offer those working in applied fields, I suggest that what Levinas does offer is just not necessarily what researchers in those fields have hoped to find. Instead of a philosophy that guarantees the ethical importance of compassion or the certainty of our responsibility to provide care for others, Levinas emphasizes the constitutive uncertainty and fragility of ethical life. If practical professions are to *make* anything practical of Levinas's thought, it is this fragility and vulnerability that must arguably become central to their self-understanding and to their appropriation of texts like *Totality and Infinity.*

LEVINAS AND NURSING CARE

Nursing was originally conceived in the West as a calling, akin to (and sometimes identical with) the calling to serve God and humanity as a member of a religious order. By the twentieth century, it had come to be seen instead as belonging to medicine as a profession, sharing in the latter's knowledge base and its professional ethos. In recent years, in an attempt to have nurses' contributions more fairly and fully valued, theorists have sought to define the profession apart from the work of doctors and other medical personnel and to demonstrate its distinctive contribution to patient health and well-being.[1] Notions of care and caring have been central to this endeavor and now inform a wide range of approaches to the philosophy of nursing.[2] Indeed, much as virtue ethics and the ethics of care came on the philosophical scene in the 1980s and 1990s and insisted on a more central role for caring attitudes within theoretical explorations of ethical judgment and behavior, so theorists of nursing have lately insisted that notions of professional decision making and the competent execution of tasks are an inadequate conception of nursing practices. But if nursing theorists are unified in looking to clarify the nature of nursing care, and if they are increasingly aware that good nursing care consists of more than the competent performance of a number of care-giving tasks, they are nonetheless struggling to give a substantive content to this *more* and thus to develop a consensus on just what care and caring mean ontologically and ethically.[3]

Levinas's writings have attracted researchers who want to give a specifically ethical content, rather than a merely affective or emotional one, to the notions of care and care-giving. And though there is likewise no strong consensus on how exactly to employ

Levinas's thought for this purpose, several points of commonality stand out in the literature on Levinas and nursing care.

First, the turn to Levinas is strongly motivated by the need to find an account of ethical life and responsibility that fits well with the concrete, holistic nature of nursing care.[4] The risk-benefit models that dominate the current medical ethics literature necessarily treat patients in the abstract, as cases or types, and are mainly concerned either with the just distribution of health care benefits or with debating the permissibility or impermissibility of certain courses of action by medical personnel. While nurses clearly share such concerns, nursing is also immediately and fundamentally concerned with the unique, concretely existing person who is here and now in front of one and in need of care. Per Nortvedt describes the situation of traditional medical ethics vis-à-vis nursing ethics as a conflict between consequentialist theories that look to maximize health care outcomes across an abstract population and the concrete, particular responsibility of care givers who must give priority to the individuals right now in their care.

Nortvedt argues that just as moral theories that demand strict impartiality fail to adequately capture ethical dimensions of personal relationships to family and friends, so too they fall short when it comes to characterizing and informing professional relationships for which care and care-giving are central. Of course, the relation of caregiver to patient is not exactly analogous to the relation of parents to children or to the relation between siblings or friends: a nurse's responsibility to and for patients is not a function of the thick emotional ties that characterize these others types of relationships. Nonetheless, it would be "implausible," Nortvedt says, to argue that "emotional and relational ties are irrelevant to therapeutic caring relationships."[5] The ethical relationship in professional care contexts is neither strictly impersonal nor fully personal. It may be better described, Nortvedt suggests, as a hybrid form in which one of the significant duties of the care professional is to develop "a sense of attachment, of feeling personally responsible for one's patient."[6]

Other theorists echo the importance of personal responsibility in nursing practices and, like Nortvedt, find resources for a theoretical articulation of this sort of responsibility in Levinas's writings. In particular, Levinas's notion of responsibility as neither universal nor generalized but *mine alone* and as a response to a face-to-face encounter with another has seemed to some a promising route for developing an account of nursing responsibility. In a paper on public health nursing in Norway, the authors invoke Levinas to argue that, "Responsibility for the Other cannot be avoided, ignored, or transferred. The nurse's responsibility is personal and infinite." This same essay goes so far as to say that "Levinas's philosophy in its entirety concerns the magnitude of personal responsibility."[7] Similarly, in an article casting Levinas's thought explicitly as an ethics of care, we read that his ethics "do not arise from moral autonomy based on a subject's rational judgment. Ethics here originate from having affection for the sick, the poor, and the alienated, and place an emphasis on an unavoidable obligation and responsibility to respond to their calls for assistance due to an interest in their faces."[8] In yet another essay with direct reference to Levinas: "According to Levinas, to take care of the other is a moral obligation, a responsibility impossible to circumvent." And later in the same paragraph: "Every person, but especially the caregiver is always responsible for the human being whom the Other represents."[9]

These theorists are searching for an understanding of responsibility that is based on a response to the concrete person before me, that carries an affective component, and that cannot be reduced to a set of duties performed in connection with a role or a set of practical ends. To understand this, we can push the analogy with personal relationships a bit further. If someone were to perform all the duties of a parent, for example, but felt no love or affection for their child, we would hardly think that they had met the ethical burden of good parenthood. Similarly, if good nursing requires a caring attitude—if such caring is the nurse's *responsibility*—then competent, pleasant performance of professional tasks may not alone meet this charge. Moreover, just as love for a child cannot be love of children in general but must be love of *this* child, so too if nurses are being urged to feel personally responsible for patients, it is these here and now, really existing (often unpleasant and fractious) patients toward whom they are to develop this attitude. A genuine and positive affective response to the other person is what is required.[10]

In tandem with the emphasis on responsibility as personal and as involving an affective response, an emphasis on embodiment is central to the nursing literature that pursues an explicitly Levinasian approach.[11] In many cases, this literature emphasizes that the body cannot be conceived separately from the person or subject: "our body is an essential part of the integrated subject that we are."[12] In part, the point once again is to turn the focus of attention from the abstract to the concrete: bodies in pain are not adequately treated when they are seen as *mere* bodies, in the abstract. Nursing care that attends to the body must attend to the full person who is here and now suffering. To put the point in terms borrowed from Stanley Cavell rather than Levinas (though there are deep affinities between the two), the patient who suffers not only needs to have it *known* that he or she is in pain, the patient needs to have the suffering *acknowledged*. Cavell suggests that knowing someone is in pain *means* acknowledging that pain, that is, knowing in this case is not just a cognitive state: "It is not enough that I know (am certain) that you suffer—I must do or reveal something (whatever can be done). In a word, I must acknowledge it, otherwise I do not know what (your or his) being in pain means." Acknowledging that you are in pain, moreover, means acknowledging that it matters to me that you are in pain, and by extension acknowledging that *you* matter. For Cavell, the other's "suffering makes a claim on me."[13] The other's suffering makes a demand that needs to be acknowledged.

There are parts of *Totality and Infinity* that can be read in line with this point of Cavell's. When Levinas says that language is a response to the being who "in a face speaks to the subject and tolerates only a personal response, that is, an ethical act," there is a parallel with Cavell's distinction between knowing and acknowledging (*TI* 219). Language is not just a matter of knowing, and speaking is not just about communicating something known: language also involves acknowledging the other as my interlocutor and this acknowledgment is not just a matter of assenting to a proposition but of responding ethically to the other through some kind of action. Anglo-American moral theories, even those like utilitarianism that make a capacity for pain central to moral personhood, have largely ignored a point like Cavell's and Levinas's. But insofar as nursing centrally involves responding to suffering, an ethics adequate to nursing practices cannot focus only on moral decision making or the cultivation of autonomy.[14] Acknowledging the other's suffering requires that nurses "develop a complex sensitivity to the vulnerability of our shared embodied heritage."[15]

Finally, much of the nursing literature that invokes Levinas emphasizes the fundamentally other-regarding nature of Levinasian ethics. Levinas is understood by a number of theorists as maintaining that "the life of the other person is more important than our own." With respect to the infinity of responsibility, one team of researchers reads Levinas as showing that "our position [is] that of being a hostage with total responsibility for our keeper, of having the power to help, but at the same time being a powerless prisoner."[16] The same essay, however, notes that this is a very challenging concept applicable perhaps only to moral saints and unlikely to be endorsed by actual nurses.

Can Levinas's thought deliver what those in the nursing professions are seeking on any of these fronts? Can his work serve as the basis for an ethics of care-giving understood as the obligation to respond personally, concretely, and affectively to patient needs, tending equally to body and soul, and putting the other before the self?

A central obstacle for those wanting to apply Levinas's thought to care-giving relationships is highlighted in the appeal to Levinas's statement that I am responsible to the other with a total responsibility, as if I were hostage to the other and the other's needs. The authors above, who rightly note the extreme character of this kind of claim, nonetheless maintain that a Levinasian ethical approach — and they appear to take his comments about being a hostage more or less literally — provides "a framework for reflection on responsibility in everyday work that may help keep the ethical dimension in focus."[17] But isn't the opposite just as likely to be true? Unless a nurse has a taste for masochism, why would he or she subscribe to an ethics where no matter what is done, it is never enough? And given that nursing is still work predominantly done by women, can we really endorse a self-abnegating ethics that plays into feminine stereotypes of self-sacrifice and self-abnegation? Further, might not this unearthly ethics ascribed to Levinas make nurses lose sight of the moral demands they face in their professional lives — demands that are not infinite and which can, in fact, be met if properly understood? If we understand Levinas as literally advocating a responsibility that is infinite in scope, wouldn't this be a recipe for the sort of defeatism or quietism that makes people lose their moral compass? If I can never fully meet my responsibility to the other, why not take a shortcut or two, ethically speaking? In effect, when read literally, Levinas's ethics seem to be so heavenly as to be of little earthly good. And, even at its best, it is very hard to see how this ethics could serve as more than a general inspiration in professional contexts, and again only for some, certainly not for all.

Beyond these practical difficulties, there are theoretical difficulties facing the appropriation of Levinas's notion of infinite responsibility for professional ethics. Namely, *what exactly* would a Levinasian responsibility enjoin the professional practitioner to do? And how would responsibility in the Levinasian sense (where it is understood as an *infinite* responsibility) be justified or grounded? To be sure, sometimes Levinas's own language makes it seem as if there are specific moral commands being issued by the face. The other's destitution, for example, often appears in Levinas's writings, especially around the time of *Totality and Infinity,* as a figure for a moral demand: "The being that expresses itself imposes itself, but does so precisely by appealing to me with its destitution and nudity—its hunger—without my being able to be deaf to that appeal" (*TI* 200). But can we read this as saying that the other's physical needs are actual or empirical sources of obligation? What would make them so? Are sentences like these meant to be read as normative claims or moral imperatives of some kind? The literature in nursing too often reads such claims as if they were unproblematically true. For example, one researcher writes, "The face…is a primordial ethical expression which has ethical orders and imperatives, such as 'you shall not commit murder.'" The same essay goes on to say that "moral responsibility for the Other is imposed…by a self's passive sensibilities influenced by the appearance of the face of the Other."[18] Another ascribes the following words to Levinas (though the essay notes the looseness of the translation): "The human face obliges each and every one of us, leaving no possibility 'to remain deaf to its appeal' or to 'cease being responsible.'" And if the whole body is a face for Levinas, this suggests that the suffering body makes a direct ethical demand, too. Thus we read, "For public health nurses, the call of the Other can be experienced in the puckered lips of the suckling infant, the untidy hair of the teenager, and the tired but contented face of the nursing mother."[19] But what exactly is this call a call to? Which responsibilities are enjoined by these faces and on what grounds?

There is a temptation in applied fields to appeal to Levinas's thought as if it constituted a constructive ethics in the same sense as other, more familiar ethical theories. For example, medical ethicists who rely on a consequentialist framework do not need to rehearse the justification for this position in any detail in order to employ it. It is enough to recall the basic principles and prescriptions of the position and then show how they can be applied to specific cases. The same is largely true of appeals to virtue ethics or duty-based moral theories. But is Levinas's work a constructive ethics in this same sense? Can the notion of an infinite responsibility be understood as an action-guiding norm or prescription? And is it supposedly grounded in an account of human nature or the nature of reason? Arguably not. I will return to this point below, but first I want to consider the case of Levinas and psychotherapeutic disciplines.

LEVINAS AND PSYCHOTHERAPY

A review of the psychotherapy literature that turns to Levinas reveals approaches and concerns similar to those in nursing, but also an attempt to use Levinas's thought to quell moral relativism. Edwin Gantt and Richard Williams, colleagues at Brigham Young University and co-editors of *Psychology for the Other: Levinas, Ethics, and the Practice of Psychology* (2002), have done as much as anyone to bring Levinas to the attention of psychotherapists. Decrying the behaviorism of contemporary psychology and critical of the discipline's methodological commitment to "reductive causal explanations," Williams and Gantt argue that psychology has been too invested in seeing itself as a science and has thereby missed the moral or ethical dimension of human action and psychotherapy's role in helping to articulate that dimension.[20] Human action, these authors argue, is "essentially" moral in character; and while they initially define moral in an exceedingly broad sense as anything or any event that "has some meaningful implication or consequence in the lives of human beings," their subsequent attacks on the relativism induced by postmodern critiques and their invocation of a contemporary cultural and intellectual crisis of meaning suggests that ultimately it is a narrower and stronger sense of ethics or morality that truly concerns them.[21] Williams's own work makes clear that his worry is with the nihilism of contemporary culture which is understood as equally affirming all values and having no way to "defend any ethical claim over any other."[22] For Williams, Levinas's work "can be thought of as a way out of nihilism, as a breaking of the epistemological log jam that prevents serious reflection on the ethical and the incorporation of the ethical into our understandings of ourselves and into the disciplines by which we have chosen to pursue such self-understanding."[23] For Gantt, the stakes of bringing Levinas into psychology are seemingly more limited. By adopting a medical or scientific model, Gantt argues, psychology has "robbed itself of the possibility for genuinely understanding the ethical significance of human suffering." A Levinasian approach makes it possible to recognize "the fundamental responsibility of the therapist to suffer-with and suffer-for the client."[24]

Gantt effectively argues for a new understanding of the therapist-client relationship, one that invests the therapist with a specific kind of personal, affective, and potentially infinite responsibility for his or her client. In this respect his work mirrors the concerns of nursing theorists who are seeking an ethics that is a better fit with the work of care-giving professionals. Like nursing theorists, Gantt is critical of his discipline's tendency to develop "abstract systems of treatment" while neglecting the need to theorize the importance of dwelling with the concrete "here-and-now immediacy" of the client who suffers.[25] More than once, Gantt emphasizes that suffering with and for a client is not being recommended as a way to produce improved outcomes for patients. Rather, his interest appears to be in reshaping the discipline's self-understanding: "suffering-with another in the very moment of their anguish is ethically prior and morally superior to any method or technique, any of which must ultimately be seen as derivative from and subservient to the call to ethical response in the face of suffering."[26] Ultimately, Gantt casts this reshaping as a way of combating certain dehumanizing tendencies that have gained the upper hand in the psychotherapeutic literature and, presumably, in the therapeutic relationship itself; his aim is to inject a fundamentally ethical dimension into both. But again there is a question of just what it means to suffer with a client. Leaving aside the question of whether this would make for good therapy, what would this suffering with and for the other look like, and what concrete actions, if any, would it require? Even more importantly, can Levinas's thought in any way be said to generate such a direct obligation? To his credit, Gantt is a more sophisticated reader than many of those who are using Levinas for applied purposes, and he emphasizes that the ethical demand as Levinas understands it is not a *fait accompli*. I can, as he says, "always attempt to uproot myself from such responsibility."[27] But the question is what exactly, on Gantt's view, this responsibility entails for the therapy professional (as, opposed say, to any man or woman on the street)? Again, there appears to be a desire for Levinas's thought to generate specific norms that would guide professional behavior, but once again the kind of norm proposed is impossibly vague.

Williams urges psychotherapists not only to a new understanding of their discipline, but to a new understanding of "our nature."[28] According to Williams, Levinas is engaged in a project that Williams terms, contra Levinas's own terminology, a "human ontology," which is to say, a description of what it means to be human. Williams argues moreover that the substantive content of this ontology is the view that the relationship to other persons is primary, or as he puts it elsewhere, Levinas shows that "what is most human about us is to recognize as distinctly human the humanity of the Other."[29] The problem here is not so much with either one of these claims, but with how Williams understands their combined force. While Levinas himself rejects ontology (as he finds it in Heidegger and in the Western tradition generally), he nonetheless is plausibly read as giving an account of human subjectivity; and if that is what is meant by an ontology, it would be quibbling over words to take issue with Williams here. Additionally, there is little doubt that Levinas does equate being human with recognizing something like the humanity of the other. The difficulty comes when the two ideas are combined in such a way that the recognition of the other's humanity is understood as *descriptively true* of what it means to be a subject, and as thus guaranteeing in some fashion that "the ethical...is intrinsic to our nature."[30]

As Williams spells out what he means by this, it becomes clear that for him right and wrong can be known immediately and intuitively—and he takes this to be Levinas's view as well. Williams asks us to consider the case of a new father who hears the baby cry and fleetingly feels he should respond before his wife also wakes, but then closes his eyes again and rationalizes his decision by saying that caring for the baby is his wife's job. For Williams, the fleeting moment in which the father felt he should respond to the baby and let his wife sleep is the truly ethical moment: "He felt the obligation to an other, to a (sleepy) face." Levinas, as Williams reads him, "would want to teach us...how much of our understanding of our experiences and of others are dependent on immediate ethical intimations and our immediate and spontaneous responses to them." It is this "immediate" response that Williams also calls "the aboriginal and most authentic voice of the ethical."[31] Elsewhere, Williams and Gantt stress that recognition of our obligation to the other does not require "cognitive sophistication, careful socialization, or arcane social construction. It is *obvious and available.*"[32] But what of all the fathers (and mothers) who hear a baby's cry and have no moment of indecision, no sense, fleeting or otherwise, that they are the ones who should respond? And what of much more complicated cases like a coworker made homeless by a flood or strangers in a far away country who lose their homes in an earthquake? Is it obvious what we must do in these circumstances? What exactly do I owe to these others? Williams's example works, if it does at all, only because the range of actions open to the father is very narrowly circumscribed and because the example draws on uncontroversial and widely shared intuitions about good parenting and kindness toward a weary spouse. But the idea that our concrete responsibilities are in every case obvious without special knowledge or deliberation is not only a gross oversimplification of ethical life, but an invitation to thoughtless repetition of the mores that dominate one's current social, familial, or personal milieu and thus shape one's moral intuitions.

The difficulties here are much the same as they were in the case of the nursing literature. Is Levinas rightly read as offering a constructivist ethics that can generate specific norms or virtues that would guide the work of therapists in professional contexts? And even if Levinas is not necessarily read as providing specific ethical directives, does he offer an account of human subjectivity according to which certain kinds of caring, compassion, or suffering for the other are normatively binding? Can he be read, moreover, as saying that some sort of ethical comportment or orientation is inherent to or essentially part of our nature? While Gantt and Williams are both worried about combating what they take to be the relativism of contemporary ethical theories, neither worries nearly enough about how the universal ethical prescriptions they propose to find in Levinas would be grounded or justified outside of a community that already believes in them. Again, the question of a *justification* of the ethics supposedly found in Levinas's work presses urgently for those who are possessed of even a little skepticism on this score.

THE FACE, NORMS, AND ETHICAL CERTAINTY: THREE PITFALLS

While nursing theorists interpret Levinas's thought along lines similar to feminist ethics of care, seeking to elevate the nurse's personal affective response to the level of an ethical responsibility, the psychotherapy literature takes Levinas in the direction of virtue ethics, advocating a way of being with clients that demonstrates ethical virtues like patience, humility, or compassion and grounds these in a purportedly Levinasian understanding of who we are as human beings. It is worth asking, however, why these theorists are turning to Levinas rather than to the ethics of care or to virtue ethics more directly? It cannot be merely that Levinas offers an alternative to forms of ethics based on adherence to rational principles. After all, both the ethics of care and virtue ethics do this as well, and in ways that are more familiar and easier to understand. I suspect Levinas's thought appeals to care-giving professionals because it gives primacy to the other in a way these alternative traditions do not. In more traditional ethical theories, even when the other person is a focus of discussion, the self is equally the center of attention. And, in many cases, the other need not be on the scene at all. For example, the virtues I cultivate, even when other-regarding, are still *my* virtues and the reasons I cultivate them are largely self-regarding; likewise care is most often understood as fundamentally reciprocal rather than only other-regarding.

When Levinas's emphasis on ethics as prior to rational principles is combined with the priority he gives to the other, this no doubt makes for much of the attraction of his work to those in care-giving fields. A passage like the following, by psychologist George Kunz, illustrates this point. Kunz writes, "The ethics described by Levinas is not reducible to a set of moral principles competing with other such sets of principles prescribed by family, church, school, government, culture. [Rather] The first principle of Levinas's ethical philosophy is the Other. The dignity of the Other immediately perceived is not an abstract principle; it is a fact. The face of the Other directly reveals herself or himself to me as vulnerable and as worthiness. This revelation is the origin of ethics."[33] Like Gantt and Williams, Kunz appears to understand the face as a demand that is immediate and undeniable, like a fact; indeed, he goes so far as to claim that it *is* a fact. Serious questions have to be raised about this kind of interpretation, which has become all too common in the literature attempting to move with Levinas into professional disciplines.

We can formulate a set of three related claims (or pitfalls) that are all too widespread in the literature on Levinas and applied ethics and that represent a serious misunderstanding of his thought: (1) that the face serves as a direct, immediate, and incontrovertible source or origin of ethical responsibility; (2) that this responsibility is of the usual sort that generates specific norms for action; and (3) that there is thus something like a guarantee of the force of ethics available in Levinas's thought. In what follows, I briefly sketch why I take this complex of ideas to be deeply problematic.[34] In the final section of this essay, I address the question of what is left of Levinas for those in practical and applied fields once these misunderstandings are taken off the table.

Regarding the assumption that the face is a source of ethical responsibility, it has to be admitted again that Levinas's own writings in many respects foster this misinterpretation. For example, Levinas writes, "the face opens the primordial discourse whose first word is obligation, which no interiority permits avoiding" (*TI* 201). This makes obligation sound unavoidable and indubitable, and it might be read as implying that the face is causally involved in producing this obligation (after all, what else would "opens" mean here?). Likewise, when he says that "to encounter a face is straightaway to hear a demand and an order" (*IR* 48), the temptation is to infer that the face directly and unequivocally "orders us to act ethically."[35] When this language of *demand* and *order* is combined with the claim that the ethical relationship precedes and exceeds comprehension or knowledge, or is "a veritable inversion of *objectifying cognition*" (*TI* 67), refusing thematization and representation, it becomes overwhelmingly tempting to think of the face as directly impacting the self at an emotional, affective level and somehow producing or requiring an equally direct and incontrovertible response.

A first objection to this kind of reading of the face comes from an empirical quarter: the claim that we are responsible in some way that is immediate and undeniable and that we *recognize ourselves as such* simply does not hold up when we consider our everyday experiences. We turn our backs on others in need all the time—we do not always contribute to famine or flood relief, even when the disaster is severe or close to home. We do not invite the indigent man who sits on our corner over for dinner or into our lives. We do not even always show kindness to those we love or take proper care of those who most depend on us. Surely these are more obvious facts than the supposed fact that we are infinitely responsible to a face that does not even appear. Were Levinas really saying that the face commands us to an ethical life in some way that is truly unavoidable, he would need an account explaining why we do not always (or even mostly) act in a manner consistent with this original ethical nature. In effect, he would need an account like the biblical one of our fall from grace or Rousseau's account of how social forces pervert our naturally ethical humanity. There is no such account in Levinas, which is one indication that he did not see himself as offering a description of some ethical nature innate to human beings. And even more to the point, reflecting on *Totality and Infinity* some years later, Levinas admits that the language of the book is perhaps still too ontological—that is, still too much in the vein of an existential analytic of Dasein—but this is because he was, above all, trying to avoid it being misunderstood as a psychological account or description.

If the face is not a physical or psychological force, can it be understood as a normative force? Some of Levinas's statements again suggest such a view: "The infinite paralyzes power by its infinite resistance to murder, which, firm and insurmountable, gleams in the face of the Other, in the total nudity of his defenseless eyes...There is here a relation not with a very great resistance, but with something absolutely *other*: the resistance of what has no resistance—the ethical resistance" (*TI* 199). A passage like this one may well encourage the reader to think of the face as something one really looks into, as if we could see the other's destitution written there and find ourselves responsible as a consequence. But how can the face do this, if it is not anything that appears? If it does not operate like a reason or an emotion, then how does it operate? Other moral imperatives we are familiar with, for example those from utilitarianism or deontology, ultimately find their ground in some familiar feature of human existence (like a capacity to feel pain or a rational principle). If the face is grounded in no such feature—if, that is, it is not grounded empirically—then it may well seem that we are on theological ground where what is involved is revelation or faith. (In fact, this is exactly what some of Levinas's most astute critics have suggested.) But a theological ground surely cannot serve as a sufficient basis for an understanding of professional responsibilities in applied fields. Here we come to an interpretive principle that must stand at the head of any attempt to take Levinas into applied fields—the face is not a solution to ethical dilemmas, it is the name for a *problem*.

Recognizing this must be the first step for those who would invoke Levinas's thought in practical contexts and is tied directly to avoiding the second pitfall: the face not only does not, but cannot provide us with determinate, action-guiding norms or rules. Although there arguably *is* an account in Levinas's thought about how it is that other people's claims register as meaningful with us, this is quite different from providing a specific algorithm (like a categorical imperative or an utilitarian calculus) that could answer the question of what one ought to do in a given case or situation. Suppose for a moment that one is inclined to see Levinas in terms of an ethics of care. If "Care for the other!" is the command issued by a face, how much should I care? At what cost to myself? Why care for this person rather than that one? The answer might come back, as it does for imperfect duties like the Kantian duty to benevolence, that you cannot be told exactly how much to care or when or where, but it is incumbent on you to care some of the time for some of the others. In the first place, this conflicts with the notion of an infinite responsibility; there the claim would be not only that I must care for some other(s), but that I am responsible for *this* other and for all of his responsibilities as well. (Which is one more reason to think that Levinas *is not* in the business of developing an ethics of care.) But even more to the point, a command like "Care!" is simply too vague to operate in contexts in which care-giving professionals need determinate answers and in which part of the task has to be distinguishing the caring that matters in their profession from more generalized notions that we should care for some of the others that populate our lives.

From the point of view of producing an accurate reading of Levinas, it has to be emphasized again that infinite responsibility before the face of the other holds only in relation to a single and singular other. In fact, as Levinas himself points out, there are *always* multiple others: "In the proximity of the other, all the others than the other obsess me, and already this obsession cries out for justice, demands measure and knowing, is consciousness" (*OB* 158). This advent of an other than the other, of a *third party*—which is technically *not* an advent, since these other others are there from the first—is the introduction of what Levinas in his later work calls politics. The responsible subject must now ask, to whom do I give priority? The ego now has to figure out what one other has done to a third, and has to figure out its own responsibility in light of these others' prior patterns of action and behavior. Thus, with this entry of the third, the ego has to develop a measured response that takes into account and balances different needs. It is only at this point in Levinas's text that we have a notion of accountability in our usual sense of a limited obligation based on actions taken in the past. Determinate norms of action that say when and where and how much to do x or y or z belong to this world of accountability and politics, and *not* to what Levinas calls the ethical relation. The face-to-face relationship neither justifies particular norms, nor overturns them; it neither provides politics with its foundational justification nor does it serve in any simple way as a corrective to political forces. In short, the function of the ethical relationship in Levinas is neither constructive nor critical; it never directly *tells* us anything specific at all.

This brings us to the third pitfall, which is perhaps the most difficult to dispel. Does Levinas's thought show us then that we are bound by ethics or by an ethical relationship? Elsewhere I have argued that Levinas's thought *is* about normativity—that is, about how and why the other makes a claim on me—but that it *is not* a normative ethics in the usual sense of generating principles or specific action-guiding norms.[36] His philosophy offers an account of the kind of pull that others have on us, but it is a pull that cannot serve to underwrite specific norms of action. Indeed, it is a pull that is exceedingly tenuous and fragile—because it defies justification—and at the same time seems urgent and even undeniable.

This becomes especially evident as we leave *Totality and Infinity* (whose language is sometimes far too definitive when it comes ethical responsibility) and turn to *Otherwise than Being or Beyond Essence* where Levinas represents the relation to the other through a series of terms—the *trace* and *illeity* principal among them—that emphasize the ambiguity and equivocation in the other's demand. No doubt this ambiguity is already there in the earlier work, most expressly in the idea that the face is not constituted for consciousness like an object accessible to a representation or concept, but the narrative structure of Levinas's presentation through the middle sections of *Totality and Infinity* (especially sections two and three) and the tone of certainty that pervades many of that work's passages tempt us to ignore the ambiguity.[37] In first presenting the ego and its interior life, then turning in a second moment to the ego's encounter with the other (through a very problematic conception of a quasi-ethical or pre-ethical feminine alterity), and finally moving to a discussion of a purportedly unavoidable command or appeal that calls the egoism of the ego into question and founds it as a freedom and a responsibility, *Totality and Infinity* gives the appearance of telling us a story about how we become ethical. The narrative form works to cultivate our sense that the ethical relation in fact happens to us and is in some manner inevitable. The reader of the 1961 text is often left with the impression that there is something like an ethical force in the face and that it generates a certain responsibility. And yet, everything that works toward certainty in that narrative of *Totality and Infinity* is turned on its head by the simultaneous claim that the other who faces me does not really appear, that the command that commands is never heard, that the imposition of ethics is not an imposition but a welcome, and so on.

Far from reassuring us that an impulse to care-giving or compassion is a part of our natural inheritance, or that a duty to care can somehow be grounded by looking into the face or eyes of the other, Levinas's work is a meditation on the fragility of such caring and compassion. In place of ethical rules, Levinas's later work gives us an ethical *saying* that is betrayed each time it is enunciated or *said*. This saying does not ring out as an authoritative command, but as a slight demand, a revelation that scintillates in what is said, blinking between visibility and invisibility, heard and unheard. It does not shine forth boldly in a face, but passes, he says, in a trace (which again is not something that appears, like a footprint in the sand, but something that appears only as the absence of such marks or signs). The ethical demand, as Levinas's later work presents it, is an *exception* in being, which is not to say that it is a rare and precious thing, like a black diamond or a shooting star that nonetheless appears from time to time. It is an exception in the sense that it breaks with the general laws of being, meaning that it *cannot* appear as such. What are we to make of this strange nonphenomenon and how could it possibly serve the needs of those looking to apply ethical theory to practice? How, indeed, can we even talk about this demand that somehow registers without appearing, and that seemingly forces Levinas's later work into figures of speech and forms of syntax that are increasingly paradoxical and hyperbolic?

In what has always seemed to me a powerful way of putting the point, Levinas says that the ethical demand forms on our own lips, in our own mouths (*OB* 147). This image distinguishes the demand, first of all, from commands that come from a source of authority that is clearly identifiable and outside of us. In this sense, the ethical demand is unlike those issued by army officers and parents, and unlike the command of a God whose voice booms like thunder in our ears. But likewise, Levinas's account distinguishes the demand from an inner claim of reason or a sentiment; it is not a product of the will or like the stirrings of need or emotion. In forming on my own lips, it comes in some way from a kind of inner space—like a voice of conscience—but in a manner that is completely unlike a volitional desire. It is almost like a Freudian slip in that it comes out of my mouth, but I am nonetheless not entirely the author of it (and neither is anyone else). With such a view of the demand, it becomes increasingly difficult to paint Levinas as someone who is going to overcome ethical relativism and give us either a firm picture of an ethical human essence or any kind of practical rules to live by.

Vulnerability and Care

So is the upshot that Levinas's work may interest abstract, theoretical disciplines like philosophy or theology but be inapplicable for theorists who are looking for ways to infuse their disciplines with an ethical focus? Is the take home message here, "Don't try this at home" if your home is in a practical, care-giving profession or another applied field? Richard Rorty once denied that the term "ethics" is applicable to Levinas's work because ethics is about adjudicating between competing interests and Levinas does not help us do that.[38] With respect to the latter, Rorty is right—such negotiations belong properly to the sphere of what Levinas terms politics (a broad term for him that includes social, political, and moral questions about who owes what to whom, under what circumstances, and so on). On specific questions—for example, about the just distribution of health care benefits or the ethical or unethical character of experimental medical treatments or psychotherapies—Levinas's thought is going to give us little or nothing in the way of direct action guiding principles. But Rorty is surely wrong in narrowing ethics to self-interest and in suggesting that the primary way we should understand our own interests is as competing with those of others. Caring relationships, compassion for human suffering, the question of what makes a life meaningful and worth living—these are equally questions of ethics and we miss the substance of them when we try to reduce them to the language of self interest or advantage, as Rorty must have been well aware.

In an essay that compares Levinas's thought with Knud Løgstrup's, Alasdair MacIntyre shares the view that both philosophies are rightly characterized as a "normativity without norms." What can be left of ethics once we subtract determinate norms, MacIntyre asks, "The answer is: the ethical demand, responsiveness to the voice that speaks to one out of the singularity of someone's need." MacIntyre further argues that the sort of moral theory Levinas and Løgstrup offer—which is not a theory in the usual constructive sense—has to be understood in historical context, specifically as a response to the aftermath of two world wars that eroded traditional moral norms and fragmented ethical life. These are not, and are not best understood as, timeless philosophies, says MacIntyre; rather the normativity without norms that both offer "is intelligible only as the end result of a history during which the relevant set of norms had lost whatever it had been that had once made those norms compelling." Thus, according to MacIntyre, Levinas and Løgstrup offer an ethics for relativist times, *not* because their thought quells that relativism but because they get inside it, as it were, and offer a description of all that remains once traditional moral supports have been eroded. And what is it that remains? Again: an ethical demand that somehow registers with complete urgency, but without recognizable or determinable foundations. Moreover, this "is an awareness and a mode of response that can only be described through phenomenological techniques." Neither Løgstrup nor Levinas are advancing an argument or expounding a system of morals; they are not laying out a set of principles that the rational agent or the empathic agent is then supposed use as the basis for making decisions or taking action. Rather, says MacIntyre, as phenomenologists they are "inviting us to an act of recognition."[39]

Part of what we are being invited to recognize by both philosophers is the failure of traditional systems of moral thought that rely exclusively on rational principles.[40] Far from being the highest expression of ethical life, as Kant or some Kantians would have it, such systems are just as likely to be a distortion of that life if they are taken to be the whole of it or even the central part of it. Such systems are decidedly of limited use where there is no shared understanding of just what reason is or what it demands, or where past understandings are under threat or undergoing significant change, which was the case at the end of World War II, in MacIntyre's view. But they are equally limited with respect to many aspects of ethical life even where there is general agreement on reason and rational behavior. As virtue theorists have long emphasized, autonomous decision making and acting in accordance with rational principles fails to capture or address the moral demands and dimensions of close personal relationships to family and friends. And as Norvedt has argued, such systems are not a good fit for the care-giving professions for the same reason. In response to this deficiency and to the breakdown in ethical categories and understandings mid-twentieth century, Levinas (and Løgstrup, too, of course on MacIntyre's view) invite us to see that regardless of the failure of traditional systems of ethics, ethical life still has a claim on us, it still pulls at us. We could explain this pull as a result of cultural brainwashing, but that too would be a distortion of what we experience.

So how can this view, which is a response to a significant breakdown of traditional norms and that does not purport to replace them with new rules or principles, work for those working in applied fields? In the first place, my hope has been to wean those in applied fields from the desire to appeal to Levinas as a *ground* for specific understandings of professional life, professional duties, or even professionalized attitudes like that of care. As I see it, there is nothing in Levinas that could serve as a foundation for any of this. And if MacIntyre is right, then Levinas's philosophy, at least in part, must be understood as arising in a historical period in which such grounds were no longer available or convincing. Those seeking a rock-solid foundation for ethical claims will thus be better off looking elsewhere. But, given that part of what is at issue for nurses and therapists alike is a recognition that traditional moral theories are unable adequately to conceptualize caring relationships, in both personal and professional contexts, then Levinas's reflections might indeed have something important to offer. Nortvedt asks, quite sensibly, "How shall the difficult philosophical language of Levinas be transposed into a language conceivable for the empirical reality we see for instance in nursing and medicine?"[41] It is a good question and one that applied theorists ignore at their peril. To make Levinas an authority who intones ethical truths will not do. And, if I am right, even a careful and nuanced reading of Levinas will not deliver ethical maxims or norms that can serve to direct professional policies or conduct. But, nonetheless, as Nortvedt again emphasizes, Levinas's words "speak to us in a very evocative and provocative way."[42] And it is here that Levinas is being used and can be used in practical fields: his work is a provocation, a call to glimpse and *describe* the other's vulnerability, to face the ambiguity that structures human experience, and to frame this as a moral experience rather than an emotional or psychological one.[43]

In effect, much of what goes on in attempts to use Levinas in applied fields is quite right. It comes from the need for a different description of ethics and ethical life—one that attends to the concrete human being whose pain and suffering demands a response rather than to generalized principles or norms. But, paradoxically, much of this literature abandons this insight by trying to make of Levinas's work a new principle or norm. It is this project that must be abandoned in order to move with Levinas into and across practical disciplines and professional fields.

SEVEN

Law, Ethics, and the Unbounded Duty of Care

Desmond Manderson

TOTALITY AND INFINITY AND THE FOUNDING OF A DUTY OF CARE

The great sundering accomplishment of *Totality and Infinity: An essay on Exteriority* lies in the way in which it reconfigured our relationship to others. It asked us to understand our responsibilities in a more dramatic and expansive fashion, and to conceive of human vulnerability as a force and a demand through which we become—more and more, not less and less—ourselves. "What is Hecuba to me?" asks Levinas. And this is a crucial legal question too. The duty of care, which is the central component of the law of negligence and of personal obligation, is unusual. It is not the outcome of an agreement founded on self-interest, like a contract. It is not a duty owed to the community, like criminal law. It describes an everyday *personal* responsibility owed to others and imposed by the law without our consent. Thus it raises, in a distinctly personal way, the ancient question, which even the Bible called "the lawyer's question" (Gen. 4:10; Luke 10:25): Who is my neighbor?

153

Am I my brother's keeper? What does it mean to be responsible? To what extent and why do I owe others a "duty of care"?[1] To speak of neighborhood, proximity, and a duty of care, is speak at once the language of law and the language of Levinas. To the extent that Levinas demands that we take this discourse seriously, thickens, enriches, and disturbs our legal complacency about it, Levinas speaks directly and with deep provocation to the law.[2]

In *Totality and Infinity,* Levinas's approach is broadly speaking phenomenological and metaphorical. He asks us to think about those experiences in our life, which belie the assumptions of totality—of the self as the origin of all knowledge and the justification for all obligation. He then treats these aspects as pointing toward a new way of thinking about what it means to be a human subject. We are asked to *deduce* the existence of infinity from the ghostly shadows and reflections it has left around us (*TI* 28). Suffering, pain, and love, are not secondary to his philosophical hypotheses any more than they are to our own: they are precisely why thinking and living matter. Levinas is not arguing that we *ought* to think more about ethics, or that we *ought* to care more about others. Levinas wishes us to see that we cannot adequately explain our own experience and existence without reconfiguring our understanding of the relationship of self to others.

Totality and Infinity offers two central moments in which things are able to affect us outside of our prior knowledge of them: the face (*visage*) and language (*dire*). Both share the features of nudity or vulnerability, on the one hand, and inequality or asymmetry, on the other. The face "*is* by itself and not by reference to a system" (*TI* 75). Because the face is irreducible to its contents, because it stands beyond representation, recollection, or possession, it presents itself to us as an entreaty (177). The face resists appropriation, but it does so in a totally passive way, as a pure vulnerability (197). Its very muteness and its inability to adequately explain or define itself constitutes the first and singular demand placed upon us. Destroy or trust?

This is the question before and beyond all words that every face asks of us.

Field for the British Isles by Antony Gormley captures the ineffable ethical demand of the face. It comprises almost 40,000 clay figurines in a vast room.[3] They are hand-baked and crudely fashioned—nothing but a rough shape, elongated and bulbous, with two indentations made with a stick before they were baked. But it is enough. Just the presence of two holes makes eyes. Just the presence of two eyes makes a face. Just the presence of a face makes a figure. These are beings. They are small—maybe knee-high—and infinitely, though subtly different. The clay and the different firing conditions have given them slightly varied colorations. The heads are slightly different, the eyes different distances apart, different sizes, angled differently. To enter a large room, crowded to overflowing with little people, clumsy and naked, is an overwhelming experience. These 40,000 unique beings *look* at you. And in that gaze there is something else: something ethical. Just by looking, they are calling for help—because that is what a face is. It looks at you. As Derrida writes, "The face is not a metaphor. It is not a figure."[4] It just *is* this demand for care. This is what is meant by a responsibility that emerges *before* knowledge or reason, not in the logic of the community or in the autonomy and symmetry of individuals. On the contrary, it is the surprise and inequality we experience—our capacity and their vulnerability—that founds the relationship. This surprise and inequality, which most theories of responsibility in the law fail to capture, seems to me precisely what law's duty of care expresses. It is not something you think about—the duty of care just *happens* to you. Before you know anything at all about another being, prior to language or any connection whatsoever, and indeed *in* the mystery of a being, there resides already a duty.[5]

This is what Levinas means by the phenomenological primacy of the ethical. It *initiates* language and consciousness itself, but the relationship does not come as a result of my free will. On the contrary, it emerges precisely as something, which comes from the other and calls me into question, asymmetrically, involuntarily. Levinas writes, "One calls this putting into question of my spontaneity by the [mere] presence of the Other, ethics" (*TI* 43).[6] What transpires from this encounter is language, again understood by the same initial inequality and vulnerability. *Le dire*, "saying," is not a sentence or a proposition; it is the foundation of all such propositions—a promise of authenticity and openness not made in return for anything, but simply as a gesture of faith, without which there could be no communication. The constitutive shocks of face and speech must be understood as events that are able to reach us while being unassimilable to the already known, to our prior rules or expectations or knowledge of the other. The self comes to consciousness therefore not as a movement from the inside out—a *choice* we make to be involved—but, surprisingly, from the outside in, as a quickening of the soul. The face, in its nudity and expectation, demands a response. The response is in the form of a "risky uncovering of oneself...and the abandon of all shelter, exposure to traumas, vulnerability," which "unblocks communication" and allows the process of self-discovery and world-unfolding to at last begin (*OB* 49). Neither are accomplished by a system of meaning of which we are the autonomous master. On the contrary, they can only be accomplished by a process of *infection* or *infestation* in which we discover that the seeds of this connection have already begun to burrow into us.

The I to whom these things happen is therefore not captain of its own identity. The other is already in me, questioning me with his vulnerability, enticing me with desire, dragging me out of my egotism. In *Totality and Infinity*, Levinas expresses this engorgement in a familiar and positive language: "enthusiasm" comes from the Greek *en-theos*, to be possessed by a God (*EI* 104–05). We certainly know that to be possessed by an enthusiasm is a gift or, if you will, a contamination that seems to take hold of us. One speaks of enthusiasm as infectious. So too "inspiration" comes from the Latin *in-spirare,* to breathe into. An inspiration is a breath from outside which fills our lung with new air (105). And again, "eccentric" comes from the Greek *ekkentros,* meaning off-center. For Levinas, particularly in *Totality and Infinity,* we are all eccentric beings precisely because our center of gravity is outside us (*TI* 290–91). If it were not, we would have no weight at all (200).

THE THIRD PARTY AND THE PROBLEM OF LAW IN LEVINAS

There is something romantic about imagining a world of only two; a world in which I am wholly for you and you are wholly for me. *Totality and Infinity* evokes that romance quite explicitly, and not only in his discussions of love, desire, birth, parenthood, childhood, and so on (*TI* 254–80). In Levinas, the one who surrenders is both host and hostage to the other.[7] And this, as has often been pointed out, is the problem. For in law and otherwise, our responsibilities do not concern one other person alone. We must *balance* obligations, weigh up the help a stranger asks of us against our duty to our families and the loved ones who are waiting at home. We live in a society in which needs clash, in which resources are limited, and where more help is sought than can ever possibly be given. For Derrida this is the real question—what then? He writes, "I cannot respond to the call, the request, the obligation, or even the love of another without sacrificing the other other, the other others....I am responsible to any one (that is to say to any other) only by failing in my responsibility to all the others, to the ethical or political generality. And I can never justify this sacrifice."[8] Any attempt to solve the problem would reduce the ethical demand to a legal formula, a hierarchy of norms and rules. And as we have seen, this defeats both the urgency and the precognitive nature of responsibility altogether. Moreover, if "every other is wholly other" (tout autre est tout autre), how could such a comparison even take place?[9] How could incommensurable obligations ever be measured?[10] Derrida says,

"Adhering absolutely to any one duty inevitably leads to my sacrificing another absolute duty, and this I do without any means of justifying my choice. And yet I choose. I choose to follow one and neglect another, to align myself with one and fight against another."[11]

Levinas is entirely mindful of the problem, and tries to address it in his later work.[12] According to Levinas, "If proximity only ordered me to the one other, there wouldn't have been any problem...it is troubled and becomes a problem when a third party enters. The third party is other than the neighbour, but also another neighbour, and also a neighbour of the other, and not simply his fellow. What then are the other and the third party for one another?...Which passes before the other?" (*OB* 157; translation modified). The recognition that the third party is *also* my neighbor brings with it the need for balance and equality.[13] For Levinas, this is why we need justice. But the birth of law in Levinas's world, particularly in *Otherwise than Being,* seems like the death of ethics. "Justice," he concludes, is all about "comparison, co-existence, contemporaneousness, assembling, order, thematization...the intelligibility of a system.... The saying is fixed in a said, is written, becomes a book, law and science" (*OB* 157–59). Levinas therefore seems to conclude that the entry of the third marks the moment at which "I am no longer infinitely responsible for the other, and consequently no longer in an asymmetrical, unequal relation."[14] Law takes over since we cannot stay with ethics.[15] But this seems to me an inadequate response, both for law and for ethics, and I believe that we can do better by staying faithful to the spirit of *Totality and Infinity.*

Totality/Infinity: Balancing and Realizing Responsibilities

In the first place, recent work on the third has suggested that our need to take into account "the other others" does not lead us to entirely abandon ethics for law. Let us return to the law of negligence, the central legal forum of this debate, which always struggles to balance the contradictory and multiple demands that responsibility lays upon us. It does so by moving from a yes/no language by which we determine those to whom we are responsible (the duty of care), to a language of reasonableness by which we determine *how* that responsibility should be fulfilled (the standard of care). Reasonableness imports a social judgment, which means that it attempts to balance what we might have done against our other obligations, expectations, and demands. But this balancing act does not entirely eviscerate the prior question of the duty of care.

The classic U.S. case on the standard of care is *United States v. Carroll Towing*.[16] There, Justice Learned Hand attempted to convert law into mathematics. The standard of reasonable care requires us, he argued, to take into account the probability of an action causing harm (P), the gravity of the injury that might result (L), and against that to weigh "the burden of adequate precautions" (B).[17] In algebraic terms he concluded that liability would ensue if $B < PL$.[18] The standard of care is to be determined *as if* the terms were commensurable: as if risk and inconvenience were able to be measured against one another. *My* B (the difficulty and cost of avoiding an accident) and *your* L (the injury you thereby suffer) both become part of the same juridical equation. This is the fundamental tenet of all forms of utilitarianism, and it is precisely the kind of totalitarian thinking that Levinas contrasts with infinity. The effect is that, as a society, we can decide whether or not my burden (the inconvenience of driving slowly, for example) is greater than your injury. Your injury becomes a cost that society will deem reasonable, if the rest of us accrue advantages from it. Not only does this absorb the two parties into the midst of a social evaluation that subsumes their personal relationship. It ultimately allows the unwanted imposition of a risk on another person if the inconvenience not just to society but *to the defendant himself* proves too great. That too would be reasonable. If the burden on me of avoiding a certain course of conduct is unreasonably great, Learned Hand's calculus allows the harm to reasonably fall on you. So here too, the two sides of the equation are treated just as if they both shared the same interests and values, as if the relationship was symmetrical and commensurable. And this misses the essence of responsibility, at least according to Levinas. We are not liable to another because the benefits and detriments of our actions are commensurable, but precisely because they are *not*.

When Levinas acknowledges the necessity of comparison and order, the necessity in other words of the calculation of reasonableness in a social context, does he thus abandon us to totality, which is to say, to politics?[19] Certainly Levinas often seems to run together "justice, society, the State and its institutions" (*OB* 159). For him, this is all the same: nonethics. But law is more complex than that. The common law of negligence, for example, takes the romantic duality of the world of responsibility— just you and I—quite seriously. In this, the law of torts is already a little closer to ethics than Levinas imagines. The question for the law of negligence is always particular, always shorn of some of its elements of expedience. We are instructed to forget the framework of insurance or of social welfare, and focus just on this singular moment and this singular relationship. For many, that gives the legal argument an air of unreality. But it also properly recognizes the foundational quality of the intimate relationship between two people and attends to its distinct contours.

In fact the law of torts does not accept the logic of *Carroll Towing*. Let us take a famous example. The notorious Ford Pinto was introduced in 1970 with very poor protection for its fuel tank. In every test carried out by Ford involving a rear-end collision over 25 mph, the tank ruptured. Said one engineer, "It's a catastrophic blunder....It's almost designed to blow up—premeditated."[20] The consequence of this design flaw was preventable death and injury: estimates range from 180 deaths up to 900. Eventually 1.5 million vehicles were recalled. Yet an internal investigation conducted by Ford as early as 1973 had concluded that vehicle modification would require a complete retooling of the assembly line and was therefore not cost effective. Taking a figure of \$200,000 as the value of a human life (a rather arbitrary number that had been adopted by the US National Highway Traffic Safety Administration), Ford determined that the cost of vehicle adjustment was \$137 million, and the benefit in injuries foregone and lives saved only \$50 million.[21] According to the logic of Learned Hand's formula (B > PL), it was entirely *reasonable and responsible* for the company to have carried out such an analysis.

Yet this is not what the Court decided, imposing instead huge punitive damages on the company just for engaging in the calculus that Learned Hand commends.[22] Clearly for most people something had gone seriously wrong at Ford in simply undertaking such a calculation, whatever the figures used. It was not merely undignified. It was not merely impossible. They had missed the point. The burden *to you* of fixing a problem is not to be weighed against the injury *to me* of leaving it, for that treats us as if we somehow shared these burdens and benefits. It is not that these things cannot be weighed, but that they should not. Responsibility for another asks us to respect our difference from each other, our fundamental incommensurability. Your gain and my loss cannot and should not be weighed on the same scale. As Levinas concedes, whether we have breached our duties involves questions of balance. Responsibility entails striking a balance between the social and the individual—we do not demand that our vehicles are as safe as they could possibly be. It entails striking a balance between the individual and the other because, as Levinas says, we are ourselves "an other to the others." In the interests of preserving our individual freedom, therefore, we are prepared to run certain risks that are neither large enough nor grave enough to warrant our attention. And it entails striking a balance between our obligations to one other and to all the others. The existence of third parties "is of itself the limit of responsibility and the birth of the question: What do I have to do with justice?" (*OB* 157). Particularly in dealing with government agencies, statutory bodies, and local authorities, the need to balance a whole range of responsibilities may limit the kind and extent of intervention that can reasonably be undertaken.[23] That has clearly been the animating concern of courts in their attempts over recent years to control the expanding liability of local councils and the like.[24] While "the Other's hunger—be it of the flesh, or of bread—is sacred... the hunger of the third party limits its rights" (*DF* xiv).

But there are limits to these limits. Responsibility does *not* entitle us to think of ourselves at the very moment when we should be thinking of the other. Levinas goes on, "the only bad materialism is our own" (*DF* xiv). Responsibility will not permit us to do nothing when we ought to be doing something, simply because doing nothing relieves us of a burden. It is not *up* to us to trade off the other against ourselves. That burden, which Learned Hand suggests can be reasoned away, is the essence of responsibility. Responsibility, like hospitality, means the welcoming of inconvenience. Our courts have not surrendered reasonableness to the calculus of cost and benefit.[25] In the Pinto case, it was held to be fundamentally wrong to attempt to balance out costs and benefits when there is a "substantial risk" to which the plaintiff was exposed. In such a case, the inconvenience or cost of protecting the safety of another is indeed your responsibility, not just an element to be considered in deciding how far it extends. Responsibility is not a question of contract, in which one *uses* another person in ways that advance some mutual project or shared interests.[26] There is a distance between us, and a *height* that, as it recognizes my power, demands of me a sacrifice in order to preserve that distance and that heterogeneity (*TI* 294). The idea of a sacrifice is just what Ford's rational system did not allow for. Instead, they traded off those who burned and died, in the interests of efficiency.[27]

Responsibility is only truly responsible when it is against my interests, against our interests, when it exceeds such calculations. If I *am* responsible for something—for the safety of others on the roads, or the welfare of the child in my care—I do not cease to be responsible when it is no longer worth it *to me*. To think of responsibility in those terms is already to be dangerously irresponsible—in a word, negligent. That is what Levinas means by contrasting "the hunger of the third party" that limits responsibility, with "our own bad materialism," which does not (*DF* xiv). Even when it is reduced to a legal system through the operation of the standard of care, responsibility thus preserves something of its essential character.[28]

THE RELATIONSHIP BETWEEN JUSTICE AND LAW

For Levinas, the infinity of our relationship to others emphasizes not only incommensurability but nonclosure—its irreducibility to prior agreements, knowledge, or rules. A relationship that respects the otherness of the other is attentive to the continuing change in our circumstances, and so continually demands something extra of us. Our responsibility grows as we find our complacent norms disrupted by "the extra-ordinary event...of [our] exposure to others" (*OB* 117). In *Totality and Infinity* Levinas writes, "The infinity of responsibility denotes not its actual immensity, but a responsibility increasing in the measure that it is assumed; duties become greater in the measure that they are accomplished" (*TI* 244). Thus, we can never be entirely settled in our duties or comfortable in our obligations. Responsibility is not a contract—we *always* get more than we bargained for.

There is nothing particularly mystical about this. Levinas's dynamic and noncontractual sense of the nature of responsibility might be describing the development of the common law of negligence over the past century. The inductive reasoning of the common law embodies the recognition that no code can ever capture the true experience of responsibility. Instead, a complex sense of responsibility has grown, gradually but inexorably, precisely *in response to* our exposure to others. Each time the law's response has been to compile a new set of rules ("a book, law and science") but never adequately or finally (*OB* 157). There is always some loose end waiting for a further case to challenge and to press it. The phenomenon of our relationship to others will always be irreducible to what we expected. Concerning each of us and in relation to the system of the common law as a whole, the duty of care is not something we choose or predict. The duty of care—like any responsibility, like love, like parenthood—just keeps happening to us.

To some this comes as a disappointment. The most common criticism of the law of negligence in recent years has been that it has become insufficiently rule-bound and dangerously unpredictable.[29] This debate achieved its greatest focus in Australia, where from 1984 to 2000 the High Court's use of the term "proximity" to describe the circumstances in which our closeness to others gives rise to legal responsibility, was an agent of radical change in the landscape of negligence while remaining, for many of its critics, frustratingly indeterminate or circular.[30] As the boundaries of responsibility expanded, the law seemed increasingly *ad hoc*.[31] A "criterion of liability," complained the House of Lords, must present an "ascertainable meaning" if it is to have "utility."[32] In Australia itself, the many dissents of Brennan CJ, which eventually triumphed in a jurisprudential *kehre* worthy of the name, made precisely this point.[33] He conceived of law as a system of rules and branded the open texture of proximity favored by expansionist judges such as Deane J as nothing but dangerous verbiage. But in making this argument, Brennan, McHugh, Gleeson, and others missed the point. Proximity was a *space* in the law, which recognized that our responsibility for others could not be reduced to the application of *a priori* rules and definitions. Proximity was not a rule but a moment of ethics. Now in relation to law Levinas makes this argument with regrettable vagueness. Not only does he confuse law with politics, as we have already seen. So too he appears to equate law, with justice, with a written code. Levinas even describes justice as "unethical and violent," saying "we must...un-face human beings, sternly reducing each one's uniqueness...and let universality rule" (*ITN* 174).[34] This might lead us to read him as separating the legal from the ethical in a rather crude way. At stake, then, are two points: the narrow way Levinas understands law, and the narrow way he understands justice.

So we need to rescue Levinas from himself. As Sarah Roberts writes, "if one takes seriously Levinas's claim that asymmetrical ethical responsibility is the origin of justice, then one must also reject Levinas's suggestion that justice involves viewing persons and responsibility as comparable and symmetrical."[35] The criticism of Levinas's conception of the meaning of justice and its relationship to law was first sounded by Derrida in "Violence and Metaphysics."[36] He then offered an extensive exploration of the legal question in his essay "Force of Law." For Derrida, there is a contrast between law, in the traditional sense of a stable body of rules, and justice: "law is the element of calculation, and it is just that there be law, but justice is incalculable, it requires us to calculate with the incalculable."[37]

The tension is not just between law on the one hand (rules and generalities) and justice (the ethics of the particular) on the other. This tension finds its expression within law itself. Every legal decision requires us to make a judgment as to the applicability of prior general norms to the necessarily different and singular situation before us. A judge trying to decide whether the current dispute fits within the established category must always confront the fact that they have a *choice*. Although hard cases dramatize it, every unique case requires us to make the same kind of decision. We must still decide if this case is the same as or different from the past, and this is of course the very choice that the past *cannot help us with*. The space of choice that judgment always opens up, then, is as much part of law as it is of justice. Both demand of us that we respect the rules in their utmost generality *and* the individual in his utter specificity; that we attend to the constructive power of the past as a way of controlling the future, and the reconstructive power of the present as a way of reinterpreting the past.[38] This complicated backward-and-forward dynamic is essential to all decision making. Thus, the moment of judgment—the answer to the question of whether and how to follow the rules, which must be singular and newly minted—is a crucial moment in which the judge is singled out and rendered irreplaceable, incapable of substitution by some mere procedure. The burden belongs only to the judge, an inescapable responsibility.[39]

Derrida situates this moment of unique responsibility within the inevitable operation of justice (and not separate from it), and within the inevitable operation of interpreting law (and not separate from it). Ethics demands an element of incalculability, irreducible to formal rules, that continually unsettles our established categories of thinking, and forces us to *question* the meaning of our rules at the very moment we apply them. If Levinas shows the necessity of this instability, Derrida shows how it is already part of something as mundane as legal reasoning. The *necessary* passage of time between enactment of a norm and its application, and the *necessary* uniqueness of the present case by comparison to prior norms, inevitably opens up something other than law itself within law.

The common law of negligence, for all its faults, is a vehicle that remains deeply committed to an engagement on these terms. Its failure as a set of rules amounts to its success as ethics. The duty of care, particularly through the language of proximity as the nonconceptual, phenomenological (Levinasian) trigger of that duty, keeps open our experience and responsibility to others. It institutionalizes change. It is part of the third or social realm but it provides space for a "never-ending oscillation" between ethics and politics.[40] No doubt such inescapable uncertainty makes the judicial role harder. Derrida writes, "This moment of suspense...is always full of anxiety, but who pretends to be just by economizing on anxiety?"[41]

For Levinas the State is always attempting to cut through the knots of discourse, and thus to destroy the interstices of ethics. Statute law and codification have something of that character, preserving law only in an eternal and coherent present. Indeed, in many jurisdictions, amendments to statutes—sometimes many a year—are now placed online.[42] While intended to be responsive to the fluidity of modern law, in practice such techniques conceal the process of amendment in a product that is always perfectly up-to-date and entirely ahistorical. In cyberspace, law loses its memory and becomes a seamless present formed out of whole cloth. But judicial decision making is different. Precedent remembers and continues to worry over the knotty problem of the past. It layers knots upon knots, imperfections upon imperfections. Certainly the court system, faced with such interruptions in its supposedly seamless thread of rules, will always attempt to gather up the loose ends and make everything neat and tidy again. That is how our institutions work. But the knots thus formed conserve the memory of that disruption and authorize the possibility of new ones to further unsettle a purely internal and conceptual system of order.[43] On one level, then, the complex jurisprudence surrounding the duty of care—in Australia but also throughout the common law world—speaks of citizens' responsibilities to one another. And as we have seen, there is an ethical obligation to articulate those responsibilities imperfectly and subject to change. Sometimes, the call of others will put the responsible citizen on the spot. On another level, law's fluidity and its receptiveness to the ways in which the hard case modifies its own rules and assumptions about responsibility, is a way of recognizing law's *own* response ability. The law, too, finds itself reminded that a responsible judgment cannot be rendered in advance; must acknowledge the imperfection of its doctrines and their openness to amendment and reflection. Sometimes the call of others will put the responsible judge on the spot. As a legal principle the duty of care testifies to the ethical engagement that connects persons. As a legal discourse it also testifies to the ethical relationship between those who pronounce the law, and those who stand vulnerably before it.

The danger of law's insistence in recent years on reducing the duty of care to a series of predetermined and concrete rules of responsibility is that it augurs the triumph of a narrower view of the nature of legal responsibility and a narrower view of the nature of legal discourse; and no view at all as to the relationship between them.[44] The context-specific subjectivity and fluidity of the duty of care, particularly as left open in the jurisprudence of proximity, did something ethical *within* the law. It set up a sympathetic resonance between the true meaning of our responsibility for others—unresolved, retrospective, nascent—and the legal forms through which that meaning was articulated. There ought to be some relationship between how the law of negligence understands responsibility to others and how it understands its own responsibility to the law. The uncertain and constantly evolving responsibility Levinas defends is, for each other of us and for the legal system as a whole, a "difficult freedom...a jurisprudence for adults."[45] The question remains whether the law is prepared to grow up.

On the Foundation and Soul of Law

In *Totality and Infinity,* Levinas inverts the established order of thinking and insists that knowledge and language presuppose ethics, and truth presupposes justice (*TI* 90–101). No thinking without already a relationship and no relationship without already a responsibility. Levinas sees ethics as first philosophy—it describes the relationship to others we need before we can have philosophy at all. So the law of negligence is first law—it describes the relationship to others we need before we can have law at all (304). The point is not just that the legal system has responded to an increasingly more complex society. More than this, the legal system has and continues to be itself a *force* in the evolution of consciousness that accompanies such complexity. The discourse of responsibility begets its own growth, by and through a language that continually reaches out beyond established frontiers. As Levinas insists in *Totality and Infinity,* responsibility "is like goodness—the Desired does not fulfill it, but deepens it" (34). Development and change is inherent to such a law. Later he writes, "The infinity of responsibility denotes not its actual immensity, but a responsibility increasing in the measure that it is assumed; duties become greater in the measure that they are accomplished" (244). The open wounds that permit others to affect us must not harden into scar tissue (*OB* 108–14). We must never dwell anywhere too securely, too unchallenged (49). It is not of course that no laws should ever be settled; it is only that ethics requires that we also find a space from which to recognize and give effect to the *necessary* unsettlement of our obligations, since that unsettlement and openness makes responsibility possible. Proximity, the duty of care, and the common law, all work—their best efforts to the contrary—to keep open these wounds. These are not just rules: they are an "optics" (*TI* 23, 78), a "rupture" we ought to welcome in the law.[46]

If this seems threatening, it is in part because of the fear of interpretative uncertainty that the positivist and Western tradition has so potently invoked. Our understanding of interpretation has always sought to maximize the objective, the impersonal, and the fixing of "right answers."[47] Adjudication is a process of settlement and determination. But the talmudic tradition from which *Totality and Infinity* clearly springs finds in the restless ambiguities of interpretation a rich source of dialogue, personal exploration, and change. That which Athens sees as a threat, Jerusalem imagines as an opportunity. It is not of course that there is some kind of choice here between the two. It is too late for that. According to Derrida, "We live in the difference between the Jews and the Greeks."[48] We are already contaminated. But our theoretical resources seem often to get thinner the more thickly complex the lives we lead. The crisis in interpretation theory we face in law is in part due to the limited tradition upon which it has tended to draw.

Courts do not or should not just choose policies because they lead to outcomes they like or because they reflect a social ideology they happen to like; if that were the case then there would be no particular reason why they could not as validly choose otherwise in order to achieve a different set of outcomes or a different social ideology. My argument has been more foundational. An expansive, organic, and self-questioning approach to the duty of care is a better understanding of how law really works. The court's focus on vulnerability, asymmetry, and unpredictability is a better understanding of what responsibility really means. And above all there is a necessary connection between this better understanding of law and this better understanding of responsibility. The duty of care embraces openness because law necessarily embraces openness, because responsibility necessarily embraces openness, *and* because law necessarily embraces responsibility. In the final pages of *Totality and Infinity,* Levinas appeals to our yearning for goodness, pluralism, and peace (*TI* 304–06). Those are law's yearnings too.

EIGHT

The Rights of the Other

Levinas and Human Rights

Scott Davidson

Human rights are the reminder that there is no justice yet.
— Levinas, "The Paradox of Morality"

This proposal to conjoin Levinas and human rights might be met initially with reservations from some Levinas scholars, especially those who would be concerned that an emphasis on human rights would betray the essential insight of Levinas's philosophy, that is, his defense of an absolute ethical responsibility for the other. Is it not a confusion to associate Levinas, the thinker of responsibility for the other, with human rights, and in particular, with their enshrinement in documents such as the Universal Declaration of Human Rights (1948) whose preamble proclaims the equality of all individuals and the goal to promote individual freedom? Perhaps such concerns would explain why Levinas scholarship has been slow to engage Levinas's writings on human rights.[1] Yet, a more careful reading of Levinas's work suggests that the so-called "rights of

man" are a topic of interest, if not direct focus, starting with
some of his earliest and continuing on to some of his last
writings.[2] Levinas, after all, does list the discovery of human
rights among the "exceptional" moments in which the ethical
emerges in Western civilization and engages this topic explicitly
in four of his later essays (*EN* 155).[3] So, even if human rights
are not taken up as a major theme in *Totality and Infinity*,
I want to suggest that they form something like the reverse
side of Levinas's emphasis on the absolute responsibility for the
other. This suggestion, if it turns out to be true, would imply
that, together with its reconfiguration of ethical responsibility,
there is a parallel reconfiguration of the traditional understanding of human rights. This too might be something Levinas
himself has in mind when, in his 1987 preface to the book's
German translation, he alludes to the importance of establishing the "source of a right of the other coming before mine" in
Totality and Infinity (198). But, even more than its import for
how that book might be read or reread, this reconfiguration of
human rights based on "the rights of the other" should be of
much interest to human rights theorists.

My primary aim, accordingly, will be to situate the Levinasian
conception of human rights within the broader context of human
rights discourse, and in so doing, to highlight the unique and
compelling features of his account. Human rights are, to be
sure, among the hallmarks of liberal political thought. In fact,
one of the primary measures of a just political arrangement, on
such a view, would be its ability to secure the rights of individual citizens, however broadly these rights may be construed.
Yet, the standard criticism of the liberal emphasis on human
rights is that it promotes an individualistic and antagonistic picture of community. Such a view, for instance, is conveyed by
Marx's famous observation that "none of the so-called 'rights
of man' go beyond egoistic man, the man withdrawn into himself, his private interest and his private choice and separated
from the community as a member of civil society."[4] The gist of
this objection is that rights talk leads people to think of their

own interests as being separate from those of others, and as a result, they become preoccupied with asserting their own interests in opposition to those of others. Levinas, likewise, rejects this egocentric and antagonistic model of community. Unlike Marx and other critics, however, this does not lead him to discard the notion of human rights altogether. Instead, through his development of a "phenomenology of the rights of the other man," Levinas reconfigures the traditional understanding of human rights in such a way that, on the one hand, it breaks free from traditional liberal justifications of them but, on the other hand, still recognizes them as an indispensible part of just political arrangements. The Levinasian account of human rights should appeal to theorists, as I will set out to show, in virtue of the unique way that Levinas answers the standard objections to them—that is, through his development of a nonantagonistic, other-centered conception of human rights (*OS* 125).

The Critique of Liberal Human Rights Justifications

The Levinasian account of human rights follows the contours of the broader critique of totality developed in *Totality and Infinity*. What makes the work of totalization problematic, on Levinas's view, is the specific way in which it relates to the other. It eliminates the separateness of the other by gathering the other under the unity of a collectivity or a single system. Setting aside the philosophical dimension of this critique of the underlying valorization of unity in Western thought, the socio-political target of this critique is clearly totalitarianism. Totalitarian political systems promote a unified conception of community that places the interests of the collective whole over the rights or interests of individual members of society. Such a conception is dangerous not simply because it undermines the distinction between the public and the private but, even more gravely, because it can be used to justify the "mechanization and enslavement" of the individual (*OS* 121). For, the state's interests do not only justify the establishment of collective goods over individual ones—they can also provide the basis for justifying the temporary or even permanent suspension of the rights of individuals. One extreme example of this is the post-World War II problem of stateless persons, so insightfully analyzed by Hannah Arendt, who lost all rights protections.[5] And, this particular situation may be at least part of what Levinas has in mind in *Totality and Infinity* when he describes the other person concretely in terms of "his destitution, his exile, and his rights as a stranger" (*TI* 76–77). Such wholesale denials of human rights would provide a prime example of the violence against the other that Levinas associates with totalitarianism, and it is against the backdrop of the totalitarian violence of his (and our) time that Levinas affirms the "pathos of liberalism" (120) with its defense of the rights of all individuals, including the dispossessed, against the interests of the state.

Although his defense of human rights puts him in common cause with the liberal political tradition, it is perhaps less obvious, but equally true, that the political dimension of Levinas's critique of the totality also targets the "possessive individualism" assumed by liberal theory.[6] Liberalism, it might be said, takes its starting point from a conception of the individual as a property owner. From this point of view, it defines individual freedom primarily in negative terms as an independence from the influence of others that leaves the individual free to hold property and to develop his or her own talents without interference. But, in this picture of community, other people are perceived primarily as a threat to one's property or talents, and so the role of government would be to protect individuals from the threats they pose to one another and to oversee their transactions on the free market. This conception of the possessive individual operating on a free market, as we are all too aware, can also enact a type of totalizing violence.[7] This occurs, for example, when the other person becomes a commodity or instrument that serves the interests of another ego or, even more broadly, the market system. Since this aspect of the Levinasian critique—specifically, his critique of the possessive individualism that undergirds liberal theory—is so essential to an appreciation of the originality of his own justification of human rights and his conception of the human rights community, I will now turn to examine in greater detail Levinas's rejection of two standard liberal justifications of human rights: the Hobbesian view based on prudence and the Kantian view based on the rational will.

The Hobbesian justification of human rights is based on the view that all human actions are guided by desire and that the most natural human desire is for self-security, which enables one to persevere in one's own being. The problem with the state of nature is that it remains unable to secure those rights. Because the other person has the power to deprive one of one's life and liberty, the other emerges primarily as a threat in the state of nature. Following Hobbesians like David Gauthier, it is out of this situation that we arrive at an agreement to respect the rights claims of one another.[8] Since I want others to respect my own rights claims, I agree to respect the rights of others to their own freedom and security, in turn. The central idea behind this agreement is that human rights are rooted in the things such as freedom and security that we, as self-interested beings, all want for ourselves. The problem with this extension of self-interest, however, is that, even if it might lead to an agreement to respect the rights of one another, it does not remove the self-interestedness of the ego. Instead, it only renders self-interestedness more temperate.

Levinas suspects, in a surprisingly Rawlsian move, that the justification based on prudence inevitably provides an unstable basis for human rights, because it still carries within itself the trace of the war of all against all. This becomes readily apparent with the emergence of inequalities of power. If power were unequally distributed, there would be nothing in the prudential view that would prevent the very powerful from justifying the violation of the rights claims of the weak and vulnerable. For, if one no longer needs the other person to attain and protect the objects of one's own rights claims, then there is no longer any self-interested motive to acknowledge the rights claims of the other person. It follows that, in the optimal situation of self-interest, there would no longer be any reason to restrict the assertion of one's own interests. Such a result leads Levinas to observe that in the prudential justification of human rights we really have nothing more than "the war of all against all, based on the rights of man!" (*AT* 147).

Also examined by Levinas is the Kantian view in which the rational will, expressed in the form of the categorical imperative, would provide the basis for human rights.[9] The central feature of the rational will, on this view, is its capacity for purposive action, which consists of the ability to select its own ends as well as to act in order to accomplish those ends. Noting that all human beings are rational agents who act in order to achieve their selected ends, Kantians like Alan Gewirth and John Rawls argue that human rights can be justified through a deduction of the conditions of the possibility of purposive action.[10] Although there is no human right to the particular things necessary to accomplish a particular end, certain all-purpose goods such as freedom and well-being are necessary for any act of willing whatsoever to be possible. Kantians can thereby conclude that these all-purpose goods—which are necessary conditions of purposive action—provide the content of human rights. But, in response to this type of justification of human rights stemming from the Kantian will, Levinas wonders: "Is it certain that free will lends itself entirely to the Kantian notion of practical reason? Does it allow itself to be totally contained therein without raising any difficulties?" (*AT* 148).

Unlike Kantians, Levinas is not so optimistic about the purity of the rational will. Recognizing that what presents itself as pure practical reason can sometimes be a mask for instrumental reason, Levinas suspects that the rational might not be able to detach itself from its own impure interests.[11] The will, in such a case, would remain susceptible to the influence of the irrational. For the powerful, this would mean that they may be in a position to coerce agreement from a weaker will, while for the weaker, this would mean that they remain under the sway of material necessities and thus, in order to fulfill those needs, may all too easily bend to the dictates of another will. Due to these ulterior motives, which can enter into the purported universal agreement of pure practical reason, Levinas asks whether the will is not rather "a principle of possible war between multiple freedoms, or a conflict between reasonable wills that must be resolved by justice?" (*OS* 122).

So, even if the discourse of human rights might trace its origins to liberal political theory, the Levinasian critique of the totality suggests that human rights cannot find adequate support there. Liberal thinkers such as Hobbes and Kant are only able to establish human rights through a process of "concession and compromise" between possessive egos. Such compromises may be better than outright violence, but they still harbor the same underlying traces of antagonism and egoism. The prudential ego, left unchecked, always threatens to undermine any compromise with others through the reassertion of its own interests over those of the other (*OS* 123). And likewise, the agreements established through the rational will can be the result of a distortion in which the will of others is trumped by a single, more powerful will. To counter the two types of totalitarian rationality—represented by liberal as well as totalitarian political systems—that are called into question in *Totality and Infinity*, the Levinasian alternative seeks to establish human rights from a standpoint that is extraterritorial, both outside of the ego and outside of the state.

This notion of an extraterritorial justice has been explored recently by Robert Bernasconi with great depth and subtlety.[12] Broadly speaking, Bernasconi examines extraterritoriality primarily in relation to liberal politics and proposes that Levinas offers a "prophetic liberalism" in which ethics is not simply relegated to the private domain but rather enters into the political sphere as an interruption and supplement to it.[13]

There Bernasconi suggests that Levinas draws inspiration from Moses Mendelssohn who, likewise, is critical of liberal political theory for its attempt to develop community based solely on the freedom of the ego. Instead of depicting human freedom in the state of nature as a condition of license for the possessive ego to do and to acquire whatever it wants, Mendelssohn characterizes the individual as being animated by a desire for benevolence toward others. The purpose of the social contract is thus not to limit freedom but to promote the development and enhancement of the pursuit of moral freedom, a view that clearly mirrors Levinas's own critique of the egoism implicit in liberal theory. This impetus toward the development of moral freedom, for both Mendelssohn and Levinas, is especially significant because it recognizes that freedom harbors both a right and a duty within itself.

Bernasconi's account of the Mendelssohnian influence on Levinas dovetails nicely with the critique of liberal justifications of human rights developed above, inasmuch as both thinkers do call into question the liberal assumption that individual freedom on its own can provide a moral ground for itself. Yet, in spite of the compelling connection demonstrated between these two thinkers, it seems to me that it is important to protect this account from a potential misreading. For, it still remains unclear precisely how the Levinasian notion of an "outside the state" differs from state of nature theorists who regard human rights as God-given. As a result of the connection drawn to Mendelssohn, readers might all too easily arrive at the (mistaken) conclusion that the extraterritorial justice provided by what Bernasconi refers to as Levinas's "prophetic liberalism" just adds God into the standard equation of liberalism. But, as Bernasconi himself reiterates in this volume, Levinas is not in any way a state of nature theorist, and his notion of extraterritoriality does not seek to redescribe the state of nature in kinder, gentler terms or to establish a religious-based critique of political institutions. What calls for further clarification, then, is the question of what this notion of extraterritoriality signifies and precisely how it differs from the traditional liberal justifications of human rights. This will require a return to the original situation in which human rights "take on meaning only in the other, as the right of the other man" (*AT* 127).

THE PHENOMENOLOGY OF THE RIGHTS OF THE OTHER MAN

Human rights, on Levinas's view, take on their concrete meaning in the face to face encounter with another person. As it turns out, there happen to be a number of interesting parallels between the status of human rights and Levinas's phenomenology of this encounter. An important starting point, in this regard, is the fact that the face of the other is not described by any common property found in either its physiognomy or its social context. In his essay "The Prohibition against Representation and 'The Rights of Man,'" Levinas raises the question of whether the biblical prohibition on representation has a broader significance than its religious one. Although Levinas does not posit a religious basis for human rights, he does point to an important analogy between the way in which both God and the other person break up representational thought.

Representational thought would disclose the face of the other through its visible form, which is to say through its physiognomic features, the eyes, mouth, nose, and so forth.[14] These visible features of the face would point to the broader horizon in and out of which they can appear, a context that might include, for example, the different varieties of animal faces, different racial physiognomies of the face, or different cultural adornments of the face. But, Levinas asserts that these representations of the face as an object enact violence against the alterity of the other, inasmuch as they serve to petrify, solidify, or freeze the other person within a horizon or a context. In this way, Levinas's phenomenology of the face, like the biblical prohibition against worshipping images of God, emphasizes that the face of the other exceeds any representations of what the other person is. Put simply, the face of the other always remains a *who* and can never be reduced to a *what*.

The above position might be described as an insistence on the extraterritoriality of the other person in two particular respects.[15] First, the other is extraterritorial in the sense of transcending every social, historical, or linguistic context in which the other might be disclosed or known. What this entails for human rights is that the other person has a standing "outside the state" (*OS* 123), apart from the other's citizenship status or group membership. This is how human rights, as Levinas puts it, "express the alterity or absolute of every person, the suspension of all *reference*" (117). Freed from all other points of reference, they remain independent of and prior to any notion of merit—tradition, jurisprudence, authority, political belonging, and so forth.[16]

Second, the other is extraterritorial in the sense of being outside the subject. Specifically, the standing of the other is not dependent on any supposed physical (or metaphysical) property belonging to human faces or persons. In *Totality and Infinity,* Levinas repeatedly asserts that the alterity of the face cannot be reduced to some type of general property that would be inherent in all the members of some genus, instead its alterity is the product of a specific type of relation between the self and other.[17] Levinas conceptualizes this relation in linguistic terms. The alterity of the other is produced concretely when the other person speaks. To be precise, what matters for Levinas's description of the other's speech is not so much *what* the other says but the fact *that* the other speaks to me. The speech of the other person, instead of appearing as a theme within a horizon (*pros allelon*), reveals the other on its own (*kath'auto*) (*TI* 65). This revelation *kath'auto* signifies an unconditioned presentation in which the other appears "from itself" and "by itself" (67; 202). This means that, before delivering any signs or any information, the speech of the other delivers a personal presence or a self-presentation, such as is the case when the other says "hello, it's me" [*moi, c'est moi*] (296). Concretely, that is to say that the alterity of the other is not realized in any particular message but in the uniqueness of the other's voice. Through this appeal that is made to me, the voice of the other person stands outside the subject. But, if this is the case, it immediately prompts an important question: How can the other whose voice is separate and unique give rise to a community of persons whose rights are universal and the same?

This paradox is not one that Levinas seeks to resolve, instead he recognizes it to convey something mysterious and remarkable about the human community. The human species is a group consisting of members who are absolutely unique, incomparable, and irreplaceable individuals. This same sense of paradox is conveyed in Levinas's observation that the singular face of the other person "attests the presence of the third party, the whole of humanity in the eyes that look at me."[18] This paradoxical presence of the other as both a unique individual and the whole of humanity sheds light on Levinas's unique understanding of the nature of human community. Levinas, to be sure, does not deny the biological connectedness of human beings,[19] but yet he does not take any physical resemblance or similarity among human beings to define it, as if it emerged like the race of humans all produced from the stones cast by Deucalion.[20] Instead of defining human beings in terms of some common feature, *Totality and Infinity* conceptualizes the human community on the model of language. The linguistic community, to put it simply, is made up of members who have the same linguistic aptitude for speech as all the others, and at the same time, who each have a unique voice that is unlike the voice of anyone else. Through the use of language, the absolutely unique voices of interlocutors enter into relation with one another. Here we have arrived at the precise difference between Levinas's notion of extraterritoriality and the state of nature. Whereas the state of nature represents an absence of or flight from community, Levinas's extraterritoriality emerges in the concrete presence of others—in the establishment of linguistic community made up of persons who are incomparably unique individuals *unlike any others* (singular) and at the same time members of humanity *just like all the others* (universal).

Without going further into all of the complex details of Levinas's conception of community, the point I want to emphasize here is just how well this linguistic model of community accords with contemporary approaches to human rights. Human rights, it is widely agreed today, are not natural or metaphysical properties of persons. Instead of expressing any facts about human beings, they are part of the fabric of our language and the interweaving of our own lives with those of others. It follows, for contemporary theorists, that their meaning should be approached through the study of the language of rights, and more specifically, the various pragmatic contexts in which language users make rights claims on one another in actual communities.[21] Human rights, from this perspective, are fundamentally linguistic claims, and the object of such claims is not to assert a fact about the world but to call on other people for specific types of treatment. Understood as claims, human rights can be characterized in terms of the following formal structure: they are claims made by someone for a certain type of treatment from someone else. Working from this starting point, many contemporary discussions of human rights discourse proceed to examine the various formal elements of these claims and the pragmatic contexts in which claims are made.

Even though Levinas's thought converges with contemporary theorists with respect to understanding human rights as linguistic claims, there can be no mistaking the fact that Levinas does not pursue a formal or systematic treatment of rights of any kind. Due to his phenomenological orientation, he would consider such an activity to be only secondary in importance and instead would find it necessary to go back to the concrete experiences where human rights originally gain their significance. Indeed, this return to the concrete encounter with the other is what sets him apart from the formal trajectory followed in most other contemporary accounts of human rights claims.

Levinas holds that human rights take on their concrete meaning, as we have already noted, within a particular type of pragmatic context, namely, one in which the other person speaks to me and makes a rights claim on me. This concrete orientation of the pragmatic context, in contrast with purely formal analyses of rights, shows why the role of the rights holder and the duty bearer cannot simply be assumed to be reversible or interchangeable with one another.

Traditional liberal justifications of human rights, as we have seen, adopt a pragmatic orientation of their own, inasmuch as they adopt the standpoint of possessive individualism. They take the ego as their starting point and thereby regard the securing of its possessions as their goal. From this perspective, the ego is a rights holder who asserts claims against the other that, if valid, the other must fulfill. Levinas's phenomenology of human rights, however, reverses the direction of this pragmatic relation, such that the other is now an interlocutor who makes a rights claim on me for a specific type of treatment, and I become the addressee who is called to respond to this claim. Within this situation, Levinas observes that human rights "manifest themselves concretely to consciousness as the rights of the other person and as a duty for an ego" (*OS* 125). On the surface, it might seem that this shift of the pragmatic context is inconsequential: it seems simply to reverse the structure of egoism and thus to transfer over to the other all of the rights that were held previously by the ego. Indeed, if this were the case, then it might be argued against Levinas that the possessive individualism of the original account remains basically unchanged and, consequently, that the ego is now put in a condition of servitude to the egocentric demands of the other. But, such a response is overly simplistic, and it can be answered by showing that, instead, what takes place here is a reconfiguration of the significance of the rights of the other *and* those of the ego.

Levinas's "phenomenology of the rights of the other man" establishes the extraterritoriality of the other, or to put it in a legal idiom, the absolute *standing* of the other. What I take this to imply is that the other has the unqualified or unconditional right to be heard and to make claims for a specific type of treatment, regardless of any consideration of his or her social status, citizenship, or group membership. Based on this unqualified standing, the rights of the other stand outside the state and go beyond any conditional terms that might be placed on an individual's standing. By establishing the standing of the stranger or stateless person in this unqualified way, Levinas provides a compelling solution to one of the pressing political issues of his times — reminding us that we have a responsibility to allow the voices of all others to be heard. But yet, this defense of the standing of claims made by all persons, on its own, cannot exhaust the full scope of the Levinasian account of responsibility for the other.

The face of the other, as Levinas describes it, includes not only its majesty and power to command but also its vulnerability and plea for help. Whereas the face's power to command would encapsulate the various types of claims made by the other, the vulnerable aspect of the face would point to a level of responsibility that goes beyond the other's actual assertion of rights claims. Understood in terms of the vulnerability of the other, it would thereby extend to include those others — such as the figure of the elderly or the child — who are so vulnerable that they cannot even assert claims on their own behalf. Taken to this extreme, the responsibility for the other would extend even to those cases where the other does not or cannot assert any claim at all. And, it is on this point that Levinas's phenomenology of the rights of the other man is most compelling — for it is precisely in those extreme types of situations that human rights talk becomes the most urgent and the most meaningful. It seems to me that only a conception of rights, such as this one, that goes beyond the assertion of rights claims and recognizes an even more fundamental relation between human beings, one oriented by responsibility for the vulnerability of the other, can account for this very important dimension of human rights.

That said, we have not yet considered the effects of this responsibility for the other on the ego itself. Some might believe that what has taken place is only a transfer of all rights over to the other, but such a view is clearly belied by Levinas's further assertion that "my freedom and my rights, before manifesting themselves in my opposition to the freedom and rights of the other person, will manifest themselves precisely in the form of responsibility, in human fraternity" (*OS* 125). So, instead of leading the rights of the ego to be annulled, the key point here is that the rights of the ego emerge from another source than egoism. That is, it is out of responsibility for the other that the ego gains its rights. Emerging out of obligation to others, they express "beyond the burgeoning of identities in their own identity and their instinct for free perseverance, the for-the-other of the social, of the for-the-stranger" (*AT* 149). The novelty of this situation is that rights are no longer the product of an egoism that asserts rights for itself but of a responsibility that asserts its own rights for the other. In its being for-the-other, the rights of the ego develop together with the rights of the other.

An appreciation of Levinas's account of human rights can thus help to counter an overly simplistic reading of *Totality and Infinity*. It is sometimes said that, while *Totality and Infinity* provides an ethics in the form of absolute responsibility for the other, it does not provide any defense of the self and thus places the self in a condition of servitude to the other. This misreading, however, can only get started on the condition of an exclusive focus on Levinas's account of ethical responsibility for the other. The defense of human rights, which remains mostly implicit in *Totality and Infinity* but becomes explicit elsewhere, suggests that there is necessarily a reverse side to the self's responsibility for the other. The responsible ego is not left without defenses or resources of its own, because it gains its own rights precisely out of its responsibility for the other. When read in terms of this codevelopment of the rights of the self and other, the account of ethical responsibility in *Totality and Infinity* takes on a dual nature: it becomes the basis for orienting the responsibility of the self toward the rights of the other and, on this very same basis, toward its own rights.

RECONFIGURING HUMAN RIGHTS

Beyond its potential interest for helping to resolve some difficulties raised by *Totality and Infinity*, I want to conclude by pointing out a few of the broader implications of Levinas's account of the rights of the other for human rights discourse. An initial point of interest can be noted by contextualizing this account in terms of the most important human rights document of this era, the "Universal Declaration of Human Rights" (1948). Each of the articles in that document begins with universal statements asserting the rights of all human beings. For instance, article 3 affirms that "Everyone has the right to life, liberty, and security," and article 4 states that "No one shall be held in slavery or servitude." But, it is important to note that near the end of this document in article 29, tucked away nearly out of sight, an abrupt shift in the discourse takes place.[22] Instead of affirming the rights of the human being, there surfaces a reminder of the limitations to individual freedoms and rights.

Article 29.1 emphasizes the importance of responsibilities to others, stating: "Everyone has duties to the community in which alone the free and full development of his personality is possible." What, then, does this emergence of responsibilities to others signify within the context of a document enumerating a set of basic human rights? The next clause, article 29.2, perhaps indicates this document's own answer to that question.[23] It suggests that the rights of others serve as a limit to our own rights, and in this respect, this document clearly bears the mark of the possessive individualism that Levinas calls into question in *Totality and Infinity*.[24] That is, it mistakenly leads us to believe that responsibility for the other emerges as a limitation of and threat to our own rights and freedoms. By contrast, we have shown that Levinas reverses the terms of this equation and leads us to think of our own rights as emerging from our responsibilities. This point of contrast should not be taken as a call to revise the document or to add a list of responsibilities to it, although the latter option was actually considered in the original drafting of the UDHR.[25] Instead, it should be noted as a different way to orient the document's meaning and purpose. Levinas helps us to appreciate that it is not vital to affirm human rights for one's own sake, instead they become meaningful partly because they are affirmed for other people and partly because they promote our own ability to be responsible for others.

Better than other justifications of human rights, Levinas's account provides a compelling response to the two most common objections against them: that they promote individual egoism and an antagonistic model of community. Against the former objection, Levinas's defense of human rights displaces egoism by conceiving rights, first and foremost, as the rights of the other. The rights of the other have an unqualified standing for Levinas, entitling the other to make rights claims independent of any characteristic, group membership or affiliation. In describing the nature of rights claims, Levinas also tries to shift our thinking away from a zero-sum game in which rights claims would assert either the interests of oneself or another, instead his notion of the self as for-the-other opens the possibility for a nonantagonistic relation to the other person or, in other words, a win-win situation in which the benefits of rights are shared. For that reason, the human rights community might be described in terms similar to those that Levinas uses for the linguistic community—both communities, it might be said, bring us together "not through what we have but what we give" (*TI* 209). As a result of this reorientation of the meaning and justification of human rights, it seems to me that they become less like the holdings of possessive individuals and more like the community that is established by giving gifts to others.

NINE

Ethics as Teaching

The Figure of the Master in *Totality and Infinity*

Joëlle Hansel
Translated by Scott Davidson

INTRODUCTION

The figure of the *master* occupies a unique place among the figures of alterity that populate *Totality and Infinity*. Unlike the *feminine* and the *child* that appear later, it emerges in the initial stage in which the "breach of the totality" occurs through discourse. Discourse describes a situation where the Same and the Other, though being in relation, remain irreducibly separated. Levinas, who began very early in the school of phenomenology, was not content with a conceptual and abstract approach. His method, in this regard, never varied: it is necessary to *deformalize* concepts and return to the concrete situations in which they take on their sense. The figure of the master is closely associated with the "deformalization" or the "concretization" of the Cartesian idea of the Infinite that, while part of the phenomenological inspiration to which *Totality and Infinity* still claims to adhere, manifests the Levinasian primacy of ethics (*EN* 197). Everything must be translated in terms of human relations because they—instead of an anonymous being or the "I think"—are conceived as the original site of meaning.

It is widely known that Levinas grants a privilege to the paradoxical figure of the other who is at once the poor *par excellence* and the master who commands me to serve him or her, albeit without domination or violence. Perhaps less attention has been given to the second sense of this term whose homonymy is exploited by Levinas, for the Other is also the master who teaches me the idea of the Infinite. Through the dual sense of the word "master"—the one who commands me and the one who teaches me—the two modalities of the deformalization of the idea of the Infinite emerge. The other who, through teaching and mastery (*seigneurie*), exceeds all my powers is the one to whom I owe everything and who I cannot approach with "empty hands" (*TI* 50). The other is also the one who gives me this idea of the Infinite of which my mind cannot be the source. Without disrupting the asymmetry that governs our relationship, the generosity of the pure gift given to the other goes along with my complete receptivity with regard to the other.[1] In order for the infinite to come to mind and for the naturally autarchic self to open to the presence of the other, it is thus necessary for the idea of the infinite to be taught to me and for a relation of the teacher and student to be established between us. In that way, teaching is given a prominent role. It can no longer be reduced to a set of methods or procedures designed to form the mind of the student or to transmit information to him or her. It is endowed with an entirely ethical signification.

This essay describes the direct link that connects ethics and teaching in *Totality and Infinity*. The figure of the master and the theme of teaching appear frequently in the texts published by Levinas in the period that begins immediately after World War II and concludes with the publication of *Totality and*

Infinity. They play an essential role in the debate that Levinas conducts with the Western philosophical tradition, whether it is his critique of the Socratic model of knowledge or his reinterpretation of the Cartesian notion of the idea of the Infinite in me. They also are a central piece of his critique of the notion of the *sacred* developed concertedly in *Totality and Infinity* and his *Essays on Judaism* collected in *Difficult Freedom.*

To understand the reason for the privilege that Levinas gives to the figure of the master who teaches, one should consider the orientation of this phase in the evolution of his thought. Although shaking the pillars of Western idealism — the hegemony of a naturally free ego and the primacy of knowledge — and seeking their justification, Levinas does not reject rationalism. The relation of the ego with an alterity that is exterior to itself and overflows all its powers — with the idea of the Infinite — does not destroy its integrity, its psychism or inner life, its position as a separated and atheist ego or even, in a sense, its freedom.

TRANSCENDENCE AND TEACHING

The first appearance of the figure of the other as a master who teaches occurs well before *Totality and Infinity.* It dates back to 1949, the year that Levinas published "The Transcendence of Words," an article devoted to *Biffures,* a work of poetry by Michel Leiris that was published one year earlier (*OS* 144–50). There one can already detect one of the axes of the critique of Western thought that will reach its culmination in *Totality and Infinity:* the questioning of the primacy of vision, whether it is sensible vision or the act of thought "that is light" (157), that "seeks the clarity of the self-evident" and that "ends up with the unveiled, the phenomenon." To the "visual experience to which Western civilization ultimately reduces all mental life," Levinas contrasts hearing and everything that results from it — sounds and words. The contrast between vision and hearing repeats the more fundamental one between immanence and transcendance. In the vision where "a form espouses a content," things are given to the eye or the mind as phenomena offered for description and understanding. "A world that is completely *here,* and self-sufficient" is constituted through visual experience. In this world bathed in the light of seeing and the concept, everything is given, everything is disclosed and revealed, "all is immanent." Unlike vision, "sound is all repercussion, outburst, scandal" (147), it marks "the incapacity of form to hold its content." It is the indication of a surpassing of the given, "a true rent" in the fabric of the world, an "overflowing," and an inadequation (148).

In an optics for which ontology is no longer fundamental, sound does not derive its transcendence from itself but from the presence of the other. In virtue of the priority that it gives to "the direct social relations between persons speaking," Levinas contrasts the "spoken word"or the "proffered word" with the silent language that vision offers for contemplation. "Reaching beyond the given" (*OS* 148) and leaving the order of immanence consists in speaking to someone. Although Levinas affirms "the privilege of the Other"—"the primary fact of existence" being "neither in being-in-itself, not in being-for-itself, but the '*for the other*'"—he does not describe the relation with the other in this article in the same ethical terms that he will use in *Totality and Infinity* (149). That said, he already conceives the fact of addressing the other—which he will later call "discourse"—as a movement of transcendence, as a departure from oneself that interrupts the autarchy of the self and the ipseity folded onto itself.[2] Thus, Levinas writes, "Expression bears within itself the impossibility of being in-itself, of keeping one's thought 'for oneself' and, consequently, the inadequacy of the position of the subject in which the ego disposes of a given world" (149). It is in this context that ethical pedagogy appears for the first time. The "living word," "destined to be heard," is presented as a teaching that one receives from the other (149). Already perceptible in his critique of vision, Levinas's distance from Platonism is made explicit in his distinction between teaching and maieutics. The other or the master whose own presence teaches the idea of transcendance is not "a midwife of minds." The other's teaching does not consist in making the ego redis-cover the truths that are immanent to itself, which are inscribed within it for all eternity, and then only have to be contemplated with complete peace of mind. The hearing of the other's speech leads beyond the world to which vision limited me. The master who teaches "wrenches experience away from its aesthetic self-sufficiency, from its *here,* where it rests in peace" (148).[3]

The Infinite and the Sacred

Between 1949 and 1961, Levinas published a number of important articles that progressively constitute the ethics that is systematically developed in *Totality and Infinity.* In the essay "Philosophy and the Idea of the Infinite" (1957), he includes his critique of maieutics in a more general argument, which calls into question the ideal of autonomy that has dominated the history of Western philosophy. In virtue of the sovereign freedom of the mind, the truth, which is foreign to the origin, becomes immanent to it after the moment it has been under-stood. Every alterity is thereby reduced and returned to an identity that constitutes the very essence of the self. In the form of the idea, the object is interior to the thought that thinks and contains it.

To this "philosophy of the Same," Levinas contrasts a het-eronomous subjectivity, which is open to a truth that always remains external to it and whose irreducible alterity it recog-nizes. While the "I think" is the incarnation of autonomous reason, the idea of the infinity in the "Third Meditation" is the purest expression of the basic heteronomy of the human mind. Levinas emphasizes the exceptional character of this idea. Unlike all other ideas, "it intends what it cannot contain and, in this precise sense, is the Infinite" (*TI* 48–49). As such, "the *ideatum* exceeds its idea" and the infinite overflows the thought that thinks it.

The exception of the idea of the Infinite is shown by a characteristic that is a direct mark of ethical pedagogy: it is the only one of our ideas that has been "placed in us" (*CPP* 54) and not rediscovered by ourselves, as the Platonic conception of maieutics would have it, by presupposing that the soul "recovers the instruction that it receives through memory" (161). It is thus an idea, which does not teach what one already knew but which teaches what one does not know. At first sight, the reason by which Levinas justifies the exceptional status of the idea of the Infinite sounds like a truism: Is not learning, by definition, discovering what one did not know until then?

To understand the singularity of the teaching of the idea of the Infinite, one must consider that the ethical foundation, which underlies Levinas's metaphysics, is that the intersubjective relation—and not the relation to anonymous being—is the source of meaning. Teaching, which gives the idea of the Infinite its exceptional character, thus cannot be reduced, as is the case for other ideas, to the transmission of a content that, though new at the beginning, ends up belonging to the world that is familiar to me. By entering into relation with the other, the other introduces an idea into consciousness that the subject, as always identical to itself, cannot derive from itself; the other teaches its own infinity, its irreducible exteriority, and its absolute alterity. It is in this resolutely nontheological sense that the notion of revelation must be understood, such as it is taken up in "Philosophy and the Idea of the Infinite" where Levinas contrasts philosophy conceived as "atheism or rather unreligion" with the idea of a truth "put into us" and not discovered by an act of recollection or acquired by self-examination (*CPP* 49).

That said, it is surprising that teaching is chosen to describe a situation in which the idea of the Infinite, or absolute alterity, enters the mind from the exterior, instead of being the fruit of what the Western tradition has glorified under the name of autonomy: "the free acceptance of a proposition," the "culmination of a free investigation" (*CPP* 48, 49). Is not the fact that an idea is "put into us" contrary to the basic principle that the good teacher is the one who helps the student to discover the truth by him or herself, through the use of his or her own understanding? Does not the contact with an exteriority that invades me—in the sense of an invasion that I have willed and the idea of which I find without seeking it out—threaten my own integrity as a subject?

This problem can become fruitful if one considers one of the major themes in the *Essays on Judaism* published in the 1950s. To the extent that education is "*action on a free being*" (*DF* 14), it must get rid of everything that can do it violence, every truth that attempts to impose itself on reason without having been the result of "collaboration" (6). In spite of the reservations expressed in this regard in 1937, Levinas does not hesitate to recognize, on this point, the virtues of the rationalism in "the moralism of the nineteenth century."[4] In spite of its "naiveté," it was able to counteract "the charm of myths and mysteries."As he writes in "Ethics and Spirit," it had at least one thing to its credit: "*it tried to interpret Judaism as a religion of the spirit*" (6).

In the *Essays on Judaism*, Levinas's criticisms have a precise target. They are aimed at two forms of "irrationality" that are especially prized by ethnology and the science of religions: the notion of the sacred and the exaltation of myth.[5] In both cases, Levinas discloses the alienating character of the contact with anonymous forces and powers that, while originally external, are introduced into the heart of subjectivity and dispossess the person of his or her identity. He is thus opposed to a relation to a divinity that would degenerate into "the numinous and the sacred [that] envelops and transports man beyond his powers and wishes" (*DF* 14). By giving rise to fear and trembling in us, "the Sacred wrenches us out of ourselves." It is the violent action par excellence, one "which we endure without at any point collaborating with it" (6–7).

Following the method that Levinas himself adopts with regard to the Cartesian notion of the Infinite, its formal schema can be retained for conceptualizing the relation to the sacred. It thus becomes the paradigm for all the situations in which something external, something that exceeds us and that we do not master, is introduced into us. In order for this situation not to turn into alienation, it is necessary to guarantee a degree of liberty for consciousness.

By reading the essays on Judaism that are contemporary with "Philosophy and the Idea of the Infinite," one thus discovers a surprising phenomenon: whereas Levinas called freedom into question in his philosophical essay, judging it to be unjust and forgetful of alterity, in his writings on Judaism he considers it to be the very essence of "spiritual life." To be sure, he does not do this without several precautions. In "A Religion of Adults," the freedom in question is heteronomous. As is the case in *Totality and Infinity,* freedom "shows itself to be arbitrary" and "appeals to an investiture" that must come from the other (*DF* 17). All the while supposing a being who is freed from the control of the sacred, education is fundamentally "obedience to another will." But, if "liberty is not an end in itself," "it does remain the condition of any value man can attain" (14).

In "A Religion of Adults," there is a further contrast with the argument developed in "Philosophy and the Idea of the Infinite." Levinas nuances his criticism of the atheism of a philosophy, which rejects "revelation"or the fact that an idea is "put into us" by an external being. To the extent that this atheism requires the destruction of idols carrying the occult powers of the sacred, "Judaism feels very close to the West, by which I mean philosophy" (*DF* 15). These differences of inflection, though real, do not mark a contradiction between the two sides of Levinas's work. In spite of his critique of the irrational—the sacred and myth—and his defense of a certain type of freedom—one that can be expressed through philosophical reflection, scientific research, or talmudic study—his Jewish writings by no means seek to justify the "philosophy of the Same" that he criticized in "Philosophy and the Idea of the Infinite."

Pursuing an idea expressed as early as 1951, reason (that is, "the rationality of the human psyche") is entirely heteronomous—it does not have its foundation in itself but outside of itself, in "the intersubjective relation" (*EN* xi).[6] By giving a place to the freedom of the ego in his *Essays on Judaism*, Levinas does not count on going back to the ideal of autonomy. He simply aims to conceive a situation in which reason has a relation with something that does not have its source within reason but does not do it violence, where "contact with an external being, instead of compromising human sovereignty, institutes and invests it" (*DF* 16). Such is the case with the idea of the Infinite. While teaching reason about the existence of an absolute alterity that founds it and while revealing the anteriority of the social relation toward the activity of knowledge, it does not destroy the integrity of the ego. Even though it is in me, this idea teaches me the idea of an alterity that remains absolutely exterior but that is not imposed on me as a force investing my entire being and taking my freedom from me. To be precise, the relation with the other tears me away from myself in a completely different sense than the contact with the sacred. To the degree that the infinite reveals itself concretely in the face-to-face with the other—in "the sight of the face"—it is not "*known*," but is "in *society* with us"; the relation with alterity is "a moving out of oneself" (10). The externalizing movement of the subject, or in other words, transcendence, responds to the exteriority of the other.

Teaching as a Welcome of the Other

In *Totality and Infinity*, the description of the relation with the other in terms of teaching appears at a central point in the economy of the book, in a passage where Levinas assigns himself the following task: "We must now indicate the terms which will state the deformalization or the concretization of the idea of infinity, this apparently empty notion" (*TI* 50). We usually envision teaching by placing ourselves in the position of the one who does the teaching, whether it is the teacher's personal qualities, training, or techniques. Levinas takes the counterpoint of this popular vision by considering it from the point of view of the one who is taught.

At first glance, the use of this grammatical form leads one to think that the self is purely passive. However, the terms used by Levinas shed light on what it means "to be taught": "To approach the Other in conversation [*discours*] is to welcome his expression, in which at each instant he overflows the idea a thought would carry away from it. It is therefore to *receive* from the Other beyond the capacity of the I, which means exactly: to have the idea of infinity. But this also means: to be taught. The relation with the Other, or Conversation, is a non-allergic relation, an ethical relation; but inasmuch as it is welcomed this conversation is a teaching" (*TI* 51). To say that the idea of the Infinite "is taught" to the ego means that it must not only be "received" but "welcomed." The sense that Levinas gives to this "welcome" of the Infinite or absolute alterity shows that the ego does not have the passivity of the wax tablets on which, according to empiricism, sense data from the outside are impressed. To describe the position of the ego who is taught by the other, one should not talk about passivity but receptivity. In this regard, one notes a characteristic feature of the complex relation that Levinas entertains with the philosophical tradition that he calls into question without ever excluding himself from it.

The harsh criticisms that he addresses to the philosphical systems stemming from the "philosophy of the Same" does not prevent him from claiming the right to keep at least "one trait" of it, although neglecting "all the details of its architecture" (*OB* 129). The points on which he rejoins the major representatives of idealism do not only touch on ethics.[7] They also concern the plane of epistemology, as shown by the passage in which he distinguishes between two senses of the word "theory." Taken in the sense of "comprehension [*intelligence*], the *logos* of being," theory refers to "a way of approaching the known being such that its alterity with regard to the knowing being vanishes." By contrast, knowledge or theory can also describe "a relation with being such that the knowing being lets the known being manifest itself while respecting its alterity" such that "in this sense metaphysical desire would be the essence of theory." By taking into consideration this sense of the word "theory," Levinas remarks that "it is not by chance that the theoretical theory has been the preferred schema of the metaphysical relation" (*TI* 42). Based on this principle, it retains the formal structure of relations that, in the domain of knowledge, connect the subject and the object in order to give them a content that is no longer epistemological but ethical.

This is illustrated, in *Totality and Infinity,* by the recourse to the notion of receptivity to conceive the position of the self to whom the idea of the Infinite is taught. In the history of philosophy, this notion is associated with Kant who uses it to describe the status of sensibility. In contrast with the activity or "spontaneity" of the understanding or the "ability to produce presentations ourselves," sensibility expresses the mind's receptivity "to receive presentations insofar as it is affected in some manner."[8] The terms Kant uses to describe this receptivity show that it cannot be confused with a pure and simple passivity. As such, sensibility is "*the capacity* (a receptivity) to acquire presentations as a result of the way in which we are affected by objects."[9]

Levinas transposes onto the ethical plane what holds for Kant in the domain of knowledge. The way in which he describes the fact of being taught or of welcoming the idea of the Infinite refers as well to the register of receptivity: "in order to welcome revelation [of the idea of infinity or of absolute alterity], a being *apt* for this role of interlocutor, a separated being, is required" (*TI* 77; italics mine). Elsewhere, he adds: "The idea of infinity implies a soul *capable* of containing more than it can draw from itself. It designates an interior being that is *capable* of a relation with the exterior, and does not take its own interiority for the totality of being" (180; italics mine). Although they are the expression of "a receptivity without passivity" (211), the notions of aptitude and capacity do not signify that the self holds a capacity or a power. They indicate that the idea of the Infinite is not given to just anybody. It is taught to a subject capable of welcoming it, to a self "separated"and "atheist"who has already broken with the totality by constituting itself as a psychism, in enjoyment or in representation.

One thus rediscovers in *Totality and Infinity* the rationalism that consists in speaking about the heteronomy of the self subjected to the other without destroying its personal identity and its inner life. In this regard, Levinas rehearses the same themes from his *Essays on Judaism* by distinguishing rigorously between the heteronomy of the self to whom the idea of the Infinite is taught from the servitude of the human being submitting to the sway of the sacred: "the infinite does not burn the eyes that are lifted unto him. He speaks; he does not have the mythical format that is impossible to confront and would hold the I in its invisible meshes. He is not numinous: the I who approaches him is neither annihilated on contact nor transported outside of itself, but remains separated and retains its as-for-me.... The metaphysical relation, the idea of infinity, connects with the noumenon which is not a numen" (*TI* 77). The self who is taught by the other or who welcomes it is thus capable of opening to an exteriority that "overflows it" without however alienating it. It is in this precise sense that "the intuition of infinity retains a rationalist meaning" by distinguishing itself radically from the sacred or from "any sort of invasion of God across an inward emotion" (211). In this regard, Levinas knows from Descartes that he has discovered, through the idea of the Infinite, "a relation with a total alterity irreducible to interiority, which nevertheless does not do violence to interiority—a receptivity without passivity, a relation between freedoms" (211).

The importance Levinas confers to receptivity and to the capacity to welcome in ourselves a truth coming from the exterior, and not from the depths of our interiority, leads him to reformulate and to deepen his criticism of maieutics. Instead of being one pedagogical method among others, it is, in his eyes, the expression *par excellence* of ontology. That is why "the primacy of the Same was Socrates' teaching" (*TI* 43). To affirm that "learning is recollection" and that the role of the teacher is limited "to simply arouse the reminiscence of former visions" does not simply have the inconvenience of proscribing the mind's discovery of the new and unheard (86). It amounts to a denial of the existence of what is outside me, of a true alterity that teaches me, by its own presence, about what I cannot derive from my own resources, "to receive nothing from the Other but what is in me, as though from all eternity I was in possession of what comes to me from the outside" (43). As in "Philosophy and the Idea of the Infinite," Levinas is opposed to maieutics or "a discourse in which the master can bring to the student what the student does not yet know" (180).

Up to now, we have discussed the attention that Levinas pays to the one who is taught, to the self that receives the revelation of the idea of the Infinite from the other. Now, we are going to turn our attention to the point of view of the master who puts this idea in me by teaching it to me. Levinas insists on the personal character of the relation that this teaching introduces between the other and me. The transmission of the truth through this idea that overflows the mind of the one who thinks it can only happen through an intersubjective relation. On this point, in spite of his criticism of Plato, Levinas feels that he is close to him: "For Plato, true discourse can come to its own assistance: the content that is presented to me is inseparable from him who has thought it—which means that the author of the discourse responds to questions. Thought, for Plato, is not reducible to an impersonal concatenation of true relations, but implies persons and interpersonal relations" (*TI* 71). Here the teachings of philosophy converge with those of the Sages of the Talmud. This is what Levinas writes in *Difficult Freedom* about the principle that prescribes a relation of the truth to the name of the one who states it: "Here I am closely akin to the famous talmudic apophthegm which announces in the same spirit: 'the day when the truth can be repeated without concealing the name of the person who first stated it, is the day when the Messiah will come.' The day when truth, in spite of its impersonal form, will retain the mark of the person who expressed himself in it, when its universality will preserve it from anonymity, is the day when the Messiah will come. For that situation is messianism itself" (*DF* 87). To preserve its personal character, it is essential for the truth to be sought in the immediacy of the face-to-face where the other teaches the idea of the Infinite to me. On this point, Levinas breaks with the Platonic model that presupposes the introduction, between the protagonists of a dialogue, of a "third term"or of mediation through abstract and impersonal Ideas (*TI* 71). He thus rejects one of the traits that he atrributed to ontology or the philosophy of the Same in "Philosophy and the Idea of the Infinite": the "recourse to the Neutral," to abstract and general concepts that provide mediations and whose role consists "in apprehending the individual which alone exists, not in its singularity...but in its generality of which alone there is science" (*DEH* 168).[10]

To mark the personal and direct character of the relation established by teaching, Levinas makes use of an expression that he had rejected in "The Transcendence of Words," judging it to be too "romantic" (*OS* 148). In contrast with what the word "idea" suggests as to abstract and pure intellection, the Infinite is expressed in the "living presence" of the teacher who faces me, in the words that emanate from a unique and singular being. Here we find a theme that appeared already in "The Transcendence of Words," namely, the superiority of oral speech over writing. Levinas evoked, in this direction, "the privilege of the living word, destined to be heard, over the picturesque word-image or sign" (149). He highlighted the contrast between writing, "disfigured words," "'frozen words' in which language is already transformed into documents and vestiges" and the "living word" that "struggles against this turning of thought into vestige" and "struggles with the letter that appears when there is no one to listen" (149).

This solidification of thought into written signs recalls, once more, a Platonic theme: the critique of writing and the defense of oral teaching. In *Phaedrus,* Socrates evokes a discourse "capable of coming to the assistance of itself," a discourse "living and animated, of which written discourse could only be called a simulacra."[11] His critique calls into question the rigidity of writing, which, unlike oral speech, cannot adapt itself to the inner disposition of the listener or distinguish between "those to whom one should speak and those before whom one must remain silent."[12] For Levinas, the Platonic distinction between the oral and the written rejoins again the talmudic rule that prescribes always citing words and teachings in the name of the one who stated them. That is why "Plato maintains the difference between the objective order of truth, that which doubtlessly is established in writings, impersonally, and reason in a living being," such that "this discourse... is not the unfolding of a prefabricated internal logic, but the constitution of truth in a struggle between thinkers, with all the risks of freedom" (*TI* 73).

Levinas often employs the Platonic expression "to come to the assistance of itself" as evidence of the virtues of orality. His reasons for justifying this privilege are quite different from the rhetorical considerations put forward by Socrates in the *Phaedrus.* They are joined to the primacy that he gives to the intersubjective relation. They are presented in a passage of *Totality and Infinity* in which he attributes the superiority of oral speech to the fact it is given a "mastery" that the written word lacks. Instead of being one quality among others, this "magisterial" character, this ability to teach, constitutes the very essence of speech. For the truth to keep its personal character, it is necessary that "ideas instruct me coming from the master who *presents* them to me." The "thematization" or "objectification" by which things become objects of knowledge can only be realized on the basis of the presence of a teacher. They "already rest on teaching" and presuppose that "we have welcomed an interlocutor" (*TI* 69).[13]

In this passage, Levinas draws fully from the dual sense of the French word *assistance*. To assist is to bring aid or to help but also to *assister à*, to be present, which includes the temporal connotations of the notions of the "present" and "presence." The oral speech of the interlocutor, the other or the master who teaches, is not only distinct from written discourse through its lack of rigidity. It opens onto a present that "is not made of instants mysteriously immobilized in duration, but of an *incessant* recovery of instants that flow by a presence that comes to their assistance, that answers to them." This "incessance" is not just one quality of the present among other ones; it "produces presence, is the presentation, the life, of the present" (*TI* 69). By situating the distinction between the oral and the written in this temporal perspective, Levinas completes the reflection undertaken in "The Transcendence of Words" where he gave the "living word" the power to " [struggle] against this turning of thought into [a] vestige" (*OS* 149). As he writes in *Totality and Infinity,* "it is as though the presence of him who speaks inverted the inevitable movement that bears the spoken word to the past state of the written word" (*TI* 69).

TEACHING AND TRANSMISSION

The privilege of orality also appears in Levinas's reflections on the Talmud. This is brought up, for example, in the following passage: "We have said that the oral Torah was written down in the Talmud. This oral Torah is thus itself written. But its writing down came late. It is explained by the contingent and dramatic circumstances of Jewish history, external to the nature and specific modality of its message. Even written down, however, the oral Torah preserves in its style its reference to oral teaching; the liveliness provided by a master addressing disciples who listen as they question" (*BV* 137). Many other passages could also be cited in which Levinas describes the master-disciple relation that structures the Talmud in similar terms to those in *Totality and Infinity*. That raises the following question: to what extent did this talmudic model inspire the ethical pedagogy developed by Levinas in his philosophical work? This question is not only motivated by the unbreakable link that connects his philosophical works to his Jewish writings. It is also due to the fact that the talmudic text belongs to a tradition in which it is the essential piece.

As a traditional text, the Talmud is the receptacle of the teachings that the Sages received from the exterior, from preceding generations. Unlike *Totality and Infinity* in which it is a characteristic of the student or the self to whom the idea of the Infinite is taught, receptivity is thus the first quality required for the teachers of the Talmud. It consists in the ability to welcome the truths that they did not find by themselves or in themselves, by calling on their own reason or their ability to remember. It is only on the basis of this initial reception that they will then be able to elaborate new and even revolutionary ideas—*hidushim*. For this reason, a talmudic text distinguishes between two successive stages in study: the first is learning, *beki'ut* (expertise, erudition), while the second, *iyun* (reflection), displays each one's originality. This distinction is expressed concretely through two central figures: Rav Yossef was called "Sinaï" because he knew everything; Raba was nicknamed "*oker harim*" (literally, the one who tears down mountains) because though having less knowledge, he was deeper.[14] In his "Mishneh Torah," Maimonides referred to the Sages as "the ones who transmit the tradition."[15] This shows that the starting point of "talmudic science" is a knowledge that comes from the exterior, inasmuch as one is dealing with an immense tradition that becomes deeper as it goes along.

The ability to receive teachings from the exterior thus takes on an eminent value in the Talmud. That said, the idea of tradition introduces a modification—or a surplus—in the pedagogical model described in *Totality and Infinity.* Before teaching oneself, any teacher worthy of the name must learn by being attentive and open to the words of those "others" who lived before and who, like the third, "regard me in the eyes of the other" (*TI* 213), in the eyes of the teacher who transmits them to him or her. In *Difficult Freedom,* Levinas expresses his admiration for the Pharisees, who are, in fact, the Sages of the Talmud: "To have an outside, to listen to what comes from outside—oh, miracle of exteriority!" (*DF* 29).[16] The division of roles between a master who teaches and a student who is taught is less sharp than in *Totality and Infinity,* where it corresponds to the complete distinction and separation between the other and oneself. This impression is reinforced by reading Levinas's other texts concerning the teacher-student relation in the Talmud. Such is the case with a commentary in which he treats the sense that the Talmud gives to the activity of "learning" (*lilmod*) and "teaching" (*lelamed*) the Torah: "Without the theoretical activity of study, without the obligation of listening and reading, without the *lilmod,* nothing can enter us. But it is also necessary to teach what has been learned in order to transmit it. Transmission, the *lelamed,* is an obligation distinct from the pure receptivity of study" (*BV* 79).

To describe the transmission or teaching through which "the fossilization of acquired knowledge" and "the congealment of the spiritual" can be avoided, Levinas employs the same terms which are evoked in *Totality and Infinity*—the "living presence" of the teacher. That said, his remarks clearly illustrate a distance from ethical pedagogy since it is not me but the other who is taught: "This congealment of the spiritual is not the same as its true transmission whose essence lies elsewhere: in vitality, inventiveness and renewal, which occur precisely through being taken up by way of tradition, or *of a lesson taught to the other and assumed by the other*" (*BV* 79; italics mine). Though constituting two "distinct obligations," learning and teaching are actually inseparable to the point that "transmission thus involves a teaching which is already outlined in the very receptivity for learning it. Receptivity is prolonged — true learning consists in receiving the lesson so deeply that it becomes a necessity to give oneself to the other." In this context, Levinas comments on the famous expression that recurs frequently in the Pentateuch: "And the Lord says to Moses: 'Speak to the people of Israel *lemor* (in these terms).'" For Levinas, the expression "in these terms" has the meaning "in order to speak." The passage thus means: "'Speak to the people of Israel in order for them to speak'; teach them sufficiently in depth for them to begin to speak, for them to hear at the point of speaking" (80).

Without breaking the asymmetry of the master-disciple relation, however, the disciple can also teach the master who teaches by asking questions. In the Talmud, the disciple has a much more active role than the receptive ego of *Totality and Infinity*, judging by this commentary by Levinas: "But if it is necessary to teach the Torah in order to perpetuate it, it is probably also necessary that the student should ask questions. The student, being both other and, generally speaking, younger, must come with questions, in the name of the future and boldly, despite the respect due to the master." Whereas the master receives teachings coming from earlier generations, the student who "will ask questions based on what the Torah will mean tomorrow" ensures their transmission to future generations. In a sense, the talmudic conception of teaching goes further than what this notion covers in *Totality and Infinity* where the teacher has the power, through his or her living word, to keep the present from changing into the past. As Levinas remarks, "The Torah not only reproduces what was taught yesterday, it is read according to tomorrow; it does not stop at the representations of what yesterday and today goes by the name of present" (*ITN* 66).

Conclusion

Due to the radicalization of Levinasian ethics, the subjectivity that is in question in *Otherwise than Being or Beyond Essence* and in "God and Philosophy" is no longer receptive but essentially passive. It is affected unto its depths by an idea of the Infinite that no longer comes to it from the exterior—from the master—but which is its own structure. To the notion of welcome that is still a "quasi-activity" (*OB* 13), Levinas opts for the notion of a *proximity*, which expresses the absolute passivity of the responsible subject. In this way, "the Good chooses me first before I can be in a position to choose, that is, welcome its choice" (122). This radicalization explains the disappearance of the themes of the master and teaching in the philosophical writings that appear after *Totality and Infinity*. By contrast, these themes do remain in the talmudic writings produced at the same time, testifying to the role that ethical pedagogy plays in the elaboration of an other rationality that opens the human psychism to what exceeds and surpasses it, or, to revelation.

TEN

Turning toward the Other

Ethics, Fecundity, and the Primacy of Education

Claire Katz

Contra the Heideggerian history of myth, the plastic image and its imitation. History is the sacred history of teachers and fathers — *teaching and fecundity* — and not of heroes. Not of political history.

— Levinas, *Carnets de Captivité*

Emmanuel Levinas returned to Paris immediately following the murderous years of World War II, during which he served as an interpreter before his unit was captured. He then spent the duration of the war, 1940–45, first in Frontstalags in Rennes and Laval, then at Vesoul, and from June 1942 until May 1945 at Stalag 11B at Fallingbostel near Magdeburg in Germany.[1] Upon his return and without delay, he went to work for the Alliance Israelite Universelle (AIU) and in 1947 became the director of the École Normale Israélite Orientale (ENIO). At an event celebrating the occasion of his eightieth birthday, Levinas made the following statement about his time immediately following his release from captivity: "After Auschwitz, I had the impression that in taking on the directorship of the École Normale Israélite Orientale I was responding to a historical calling. It was my little secret.... Probably the naiveté of a young man. I am still mindful and proud of it today."[2] This celebration brought together several of his former students from those years at the ENIO and issued in a small publication, *Levinas—Philosophe et Pédagogue,* which collected several short essays about Levinas as a teacher, talmudist, and philosopher.[3] The collection comprises just a select few of the commentaries offered by Levinas's own students, yet even they provide a glimpse of Levinas as both a teacher and a philosopher of the highest order. One statement in particular stands out in its unique character.

Ady Steg, who was the president of the AIU at the time of the celebration, offered a fable speculating about the time when Levinas would stand before the Heavenly Throne.[4] To summarize, the Eternal One asks Levinas what he did with his life. With each answer—"I believed in the Good, about which I wrote"; "I studied with Husserl and Heidegger"; "I studied with Chouchani"—the Eternal One replies—"And?" It is only when Levinas mentions that he directed the ENIO that the Eternal One is impressed and replies, "Director of the school, you, a prestigious philosopher?" After this response the Eternal One seems satisfied and sends Levinas on his way.

The response from the Eternal One, while it runs counter to the prevailing attitude toward education, also betrays a sense of surprise—a philosopher of such great prestige would direct a day school? While the Heavenly Throne considers this particular task to be of the greatest importance, this surprise reveals an awareness of the possibility that not everyone would see things in the same way, thus making Levinas's devotion to the school all the more admirable. The Eternal One's surprise indicated by his question—"You, a famous philosopher [directed a school]?"—clearly indicates that in spite of Levinas's academic accomplishments, he was not too proud or arrogant to devote himself to the education of the younger generation.

Nonetheless, the Eternal One's added question—"you, a famous philosopher?"—spoken with more than a hint of doubt or suspicion, betrays the more common negative sentiment toward education and those who educate. The view that "those who can't, teach" is still prevalent today, and the attitudes toward education range from resentment—teachers are paid too much (?!) for such cushy jobs—to outright cynicism and contempt regarding the educational system and what it promises. This range of negative attitudes creates a powerful force pushing against education, hindering any possibility of real reform: no one believes that education produces anything positive; only those who are not good at anything else would go into teaching; and teaching is so easy that teachers should not be compensated adequately for doing such a job. In contrast to the negative view about teaching, Levinas saw it as fundamental to any hope for the future, certainly for the Jewish people and I contend for the rest of humanity. The future of the world rests on how we educate our young people. Ady Steg's fable is certainly written for effect. Yet, it is not lost on any of his students from the ENIO or anyone who reads his essays on Jewish education that education is not a side hobby in which he engaged.

Totality and Infinity was published in 1961, 15 years after the lecture course that was published as *Time and the Other*. While it does seem to be the case that many of the themes from the earlier work are given new life in his 1961 book, *Totality and Infinity* cannot be reduced simply to an expansion of the themes in *Time and the Other*. For example, although Levinas gestures toward the ethical relationship in *Time and the Other*, he does not name it in that book. Additionally, the references to teaching that are so frequent in *Totality and Infinity* do not appear at all in *Time and the Other*. Although I am unaware of the exact years that Levinas was writing *Totality and Infinity*, it should be safe to say that one reason for this particular difference—the references to teaching that are absent from those earlier writings—is that he was working through these themes in the 1950s, the years when he was also the director of the École Normale Israélite Orientale (ENIO), the branch of the Alliance Israelite Universelle that coordinated the actual teaching in the schools and trained future teachers. We should not be surprised then that references to teaching peppered the philosophical project Levinas was developing at the same time that he was in the trenches teaching the Jewish youth and concerned with crises for which he saw education as the solution.

More interesting to note is the similarity in themes that concerned him in both the Jewish writings and the philosophical project of that time period. In both sets of writing he identifies a crisis in humanism for which a new subjectivity is needed. But, he describes this new subjectivity in different registers in his Jewish writings and in *Totality and Infinity*. The present essay takes a developmental approach to Levinas's project and considers what it means that *Totality and Infinity* was published after he had been the director of the ENIO for 15 years and that it was written during the same period he was concerned with themes that covered the failure of assimilation, the question about the relationship between the universal and the particular, and the promise of education found in his writings from the 1950s, which were published in *Difficult Freedom* ten years prior to the publication of *Totality and Infinity*. For this reason, it would be more surprising if references to education and teaching were not found in this text. Nonetheless, the place of *Totality and Infinity* within the context of his writings on Jewish education has *not* been studied adequately, if at all.[5] With this chronology in mind, it becomes increasingly difficult to think of his references to teaching as a mere trope or metaphor. Those references are fleeting, but not insignificant. Teaching is not a simple trope but rather the key to Levinas's philosophical project in *Totality and Infinity*. In fact, his interest in education is not only related to the development of his ethical project, but it is also fundamental to the project's coherence.

The Primacy of Education

In 1951, only six years after he was released from the German POW camp, Levinas published "Reflections on Jewish Education," in *Les Cahiers de l'Alliance Israélite Universelle* (*DF* 265–68). He opens this essay with the following assertion: "The existence of Jews who wish to remain Jews...depends on Jewish education." The statement should be neither surprising nor provocative. Permeating all of Judaism is an emphasis on education, commandments "to teach these things to your children," rabbinic readings that are meant to teach, and so forth. For Levinas, if Judaism is about anything, it is about education and in the very next sentence he clarifies his statement: "religious instruction in the sense in which it is understood by Catholics and Protestants, is insufficient as a formula for Jewish education" (265).

Levinas's point in drawing this distinction is to emphasize that Jewish education is not about teaching the lessons of a Catechism. Importantly, Levinas links this distinction to his emphasis on the importance of learning Hebrew. He underscores that the most ancient of the modern religions cannot be separated from its ancient language, the peculiarities of which can be understood or recognized only if one reads the language. He holds that by being able to read the Jewish texts in the original Hebrew, students come to understand that the conversations that surround the Jewish sources animate the text; these are living conversations that keep the text dynamic rather than static. The structure of the Hebrew language inherently keeps the text animated, and thus prevents Jewish education from becoming simply learning catechism. His worry is that Jewish education will become precisely that if Hebrew is not taught—without the original language, which opens the text up and allows the multiple voices and interpretations to emerge, the teaching of the Jewish sources runs the risk of teaching dogma.

It is this seemingly small but crucial distinction that guides the rest of this essay—without the Hebrew language, Jewish education will lose that which makes it unique. Judaism remains a minority in all parts of the world. The Hebrew language and the distinct way that this language inspires the rich commentary on the texts is precisely what allows Judaism to survive within a broader world that seeks to assimilate it into its own homogenous culture. If the religious teachings are detached from the ancient language, it is as if Jewish education has been reduced to a catechism and the very life that animates the words will have been removed and hidden, with no means for the students to recover it: "In a world in which nothing is Jewish, only the text reverberates and echoes a teaching that no cathedral, no plastic form, no specific social structure can free from its abstract nature." Conversely, Levinas describes Christian religious instruction as being able "to content itself with summary notions because Christian civilization is here and present, giving these notions a concrete meaning and confirming them everyday" (*DF* 265). For example, Christianity shapes the very calendar that governs the cycle of our lives. With these forces working against Judaism's survival, sheer luck and family narratives have allowed Judaism to stay alive in the 150 years of years of emancipation—what Levinas would refer to as assimilation. Yet, even with this apparent survival, Levinas notes that family memories do not replace a civilization, and this luck might have run its course.

Repeating many themes from this 1951 essay in his 1956 essay, "For a Jewish Humanism," Levinas reassures his audience that the Jewish school does not betray the ideals of the secular school. By supporting what he calls "Jewish humanism"—"that which cannot remain indifferent to the modern world in which it seeks a whole humanity"—the Jewish school lends support to what gives meaning to Judaism in the modern world (*DF* 273–76). The aim of the Jewish school, then, is not simply to maintain Judaism as a religion, instead its aim is to reinforce the Jewish humanism found in and promoted by Jewish texts.

Citing Mendelssohn, Spinoza, and Maimonides, Levinas corrects the view that monotheism is a revealed religion and instead calls it a revealed Law, indicating that its truth is universal—like reason (*DF* 274). This monotheism, however, is not concerned with preparing individuals "for a private meeting with a consoling God; but in bringing the divine presence to just and human effort.... The vision of God is a moral act. This optics is an ethics" (274–75). Rather than lead us to God, this religion leads us to humanity and thus Levinas emphatically states, "Monotheism is a humanism." And he reminds his readers that quietly motivating the Jewish rejection of conversion is the belief that the human truths of the "Hebrew Bible were being lost in the theology of the New" (275).

Levinas concludes this essay by identifying the problem with assimilation—the homogeneity that Jews desired and for the most part achieved has resulted in the loss of that which made them unique: "the secret of their science." Once again, he emphasizes, "the Hebrew language—and the texts, to which it is substantially linked and which are revealed only through it—is the vehicle for a difficult wisdom concerned with truths that correlate to virtues. The unique nature of Judaism itself is that it consists in promoting as one of the highest virtues the knowledge of its own sources" (*DF* 275). Judaism's uniqueness consists not only in that it commands the teaching of itself, but also that this teaching has built into it the discovery, preservation, and enactment of a Jewish humanism—and this uniqueness derives in part from the Hebrew language. As a result, Levinas does not see Judaism as parochial or separate, but as precisely the opposite—as that which is "indispensable to human harmony." It should not surprise us then that "the discovery and preservation of Jewish humanism would already be one sufficient *raison d'être* for the Jewish school, in a world in which we want above all to see an education that does not separate men" (276). Thus, Levinas identifies the Jewish school as the primary space in which Jewish humanism will be kept safe. Nonetheless, he admits early in the essay that while the notion of a Jewish humanism remains secular—and thus can be universal—Judaism itself sits at the crossroads of faith and logic.

In the same year that Levinas published "Reflections on Jewish Education" (1951), he also published the essay, "The State of Israel and the Religion of Israel," in which he identifies that which makes the State of Israel unique from all other modern political states (*DF* 216–20). Here Levinas tries to differentiate not only the State of Israel from other states but also the religion of Israel from other religions. He refers to a collection of essays brought together by the Labor Zionist, Chaim Grinberg.[6] Levinas comments that he is struck by the ease with which the essays make the move from religion to ethics. He adds that he does not "get the impression of a morality being added to the dogma, but of a 'dogma' that is morality itself" (218).

He summarizes the collection with the affirmation that belief in God does not *incite* us to social justice; it is the "institution of that justice." This justice is not an abstract principle. Anticipating themes that will appear in full force in 1961, he asks if the whole aim of religion is not "ultimately to bring about the very possibility of Society, the possibility for a man to see the face of the Other?" To his own question, he boldly replies that "the thing that is special about the State of Israel is not that it fulfills an ancient promise, or heralds a new age of material security (one that is unfortunately problematic), but that it finally offers the opportunity to carry out the social law of Judaism." Again, emphasizing the ethical dimension of Judaism, the Jewish people, and the State of Israel, he writes, "The Jewish people craved their own land and their own State not because of the abstract independence which they desired, but because they could finally begin the work of their lives" (*DF* 218). The "work of their lives" is the work of ethics.

Returning to Grinberg's collection, Levinas finds an answer to his own question, "But how are we to read these [great] books?" It is the Torah, after all, in which we find the values of democracy and socialism, and the inspiration for an "avant-garde state." But why remain tethered to the Torah? Is the Torah not out of date? What can it teach us today? For his answers, he refers to Yeshayahu Leibovitz's essay, "Religion and State," which Levinas summarizes thusly: "The social and political situation described by the Bible and the Talmud is the example of a given situation that is rendered human by the Law. From it we can deduce the justice required for any and every situation" (*DF* 219). Here, Levinas distinguishes Judaism from its religious counterparts and emphasizes, "*The relationship between the Jewish State and the Jewish religion*—we dare not to say Church—*is one of study*" (219–20; emphasis mine; translation modified).

These essays on Jewish education draw out the connection between Judaism and the ethical, or the impulse to social justice, the universality of this dimension of the religion, and the relationship this particular practice of the religion has to education. That is, Levinas accomplishes several tasks in this set of essays. First, he emphasizes that Judaism is first and foremost about ethics—seeing the face of the other—and that this ethics, while fundamental to Judaism, maybe even original to it, is also universal; that is, one need not be a practicing or observant Jew to be ethical in the way that he describes. Second, the essays are intended to remind his readers that Jewish education is the best way to reclaim this ethical tradition that has been forgotten in Judaism's quest to assimilate. There is something unique about Hebrew and its relationship to Torah and Talmud that develops both the creative mind and a response to the other.

The Jewish texts are infused with the message of responding to the suffering of the other but they do this not by preaching dogmatic principles but by engaging the individual in an educational endeavor that practices this very idea. He states emphatically that what has been lost in Jewish education and thus also in the religion is the way in which we let the texts speak to us—the way in which we allow the text to teach us. We must, therefore, "return to what was strongest in rabbinical exegesis. This exegesis made the text speak." To practice Judaism in its original spirit and to read the text as a Jew is not to take the text as a thing but to see the text as "a source of teaching" (*DF* 220). Only six years after the war had ended, Levinas's writings reflect a firm commitment to Jewish education as the means to reclaim the Judaism that emphasizes the obligation to the other and the humanism that can apply to everyone.

Turning toward the Other

The question of how one becomes a Levinasian subject—a subject that can see the face of the other and respond—is a question that haunts Levinas's project and always seems to lurk in the background of many commentaries on and criticisms of his ethics. However, this problem can be largely alleviated through careful attention to Levinas's scattered references to teaching, while few and undeveloped, in *Totality and Infinity*. For just as Levinas called for the Jewish community to return to Jewish education as a means of reclaiming the ethical tradition that is unique to Judaism, so too, Levinas employs a model of education—of teaching—for the self to become an ethical subject.

Levinas's references to teaching in *Totality and Infinity* can be placed into three distinct categories. The first is the set of references early in the text where Levinas describes the Other in terms of a teacher or as my master. That is, this first set of references to teaching establishes the relationship to the Other as a teaching relationship. One of the earliest references appears in "Transcendence as the Idea of Infinity" (*TI* 48–52), a subsection of "Metaphysics and Transcendence," in the first part of the book. He writes, "The relation with the Other, or Conversation, is a non-allergic relation, an ethical relation; but inasmuch as it is welcomed this conversation is a teaching [*enseignement*]. Teaching is not reducible to maieutics; it comes from the exterior and brings me more than I contain" (51). Here the relation with the Other is referred to as a conversation, thus it is characterized in terms of speech—the other speaks to me. By occupying a position of an interlocutor, the Other also teaches me. Levinas clearly intends to distance the ethical relation, where that which comes from outside is emphasized, from the pedagogy of Socrates, where truth is pulled out from one person by a series of questions being posed. The relationship to the Other, will always exceed any knowledge that can be brought forth from within.

This description mirrors the one Levinas offered 12 years earlier in his 1949 essay "Transcendence of Words: On Michel Leiris's *Biffures*," where he writes, "The presence of the Other is a presence that teaches; that is why the word as teaching is more than the experience of the real, and the master more than a midwife of minds. He wrenches experience away from its esthetic self-sufficiency, from its *here*, where it rests in peace. And by invoking it he transforms it into a creature" (*OS* 148). This comment follows his discussion of Robinson Crusoe, in which Levinas shatters the mythology of Crusoe as an insular individual who lived a solitary life by recalling the character "Friday" and emphasizing the role that language—speech—played between Crusoe and Friday.

The second set of references is found in the section called "Ethics and the Face" (*TI* 194–219), where the face of the other is described in terms of the ethical relation. Because Levinas has already cast the relationship to the Other as a teaching relationship, the ethical relation can now be seen as a relationship of teaching. This move is specifically the move from a phenomenological description of the other to a description of that relationship as fundamentally normative. The move is neither obvious nor inherent—it must be established. But insofar as Levinas carries the teaching relationship forward, we can see the parallel he draws between the ethical relation and the teaching relation. The ethical relation is always already a teaching relation.

In these references to teaching, Levinas binds the relationship the I has to the Other to that of teacher and student. Recalling the discussion of education in the first part of the essay, we can see the significance of teaching to the Jewish tradition. The teacher is not only valued, but is valued more highly than the parent. Teaching is fundamentally part of the tradition, which sees itself as commanded to teach itself to the next generations. Repeatedly, these references to teaching are found throughout the biblical tradition, and the role of teaching is taken up again in the rabbinic commentary, which makes the Hebrew Bible Jewish.

These two sets of references feed the third category, which we find in the final section of the book, "Beyond the Face" (*TI* 254–307). Here, we also see how Levinas reverses the way we might typically understand the teaching relation. As Levinas characterizes the relation, the Other is the teacher. We see this point most clearly in the description of filiality and the relationship between the father and son. Typically, we think of the parent as the teacher, and of course, in many ways this is the case. In his discussion of fecundity, Levinas characterizes the child as a Stranger (Isa. 49)—and throughout *Totality and Infinity,* he repeatedly proclaimed his responsibility to the Stranger (267; cf. 13, 39, 49, 75, 213, 251). In this description, then, it is the son, cast as Other, who teaches the father.

Here, the lesson that the child teaches the parent is of a different order—it is a lesson that calls the parent to ethical responsibility, to place the child before the parent; it calls for the parent to set aside his or own ego and turn toward the child, just as the I must turn toward the Other. The birth of the son turns the father not only toward the son in responsibility for him but also outward, toward the community, toward the other others. Here the father is responsible for his son but also for his son's responsibility—the child cannot exist on his own and thus "he can be brought up, be commanded, and can obey" (*TI* 279). Part of the responsibility that the father has to the child is in turn to teach the child, to bring the child up to be responsible for other others—and this point was made clearly in my discussion of Levinas's essays on Jewish education in the first part of this essay.

This is where I see the connection between Levinas's references to teaching in *Totality and Infinity* to his earlier discussions of Jewish education in his essays of the1950s. It is clear from those essays that the school, the teacher, and the parent have a fundamental role to play in the cultivation of an ethical subject. Certainly we could argue that his view only applies to the Jewish community, but that would not be supported by his own references to teaching and parenting. Indeed if we recall the epigraph for this essay, history is the "history of teachers and fathers, teaching and fecundity."[7] By importing the trope of teaching into his philosophical project—into the language of the Greek universal—what I contend Levinas has done is import the significant role that teaching plays in the development of the ethical subject in Jewish education to a wider non-Jewish audience. It is not only that he has attempted to translate the notion of Jewish ethics from the Hebrew to the Greek; he is also attempting to translate the method by which one can accomplish the task. It simply cannot be the case that although Jewish children need to be reared to turn toward the other, everyone else simply needs to read a book and make a rational choice to do this. Among other problems, this view would run completely counter to the very way in which Levinas describes ethical subjectivity. My point is two-fold. First, in his essays on Jewish education, Levinas argues that education is the key to forming this new (old) subjectivity. But it cannot be that he believes Jewish children are the only children who would need an education of this kind. Thus, if others are also going to adopt this new subjectivity, then those children need to be reared similarly, using a model of education similar to the one Levinas calls for in his essays on Jewish education.

Although Levinas's discussion of eros, fecundity, and filiality have been criticized from all angles, and while many of the criticisms are certainly with merit, this reading of education helps us to understand why they tend to miss the point.[8] In order for the phenomenology to work, the child needs to have been introduced to some kind of moral upbringing. The Levinasian subject does not enter the world *sui generis.* Just as Merleau-Ponty's ontological structures regarding the other can be traced back to his essay describing the child's relations with others, so too, Levinas's ethical subject assumes some kind of introduction to morality, however that term might be construed.

Even in *Emile,* Rousseau acknowledges that an innate capacity to see the suffering of the other is not enough, for the child could develop in one of two ways. The child could develop such that an aversion to suffering compels him or her to want to bring that suffering to an end and thus help the other person, or the child could develop into a person whose aversion to the suffering compels him or her to do everything to avoid it, what I call "the gated community syndrome." Only through a proper education (though certainly we can raise questions if the one Rousseau proposes is proper) can the path of wanting to help the suffering other be secured. Thus, Levinas's turn to the family structure, though problematic, does get at a fundamental problem in his work: how does the individual grow into the subject who can be interrupted by and respond to the other? While it might not be the case that we all raise children, it is indeed the case that we were all raised by someone—for better or for worse—and we were introduced to the moral world at the same time as that parent or caregiver was called to ethical subjectivity by the child.

In the collection of interviews published under the title *Ethics and Infinity,* Philippe Nemo asks Levinas, "You see in [filiality] a properly ontological feature and not merely a psychological accident or perhaps a ruse of biology?" Levinas replies, "I believe that psychological 'accidents' are the ways in which ontological relations show themselves. The fact of seeing the possibilities of the other as your own possibilities, of being able to escape the closure of your identity and what is bestowed on you...this is paternity" (*EI* 70). Levinas then adds, "It is not necessary that those who have no children see in this fact any depreciation whatever; biological filiality is only the first shape filiality takes; but one can very well conceive filiality as a relationship between human beings without the tie of biological kinship. One can have a paternal attitude with regard to the Other. To consider the Other as a son is precisely to establish with him those relations I call 'beyond the possible'" (70–71). For Levinas, then, the *first* moment of the ethical relation is found within this erotic and then parental relationship. And we see here the movement from ethics to politics, from the original microsociety of a family to larger formations. Levinas refers to the Other in the ethical relation in *Totality and Infinity* as his teacher and he refers to the ethical relationship par excellence—that of father and son—a relationship of teaching. In his interview with Philippe Nemo, Levinas responds precisely to this point: "Filiation and fraternity—parental relations without biological bases—are current metaphors of our everyday life. The relationship of master to disciple does not reduce to filiation and fraternity but it certainly includes them" (71).[9]

In his writings following *Totality and Infinity,* Levinas appears to drop the familial references, with the exception of his use of "maternity" most notably in *Otherwise than Being* (1974). My argument is that Levinas turns to a stronger view of the ethical subject than the one that he initially describes in his 1961 work and that this subject is dependent on an educational process that shapes her. The claim that Levinas's 1961 project fails is partially correct. Instead of a complete failure, however, Levinas exchanges the father-teacher for the teacher, even if not stated as such. What becomes clearer in the writings after 1961 is Levinas's emphasis on an ethical subject that is not simply "interrupted" by the Other, but who is also shaped in such a way that the subject is willing to cede his or her position to the Other.[10]

Returning to the essays on Judaism and in particular Jewish education, we can see two significant points. The first is that Levinas is naming the inhumanities of the twentieth century a crisis in humanism, which he then reformulates as a loss of ethical subjectivity. He is calling on the Jewish community to return to Jewish education in order to reinvigorate Judaism with this Jewish humanism—this ethical subjectivity. And notably, this ethical subjectivity is not only for the Jews; it is the universal part of Judaism and it is the obligation of the Jews to share this part of Judaism with others.

I maintain that *Totality and Infinity* is Levinas's first attempt to do precisely this—to articulate this Jewish humanism, this ethical subjectivity, in Greek, a philosophical language that can be understood and appreciated universally. Levinas appeals to the Jewish community that they return to Jewish education and that they need to raise the youth differently. Similarly, his description of this new ethical subjectivity relies on cultivation, on child rearing, and on education. It is not the case that one reads Levinas and makes a decision to become Levinasian—this, in fact, would be all too Kantian, a choosing of duty over inclination or an exertion of the will. Rather, the philosophical intention is to reorient its readers to a new subjectivity, one that counters the antihumanism that held sway over twentieth century intellectuals for far too long. Can this be done simply by reading his philosophical work? I cannot say for sure, but my guess is that it cannot. This is not to say that Levinas is more like Arisotle and less like Kant—Aristotle, though he recognized the need to cultivate good practices, was interested in the cultivation of a virtuous person. Levinas is not concerned with moral perfection but the development of an ego that is for the other—and this cannot be a rational choice.

If considered between the writings in *Difficult Freedom* and the essays collected in *Humanism of the Other,* Levinas's ethical subject is one that is developed — taught, if you will. And while I am sympathetic to this view of the subject, I am not without concerns. Like a Kantian system that seems to rely on an already ethical community — lest one need to lie to the Nazis when they come asking for the Jew hiding in the attic — the Levinasian subject is one that seems nearly self-sacrificing. To turn to the other, to cede one's place in the sun, will prevent wars if all are successfully educated — and I think this is what Levinas has in mind. Yet, I can imagine the hesitation — "I'll do this, if you do that" which begins to sound more like a social contract, an exchange of favors, rather than the pre-rational turning to the other he describes.[11]

My point here is not to say that I think Levinas is wrong in his promotion of a new subjectivity — but that a Levinasian ethics is difficult, if not impossible. My worry is that commentators have made Levinas's ethics seem easy or natural, as if it were part of who we already are and as if we had just simply ignored it or covered it over. I think Levinas is saying something far more complex and difficult to achieve, and it involves a commitment we might not be ready to make. We cannot simply read his books and then "become Levinasian"; nor can one be Levinasian, whatever that might mean, without consequence.[12] To become a subject in the way that Levinas describes requires a commitment by those who parent and teach — and it is not a commitment made lightly. While it is true that Levinas does not prescribe moral rules such as the Ten Commandments or even a categorical imperative, it is not the case that there are no prescriptions — first and foremost, the face of the other commands me not to murder. But even if I bracket this point, he is not simply describing but also prescribing a different subjectivity, one that implies a different way of being, as it were, with another. He comments repeatedly about the widow and the orphan, about tending to the misery or suffering of the other.

In the end, Levinas describes the ethical relation with terms like interruption, and yet his essays on education seem to state rather clearly that in order to be interrupted and respond to that interruption, the subject needs to be cultivated—and that implies an education that turns the subject toward the other.

My hope is that 50 years after its publication, readers of *Totality and Infinity* might situate it within a historical trajectory of Levinas's writings—not simply as the major book that follows *Time and the Other* and *Existence and Existents*—connected also to his writings from the 1950s while he was director of the ENIO. If readers will consider Levinas's ethical project, as developed in *Totality and Infinity*, within the context of Levinas's own dedication to education (specifically Jewish education), we might be better able to address some of the questions that continue to haunt us about his work.

ELEVEN

Future Interval

On Levinas and Glissant

John Drabinski

> It is a question of a nothingness distinct from the nothingness of anxiety: the nothingness of the future buried in the secrecy of the less than nothing.
>
> — Levinas, *Totality and Infinity*

I begin my reflections here by evoking two moments in the cinema of catastrophe. A first site: in *Life and Nothing More,* the second volume of Abbas Kiarostami's "Earthquake Trilogy," the film director is diverted off the main highway, sent along small, winding roads through rural Iran. The dirt roads are lined with the rubble of a devastating earthquake. People mill about, walk the highway with everything from melancholic expression to bundles of daily items. Kiarostami theorizes, alongside these roads, what it means to recover from trauma: we see a wedding, marking the renewal of folkways and familial bonds, but also a man carrying a toilet seat. After a disastrous event, matters deep and mundane call to us from, but also toward, the future. Life

goes on. *The future holds open renewal, but always on the ground
of rubble and ruin.*

A second site: the close of Claude Lanzmann's *Shoah,* that
moment in which the documentary is brought back to the
bombing of the Warsaw ghetto. After a handful of hours docu-
menting trauma, memory, and the mechanism of mass death,
Lanzmann comes to a small fragment of resistance. *Shoah* closes
with the uprising in the ghetto, which of course comes back
around to mass death. In the last utterance of the film, the witness (Simha Rottem) remembers the moment he emerged from
the sewers: "I didn't meet a living soul. At one point I recall
feeling a kind of peace, of serenity. I said to myself: 'I'm the last
Jew. I'll wait for the morning, and for the Germans.'"[1]

Catastrophe destroys the world, completely. The world
ends. Rottem emerges from the completeness of disaster to re-
enter the world because, even at the end of the world, there is
another time: the time of the future. Life goes on. *The future
holds only the final remnant, which resists, ever precariously, complete absence.*

These cinematic events raise a fundamental philosophical
question that crosses the philosophy of history with the existential drama of massive human suffering: how to begin again after
catastrophe? Kiarostami and Lanzmann envision that beginning
in the midst, not after the clearing, of ruins. When everything
has been lost, ruins remain and only alienate. These ruins never
edify because they are encountered before resolution and the
reinvention of the past—the sort of transformation of the past
made possible after a future has been full revisioned. We can
see, then, how, in theorizing disaster, the question of beginning
so often takes on an urgent and melancholic character. With
the present reflections, I want to sit in this between-space, this
interval, in order to catch sight of two thinkers—Emmanuel
Levinas and Édouard Glissant—making the quirky, even near
impossible, transition between catastrophe and the future. Or,
to put it another way, I want to ask how we make sense of
disastrous events in the crossing of philosophy of history and

the (collective) existential transformation of the meaning of being in the world. That sense-making is located in the interval between a past torn apart and a future yet to be articulated.

How does philosophy theorize beginning after everything has been lost? Philosophy, after all, does not theorize from a nonplace. Philosophical meditation—and so notions of space, time, meaning, language, and so on—is embedded in place and places. Historical experience informs the formulation of philosophy. The question "How to begin?" is therefore a matter of reckoning, explicitly or implicitly, with the historical and existential exigencies of the moment. This old question is especially appropriate to the twentieth century and so many of its attendant anxieties. Whether it is the end of domination in postcolonial struggles, the closure of metaphysics and the old world of philosophy, or unprecedented internal and external violence, the just-ended century is in many ways one long witness to the anxiety of beginning again. Catastrophe is nearly synonymous with the long twentieth century. From the ecstasy of Frantz Fanon's imagination of life after revolution to the persistent call to renew the vocation of philosophy to projects of complex retrieval, beginning is made anxious by a loss that seems, at first glance, just so total. Loss is surely devastation, but there is also a tradition of seeing in loss fecundity and new possibility. Recall, for example, how in Martin Heidegger's long meditations on beginning, meditations that (among so many other things) sought to reinvest Husserl's project of perpetual beginning with historical sensibility, the problem of loss is prominent and decisive. Heidegger's famous remark on the Greek temple in "The Origin of the Work of Art," for example, where he notes that we encounter only the having-lost god, never the god's presence or presence in absence, locates the problem of philosophy's beginning in the experience of loss. But Heidegger's loss is always a loss of a previous abundance that is eclipsed in the shifts and rifts of subsequent epochs. There is always so much to say, by way of retrieval, about the pre-Socratic words for being *precisely because they contain*

productive remnants of an abundant past. There is no total
catastrophe. There is never total loss. In its own small way, this
is a manifestation of Heidegger's all too familiar forgetting of
the violence of Europe's twentieth century.

Levinas's philosophy tells a peculiar story about ethics, first
philosophy, and the fate of every thinking (save for those few
ruptures and accidents) preceding the thought of *autrui*.
Levinas's story about the history of philosophy-as-totalitarian-
ism has been told many times—sometimes with wild skepticism, sometimes with uncritical adherance. What has rarely been
told, however, is the story of beginning. How does Levinas's
philosophy begin? How is beginning related to catastrophe?

In what follows, I explore these questions through a rereading of the problem of futurity in *Totality and Infinity*. Despite
the absence of the particular word or phrasing, *Totality and
Infinity* is fundamentally a book about beginning again, after
catastrophe. But that is only part of my question. I am also
interested in putting Levinas into conversation with that other
great Francophone thinker of beginnings, the Martiniquan
poet, novelist, and literary critic Édouard Glissant. Glissant
also thinks disaster and beginning at one and the same time,
conceiving the problem of theorizing the Americas as a moment
of reckoning with the Middle Passage, the plantation, and
colonialism.

I put the two thinkers in proximity in order to accomplish
two tasks. First, I hope to show how the problem of futurity—
a theoretical and existential problem of how to make the
world meaningful *again* or *for the first time*—is crucial for
any thinking of beginning after catastrophe, and that Levinas's
articulation of the terms and stakes of beginning again are
indispensable for imagining another possible world. Levinas's
account of fecundity works with the very little, almost nothing,
that remains after Europe's murderous past century. When read
with Glissant, whose ethical sensibility matches that of Levinas
so well, a fuller sense of the project of an ethical metaphysics
of the future emerges as a globalizing and globally entangled

imperative. Martinique, after all, *is* France—an insight whose own futurity we will explore in a Levinasian register. Second, and perhaps most searchingly, I locate the particularly European tenor of Levinas's project and ask, in a critical voice, how that tenor might limit our appreciation of the entangled responsibilities of moral life after modernity. That is, I do not simply charge Levinas with the rather common thought crime of Eurocentrism (though that is not nothing). Rather, Levinasian responsibility—when thought in the interval of catastrophe, beginning, and futurity—always exceeds his construal of the scope and character of our moral consciousness. To *be* responsible in historical experience is to engage, always, the entanglements of conscience—global and local. Conscience is linked to beginning after catastrophe, so our interrogation of how the world is made meaningful *again* or *for the first time* must be de-linked from the still colonial reliance on European models of historical experience.

An Ethical Metaphysics of the Future

In "Signature," Levinas offers an at times predictable, at other times engaging and surprising, account of his life in a sort of intellectual autobiography. I say "sort of intellectual autobiography" because Levinas in many ways repeats old lists and common characterizations of his work—the sorts of comments we find well before the retrospective piece is published in 1970. The remark that strikes me as most surprising and certainly most important for this essay is the claim Levinas makes about the Shoah. It is obvious that the Shoah was a transformative event for Levinas, as it was for every Jew and Roma, and indeed for every European. What is less obvious is how that event functions in relation to Levinas's own writing, which is dedicated first and foremost to the infinity of obligation, to the singular other, and so to the nonracial or nonethnic character of the human. Did the genocide of European Jews (and Roma, though Levinas does not note this—joining most theorists of the Shoah) impact Levinas's thinking? Or is it simply part of his biography, while his philosophy stands well apart, independent of the historical experience of disaster? Though Levinas has written very little on the Shoah, the opening remarks in "Signature" invite speculation and rereading. As a general characterization of the essay, he writes simply, "This disparate inventory is a biography. It is dominated by the presentiment and the memory of the Nazi horror" (*DF* 291). How are we to read this statement? What is the relation between biography, philosophical work, and presentiment?

With this statement in view, the memory of the Nazi horror has been read as formative for Levinas's work. This reading sets out an important claim, were we to explore all of the consequences. It would require that we think of Levinas's work as post-Holocaust theory, which in turn would require a systematic rereading of that work as less a phenomenology of obligation than an elaborate exploration of traumatic memory. Perhaps Levinas's work has *always* been a response to Nazi terror and the Shoah, seeking an ethics after the catastrophe? Such a reading would frame Levinas's work as a memory project against history and narrative. A memory project, yes, but one that seeks to redeem humanity with the pure simplicity of the vulnerable face.

I have always been suspicious of this claim about Levinas's work as post-Holocaust theory. Apart from the dedication of *Otherwise than Being*, which is given over to the memory of the murdered in the death camps, the Shoah almost never appears in Levinas's work. Beyond predictable critiques of Husserlian and Heideggerian conceptions of memory and time, Levinas does not offer much for those interested in the relation between history and memory (one of the signature concerns of post-Holocaust memory projects). If we consider other thinkers for whom the Shoah functions as the decisive event—such as Adorno and Horkheimer, as well as Arendt, Jaspers, and many others—then it becomes clear just how little Levinas engages with the central issues of post-Shoah theorizing: the structures of modernity, bureaucracy, eliminationist culture, collective guilt, and so on. To be sure, Levinas's hyperbolic rhetoric equates ontology and certain epistemological orientations as totalitarian, which can easily be inscribed in post-Shoah discourse, but that is hardly a sufficient engagement of the vast and deep cultural conditions of genocide. Nor does Levinas explore with much (if any) depth the traumatic experience of loss, even as the language of trauma and persecution comes to dominate his work in the mid-1970s and after. So, what is the Shoah to Levinas, beyond terrifying autobiography?

Let me propose an answer by giving away, ahead of the analysis, a sort of conclusion: Levinas's account of beginning and futurity in *Totality and Infinity* is his one and most sustained exploration of the philosophical consequences of catastrophic loss. The name of the father—here the surname, not the Lacanian motif—functions as the ruin after catastrophe, the cindered trace capable of carrying memory and identity into a future torn apart by violence. The fecundity of the (sur-) name gives to the future a meaning and continuity that survives loss—very little, perhaps, but not nothing.

Two sites frame our initial reading of Levinas and the problem of beginning and futurity in *Totality and Infinity:* the opening passages in the preface, toward which we can only gesture here, and the concluding section on futurity, fecundity, and reproduction, "Beyond the Face" (*TI* 254–307). The opening paragraphs of *Totality and Infinity* have occasioned more than a few comments, mostly concerning the elevated and historical terms of Levinas's programmatic motif. Levinas asks the biggest question, one to which *Totality and Infinity* by itself could never comprise a full answer: are we duped by morality? Levinas, in a tone wholly appropriate to the middle of Europe's twentieth century, wonders if the seeming permanency of war is inevitable and worthy only of calculation in response. Morality is at stake in this wondering, for it is morality that holds out for another possible world, or at least an interruption of war's dominance over the world. What becomes of *Totality and Infinity*'s opening query? Are we duped by morality? If so, what does that mean? Where is the duplicity located and how is it possible to contest the state of war? And why this strange and hyperbolic beginning to the book?

The problematic of futurity emerges as crucial in the midst of these questions. Morality has duped us insofar as morality is inevitably and perhaps even invariably duplicitous when it operates under regimes of totality. Duty, virtue, and so on, all for Levinas fall under suspicion not only because he objects in simple principle to the occlusion of singularity, which is absorbed by generalities of law and habit, but even more importantly because conventional models of morality service totalitarian violence with barely a hiccup. Duty has long been identified by thinkers like Arendt as a prominent feature of the National Socialist machinery of death. Part of Levinas's alternative evokes the language of first philosophy and what has been called the transcendental dimension of Levinasian ethics, as when he writes in *Totality and Infinity* that war "presupposes peace, the antecedent and non-allergic presence of the Other; war does not represent the first event of encounter" (*TI* 199). If peace is presupposed by war, then an appeal to the possibility of the ethical—however remote, with whatever tenor of desperation—has real grounds. First philosophy secures, however precariously, a sense of hope.

With this cast, Levinas has given the *history* of the West the form of ceaseless war and violence. Obsession with being and knowing, those signature features of Western philosophy, explain war as a total cultural and historical event. War is not only possible, but necessary. Yet, hope does not disappear into the theory, then practice, of violence, for another world is possible—even if only in glimpses and occasional interruptions. *Only the future can save us. The past is comprised of the terms of violence, so retrieval of the past only promises the repetition of violence. The future must be new and other possibilities must come from that newness.* But, in a particularly disconcerting turn, Levinas notes that even the future has been colonized by totality.

He writes, "The meaning of individuals (invisible outside of this totality) is derived from the totality. The unicity of each present is incessantly sacrificed to a future appealed to in order to bring forth its objective meaning. For the ultimate meaning alone counts; the last act alone changes beings into themselves. They are what they will appear to be in the already plastic forms of the epic" (*TI* 22). In this passage, Levinas announces the important figurative distinction between the Homeric epic of Odysseus's return and the biblical tale (epic?) of wandering and nonreturn. So much is at stake in this distinction. Is the meaning of historical time explained by arrival? That is, does human or divine theodicy make sense of our experience of history? Or is the moment, whether in the present or in the past, punctured by what lies outside of it? The place of the Other is at stake in this question about time and its figures. Indeed, only two years later in "The Trace of the Other,"[2] the distinction between Odysseus and Abraham—the Greek and the Hebraic—will prove crucial in Levinas's ongoing attempt to break with totality. The claim is straightforward, if the future is only sacrifice to a preconceived idea (the human and divine versions of theodicy), then the future is no future at all. So much, perhaps everything, hangs in the balance.

Totality, violence, and war are projective, providing ideological justifications for destruction. The future is set out as repetition unless there is interruption. Ethics and the face open the possibility of interruption, and so a different future, one that Levinas later rewrites under the rubrics of messianism and the prophetic. But those articulations of the future, even when they appear in *Totality and Infinity,* seem less attuned to life after catastrophe than reflective of the hopeless hope we find in late- and postmodernity. That is, rubrics of messianism and the prophetic offer only interruption, never continuity, whereas life after catastrophe always keeps continuity in view, *even as interruption does its deconstructive work.* Levinas's work on the future is inseparable from (and crucial for thinking about) the destruction *and* the survival of Judaism after the

Shoah. That is, precisely because Levinas's philosophical work on the idea of Europe, the meaning of culture, and the general productivity of time for meaning crosses philosophy with the religion, we ought to (or at least *can*) see part of his project as concerned with the meaning of Judaism after disaster. Indeed, one reply to criticism of Levinas's incessant concern with Europe (his Eurocentrism in the most sympathetic sense) *might* be that the future of Judaism is at stake, and so is worthy of its own consideration. With this in mind, then, how does Levinas conceive futurity with remnants of continuity? And, thus, how can we read his account of futurity in the frame of living after catastrophe?

Catastrophe changes everything about beginning, initiating not just the urgency, but the necessity of beginning again after violence. Beginning, that is, with a new relation to the Other and a robust sense of how the various manifestations of otherness—the cultural Other, the political Other, the Other as neighbor, even familial—make futurity possible. Levinas's various names for this new relation—the ethical, justice, fraternity—are grounded in what is absolute and, paradoxically, in what is always groundless. And so the new relation is always fragile and precarious, subjected to the often-dispiriting vicissitudes of action and commitment. Not even love is sufficient, for lovers shirk their responsibilities in the bordered intimacy of the one-to-one relation. Responsibility is difficult. It always exceeds what love finds and that to which love grafts itself.

But not all love is insufficient. In the final section of *Totality and Infinity*, Levinas's treatment of fecundity, paternity, and the son rewrites love against propriety and borders. This rewriting re-imagines a future in which there is continuity and disruption, identity and difference, borders and infinity. Time itself is exploded at the very same moment time keeps the past alive into the future. "Fecundity," Levinas writes, "is to be set up as an ontological category.... The son is not only my work, like a poem or an object, nor is he my property. Neither the categories of power nor those of knowledge describe my relation with the child. The fecundity of the I is neither a cause nor a domination. I do not have my child; I am my child" (*TI 277*). The ontological moment in time lies in the identification of the I and the child. This identification is ethical and ontological at the same time; the child renders the father in the accusative, setting up at the same time a relation of the me and the child. Paradoxically, then, fecundity's relation to the future is both within and outside being without contradiction. The paradox names intersection, folding, and a healing rupture. And so Levinas continues, declaring the paradox of the future in writing that "in this transcendence the I is not swept away, since the son is not me; and yet I *am* my son" (277).

The fecundity of the father-son relation produces beyond what Levinas calls the *unique* son—the son who, in Levinas's particularly patriarchal formulation, is only my own *in both name and identity*. Rather, the chosenness of the son by the I and the I by the son is transformed into—or perhaps just already implicated in—the chosenness of fraternity. Chosenness moves the future from the model of sequentiality, and therefore countability—toward infinity. Difference is set out into the future without borders, but one that maintains the continuity of the paternal line in the name: *multiplicity, difference, and identity all at once.*

In this account of futurity, we can hear an echo of the problematic of beginning after catastrophe. Perhaps Levinas gives us something akin to a transcendental account of beginning again, those conditions under which it is possible to make collectivity *again* after filiation. If we read Levinas on fecundity and futurity in this register, then we can revisit the famous remark at the beginning of "Signature" and reopen the problem of reading Levinas as (at least in part) a post-Shoah thinker. That is, the Shoah was not just an event of singular suffering. It is also a complete and total cultural loss. After World War II, the category "European Jew"—so constitutive of European history across the range of intellectual production to political negation—ceases to exist in any significant way. Whatever the sedimentation in culture and history, whatever the remaining numbers, and whatever the fantasized version of Israel that remakes it a kind of European nation, the Nazi genocide changes everything about history. And so beginning again cannot summon the fullness of the past in the present. This is Levinas's moment of rewriting Heidegger's remarks on the Greek temple, when the absent god of the Greeks is replaced with the absent community after catastrophe. Yet, there is always the future.

What can that future mean? Fecundity gives us just that clue, if not explicit treatment. What survives catastrophe, in the context of the Shoah, is *the name*. The name is the name of the father, which becomes the name of the son, which then becomes the name that makes fraternity possible. The name survives catastrophe, exceeding genocidal violence with a fecund survival. With a name, a people survive with more than bodies; cultural forms and possibilities are carried with a name. Just as there is a son—or perhaps *because* there is a son—there is continuity *in name* for Judaism after the disaster. Not because the name wills the future come, but because the future happens to subjectivity, collective or singular, in the interval named fecundity.

THE (OTHER) OTHER'S PAIN

In the very same year Levinas published *Totality and Infinity*, the global south was galvanized by the publication of arguably the most important anticolonial manifesto: Frantz Fanon's *The Wretched of the Earth*. It was also the penultimate year of Algeria's brutal struggle against French colonial rule (which claimed hundreds of thousands of Algerian lives) and, in particular, was the year French police massacred peaceful Algerian protesters in the so-called Paris Massacre of 1961. While many of the key figures in French intellectual life gave complicated and at times controversial thoughts on the Algerian situation (as well as the other colonies involved in anticolonial struggle), Levinas seems to have been all but oblivious to the world-changing conflict surrounding France and other European powers.[3] And by 1961, Fanon's home country of Martinique had been one of the newly established Départements d'Outre-Mer for a decade and a half.

In other words, *Totality and Infinity* was published in interesting times. Whatever the interesting times, Levinas's work shows no signs of engagement with these events, nor does his work seem especially attuned to the experiences of mass suffering just outside of (or technically within) French borders. I do not say this to somehow shame Levinas for his insularity or insensitivity (though such shame would be refreshing to read in Levinas scholarship from time-to-time), but rather to underscore the intimacy of the problem of beginning, catastrophe, and futurity with the *other* Other's moment on the world stage. Catastrophe *as such* dominates the middle of the twentieth century and, in the moment of anticolonial struggle, the problems of beginning and futurity are raised with every bit the same urgency as those in a specifically European context.

For Édouard Glissant, the historical experience of catastrophe haunts the problem of beginning in the postcolonial moment—a moment exacerbated and prolonged by the arrangement of departmentalization, which perpetuates the functional *and* existential relationship with the colonizer. Glissant's postcolonial question becomes how to re-render that historical experience so that the pain of history becomes productive and not just debilitating. Put in relation to Fanon, whose shadow cast over Martinican thought cannot be overstated, it is a matter of imagining the collective out of the inferiority complex by way of an affirmation of the Caribbean's composite cultural life—Glissant calls his method *Antillanité*—without recourse or return to an elsewhere.

Beginning with historical experience also means an honest reckoning with the pain of history. For Glissant, historical experience discloses a sense of futurity that translates pain through an engagement with composite cultural forms, into another *imaginary*—his term for the imagining and re-imagining of the meaning of the world. Glissant's *Poetics of Relation*, perhaps his greatest theoretical work, brings four decades of reflection to bear on questions of beginning, globalization, and futurity. How does *Poetics of Relation* begin thinking about pain, trauma, and beginning?

"What is terrifying," Glissant writes, "partakes of the abyss."[4] With that remark, Glissant initiates his long meditation on the relation between traumatic historical experience and beginning. Beginning in the Caribbean context is structured by a three-fold sense of the abyss. The abyss in general is produced in the trauma of the forced migration of the Middle Passage, but with nuanced shifts in sites; the traumatic event has three distinct moments of transformative pain. Glissant's account traces three moments of forced migration: departure, passage, and arrival. The first abyss, the loss and vanishing of memory, is initiated when "you fell into the belly of the boat. . . . Yet the belly of this boat dissolves you, precipitates you in a nonworld from which you cry out. This boat is a womb, a womb abyss." "The next abyss," Glissant writes, "was the depths of the sea. Whenever a fleet of ships gave chase to the slave ships, it was easiest just to lighten the boat by throwing cargo overboard, weighing it down with balls and chains. These underwater signposts mark the course between the Gold Coast and the Leeward Islands."[5]

The second abyss names passage itself and provides for Glissant the figure of loss: drown memory. The bodies thrown overboard carry with them the memory of passage, marking the passage with signposts of radical absence—abyssal absence, drowned presence. We should note an important difference here, one that will become more significant below, between the figures of loss in European discourse on the Shoah and in theorizing the Middle Passage. Rather than ashen memory and the cinder, there is the ball and chain at the bottom of the ocean. Not the body or its remainder. Only what drowned the body at the bottom of an unfathomable sea. Memory in the second abyss figures loss differently, and that figure is far from just literary. Rather, the drowning of memory is also the drowning of the name, a loss that is perhaps more total than ashen memory. With ashes, there is the trace remainder of the past, something we can place in Levinas's account of the name. Ashen memory figures a thread of meaning that holds the past to the future, even if that thread is disrupted by the demand to break from the past. But drowned memory is fundamentally different.[6] The Middle Passage, on Glissant's account, does not leave threads and traces. It is the moment of painful birth, not rebirth; there is never doubling back to the past. Beginning's abyss is abyssal without compromise. The melancholic beginning of composite culture begins by fiat and necessity, not because Glissant wants to name resistance or anticolonial struggle, but because the drowning of memory leaves nothing to thread the past to the present and future.

The third abyss is the moment of arrival. The moment of arrival is defined by the disorientation and trauma of plantation violence, but it is also defined by the absoluteness of forgetting. What is drown in the second abyss arrives without name. The "mass of water" becomes the nameless surge of arrival. Glissant writes, "Paralleling this mass of water, the third metamorphosis of the abyss thus projects a reverse image of all that had been left behind, not to be regained for generations except—more and more threadbare—in the blue savannas of memory or imagination."[7] Arrival confirms forgetting. The first two appearances of the abyss sever the memorial tie, which would *seem* to give nothing to the future except melancholic loss. Without the name, continuity is drown rather than broken or made ashen. The very notion of retrieval is therefore set in the blue savannas of memory—which is to say, no memory at all. Thus, arrival remaps a wholly new, wholly fractal geography of cultural production, striking the final traumatic blow against the past. Arrival's disorientation does not reroot according to an atavistic logic of origins (in whatever ruined form), but instead reroutes according to the nomadic and rhizomatic logic of Chaos. It would be enough to theorize the catastrophe as mass death and suffering. But for Glissant, the forgetting of origins widens and deepens disaster by tearing apart and dispensing with European narratives of loss, recovery, and futurity.

The abyss, in its three-fold claim on life, makes "one vast beginning, but a beginning whose time is marked by these balls and chains gone green."[8] *Time is marked.* That is, time is fundamentally transformed—to the point of curvature—by the catastrophe of the Middle Passage. By the curvature of time, Glissant, in appealing to Einstein's physics, wants to make an absolute break with those models of sequentiality that dominate the European model of trauma and loss. We can see this clearly in relation to Levinas's work, where even the traumatic break with atavism does not, in the end, dispense with the name. *That* beginning begins with the thread of the surname, giving a future that is at once alienating and intimate, both wholly Other and wholly me. The figure of drown memory changes this story dramatically and also underscores Glissant's great distance from Negritude. Abyssal beginning is not simply a story of the first Africans in the Americas. Rather, abyssal beginning is *another* beginning, a first and new beginning of history. Loss is just that total and absolute, recasting the African past as blue savannas of memory and imagination. And yet there is also an important distinction in Glissant's work on the trace. Rather than a question of identity, the trace functions in the play of imagination. That space of play is less continuity than it is a force without name, but with effect and animation. Africanness is not a question of identity, for Glissant, but instead an imaginary component, animating what is *first* (and thus not secondary or tertiary) a composite culture and its productions.

Abyssal beginning changes the meaning of alterity in the New World context. So, we should not be surprised at the ethical language that comes to the fore in Glissant's later work. The Levinasian motifs in *Poetics of Relation* are evident from the tropes of the Other and opacity, both of which signify the ethical core of Glissant's theorizing the Caribbean and are derived from the fundamental fragility and vulnerability of composite cultural forms. The historical experience of conquest and the slave trade, after all, seals fragility and vulnerability in the margins of the global system of cultural formation. Without atavistic roots, everything is precarious. As well, and this is crucial here, composite cultural forms are *ex vi termini* comprised of relations with the Other that implicate Levinasian epistemological, ontological, and ethical themes. Otherness, of course, can play many roles that place the Other outside the peculiar economy of the Levinasian ethical. In this register, Glissant carefully marks out the distinction between what he calls "the thought of the Other" and "the Other of thought." The former is still bound by the structure of knowledge, suggesting the primacy of *comprendre*. Glissant employs *comprendre* as a troubled term in order to evoke senses of seizing upon or capture in conventional epistemology—senses that resonate with an historically terrifying specificity in an Africana context. But the Other suggests something else, something that makes the work of composite cultural formation vital, intense, and imaginative. He writes that the

> thought of the Other is sterile without the other of Thought. Thought of the Other is the moral generosity disposing me to accept the principle of alterity, to conceive of the world as not simple and straightforward, with only one truth—mine. But thought of the Other can dwell within me without making me alter course....The other of Thought is precisely this altering. Then I have to act. That is the moment I change my thought, without renouncing its contribution. I change, and I exchange. This is an aesthetics of turbulence whose corresponding ethics is not provided in advance.⁹

For Glissant, then, the explosion of thought by the Other, which breaks alterity out of the seizing grasp of consciousness, sets thinking into the Chaos of Relation. From this sense of Relation, an "imaginary [is] rekindled by the other of Thought."¹⁰

With the term "imaginary," Glissant wants to retain the idea of knowing without putting the Other at risk in knowledge. Abyssal beginning, after all, changes so much of what it means to know. *Comprendre* and comparison import both the figures and practices of imperial force. Seizing and grasping figure what is made political and cultural practice under colonialism. But there is also the composition of knowing and contact *outside* the totalitarian economy, a sense of relation that keeps the opacity of the Other safe without insisting on simple separation. Opacity, contact, *then* composition—this is the ethical movement of making the world meaningful. The composition of knowing in a composite cultural context crafts meaning in the imaginary—the precarious aesthetic sphere of knowing and being that structures a relation to the world—out of fragments of the past and present that bear no atavistic relation to a rooted past. The Caribbean imaginary is this unrooted Chaos of knowing that is never fixed and never a struggle for domination, but rather a constant figuration, *mise en question,* and refiguration—a knowledge that *becomes.* Indeed, the opening intertext to *Poetics of Relation* makes this clear when Glissant writes, "Thought draws the imaginary of the past: a knowledge becoming. One cannot stop it to assess it nor isolate it to transmit it. It is sharing one can never not retain, nor ever, in standing still, boast about it."[11] Glissant's vision of the Caribbean is that of a form of knowing as irreducibly becoming, moving across the dynamic space of thinking and its other without cessation. This dynamic space maintains, and is even kept vital and urgent because of, the opacity of the Other. The Other of thought makes thinking compatible with radical alterity and an ethics thereof.

This vision of knowledge is crucial for understanding Glissant's conception of the future. Because becoming and knowing are generated by a relation to the past (the space of beginning), the traumatic production of the abyss de-links the future from a rootedness in the past. For this reason, Glissant repeatedly turns to Deleuze and Guattari's figure of the rhizome in his later work while arguing against atavistic conceptions of culture and meaning. The abyss, informed by the rhizomatic conception of relation and identity, gives becoming to being, disassembling the totalitarian pretensions of identity with the other Other's historical experience. *After the Middle Passage, there is not even the continuity of the name.* And yet there is knowing. In the opening section of *Poetics of Relation,* Glissant makes the relation between the abyss and knowledge clear when he writes, "Thus, the absolute unknown, projected by the abyss and bearing into eternity the womb abyss and the infinite abyss, in the end became knowledge.... For though this experience made you, original victim floating toward the sea's abysses, an exception, it became something shared and made us, the descendants, one people among others.... This experience of the abyss can now be said to be the best element of exchange."[12] This is a peculiar and even unexpected twist in the treatment of catastrophe. Not unlike Levinas's shift from the dispiriting philosophy of history as totality and war to the fecundity of the name and identity, Glissant sees the opening of the future as a break from catastrophe—not as redemption, but rather as the persistence of time. The persistence of time manifests in the making of a people—a future made out of the abyss, which is a womb and bequeaths no name, yet still bequeaths time. That is, it is not just that descendants survive. Descendents *become* a people, creating through contact, what Glissant calls, Relation—a nomadic, rhizomatic identity.

Without the persistence of the name, we get an important shift away from Levinas's response to our opening query: how to begin after catastrophe? The ashes of memory leave a certain continuity intact, so loss is not total *insofar as one retains rights to loss.* By "rights to loss," I here mean a sense of connection to the terms of loss and the narration of its meaning. The name persists, which gives an important contour to loss; we can narrate the terms of loss, what it puts in crisis, and so what it means to begin again, after disaster. In a certain sense, we can see Levinas's conception of futurity as a rewriting of Heidegger's conception of language and retrieval—loss *is* loss because we catch sight of continuity and its breaking up. The drowning of memory is very different, though, as what is lost is the name itself. Atavism vanishes in the second sense of Glissant's abyss.

This is a total vanishing; fragments and traces bear no threaded relation to the past, nor to an original. Originless beginning begins again without the rights to loss. Narrative fails before it begins. How could it be otherwise after the catastrophe of the Middle Passage, after the threaded relation to the African past is drown in the sea? And yet there is always the future on the ruin of the shoreline—a new language, a new identity, and so a new sense of the historical experience and existential drama of beginning. In this drama, the word, language as such, and so too the name, is first, wholly new, and always *creolized*—that linguistic event that marks with such clarity the intersection of the Middle Passage with the fact of survival in the composition of composite culture.

Composite culture denotes that most complex and most compelling moment in Glissant's thinking of the new. Composed of fragments, the new is not a site of resonance of the past; traces *after the Middle Passage* do not speak with an assertive, atavistic (or trace-atavistic) voice. Rather, the new is wholly new in that the component parts of composite culture are set in a Relation that is defined by Chaos and fractal assemblage. The new emerges here out of a *curved* temporality, never *ex nihilo*—even as the trauma of the Middle Passage and arrival in the New World drowns memory. Out of fragments, chaotic and fractal formations of the new emerge—an abyssal beginning.

Future and Catastrophe after Europe

For both Levinas and Glissant, the problem of beginning, then place, is set against the devastation of history. And yet, unlike, say, the historiographic argument of Walter Benjamin's "Theses on the Philosophy of History," which imagines telling (or the impossibility of telling) history from the sadness of the victims, Levinas and Glissant emphatically turn to an analysis of the future. The past is sealed in its immemoriality in both structure—neither thinker can theoretically justify awakening the absent—and by a certain urgency of the future. Survival is not enough. To have survived simply means that the immemorial is not all that remains; there is always the matter of *how* one is to survive, *how* the collective remains so across the interval between catastrophe and an accomplished living-after.

This means in part that we read Glissant against the sorts of sentiments Aimé Césaire expresses in the famous line from *Discourse on Colonialism*, where he writes that what Hitler did to European enemies was "the same" as what Europe had been doing to Africans and indigenous peoples of the Americas for centuries. To be sure, Césaire makes an important point. One ought not be astonished at the severity of internal violence—genocidal and otherwise—in Europe across the two world wars. After all, Europe had already proven itself to be a machine of death and suffering in other parts of the globe—most of the globe, in fact. So the catastrophic violence in the first half of the twentieth century seems, with a bit of perspective, completely consistent. And there is a bit of continuity between Césaire and Levinas on this very point, insofar as both see a *form* across violence that points to an inner identity. Just as Césaire writes about the slave trade and colonial violence across the collapse of Europe through internal spasms of mass killing and genocide, Levinas gestures toward the inner identity of violence in his account of totality as the transcendental of war.

The shift in figures of beginning, however, changes everything. Beginning does not proceed from one and the same catastrophe. Rather, the figure of loss as cindered or drown prefigures the terms of beginning—and so also of futurity. This very difference is nicely captured in how Levinas and Glissant both use the motif of *curvature*. For Levinas, curvature describes the transformation of space in the (non-) relation of separation. The truth of exteriority produces a surplus exceeding all ideas, locations, and therefore any mapping of the relation(s) constitutive of moral consciousness; Levinas calls this the curvature of the space of relationality. Intersubjectivity is transformed from a grid underpinning theories of objectivity—the service to which Husserl put intersubjectivity in the Fifth of the *Cartesian Meditations*—into the strange, infinite quasi space of obligation. In *Totality and Infinity*, Levinas writes, "This 'curvature' of intersubjective space in which exteriority is effectuated (we do not say 'in which it appears') as superiority must be distinguished from the arbitrariness of 'points of view' taken upon objects that appear.... The 'curvature of space' expresses the relation between human beings" (*TI* 291). Separation is not perspectivalism infused with moral language, of course. This is such an important distinction in Levinas's work and the complexity entailed in it cannot be overstated. But here it is enough to say that Levinas conceives curvature as fundamentally spatial.

Glissant also turns to the motif of curvature in describing the relation of Same and Other in *Poetics of Relation* and *Introduction à une poétique du divers*, but with an important shift. For Glissant, catastrophe produces a curvature of *time*, not space. The curvature of time breaks with sequentiality absolutely, without remainder or retention. And so memory functions otherwise than fracture and separation. Curvature, in Glissant's text, evokes Einstein's relativity theory, removing all senses of measure from the experience of historical time. Time does not happen in sequence; one's position in the unfolding of temporality bends time such that it does not unfold as such, but instead twists erratically according to the (perhaps chaotic) specificity of historical experience. Rather than being measured by a hastily universalized European experience of time, which has its marks and fractures and fissures, and rather than the experience of the loss of the African root as the defining feature of Afro-Caribbean life, Glissant's account of the curvature of time clears the space for thinking trauma, beginning, and futurity on its own terms. If living after disaster entails a certain bit of intractable melancholy, then the time and space of that

melancholic resonance needs accounting in specifically historical terms. That is, we need an accounting in terms of both the
decidedly *nonuniversalizable* sense of a connection to and historical experience of place: root or rhizome? And what kind of
rhizome, for what sorts of reasons?

We can now return to the opening remarks of the present
essay. It is not enough to simply note that Levinas's work is
exclusively concerned with European thinkers (true) or that he
makes immensely troubling remarks when his thoughts wander
outside the borders of Europe (also true). Rather, it is necessary to think about Levinas's work as structured from within
by his Europeanness, which, in the case of the present reflections, is another way of saying that Levinas's concern with the
fecundity of the Jewish name and future fraternity of the Jews
as a people turns on a Eurocentric concern with a certain kind
of catastrophe, a particular problem of beginning, and so a very
specific form of futurity. This concern is itself fecund. For atavistic cultural forms and traditions that bear the memory of
disaster (conquest being chief among those memories in the
New World), Levinas's account of beginning and possible futu-
rities conjoins questions of retrieval, productivity, and responsibility to wider issues of history and language. In certain colonial
and postcolonial contexts, such as those explored by Spivak,
Bhabha, and others, Levinas's work is both deeply connected
and consistently important. But that very work presupposes
continuity in order to address the *particular form* of discontinuity and fracture that too often gets discussed as a general
sense of trauma, loss, and separation. Glissant's work on the
same interval between catastrophe and fecundity exposes a fundamental monolingualism at the heart of Levinas's ethics of the
future. We see this monolingualism in the function of the name
as a thread of continuity and continuation, holding close to
what is broken apart and the pain of history, while at the same
time promising a future to the fraternity to come — *to a people.*
Perhaps this reveals an inner connection between Levinas's
conception of time and a theory of ruins.

Glissant's commitment to Caribbeanness begins with a space already dispossessed of the kinds of ruins that prove productive. Beginning without ruins initiates a movement without root-edness in the past. However precarious those roots become after catastrophic violence, there is only abyss. The melancholic moment in this story is obvious and it leads Glissant to remind readers of the necessity to "remember our boats."[13] Memory of pain persists, without ruins, as drown memory, but so too does the future. The future is absolute mixture in that chaotic curvature of time Glissant calls "creolization." Creolization mixes without circulating around a single root, and yet also and always mixes in order to set multiple roots—none of which alone sustain the life of a people, but which, as a composite, do in fact give the identity of a people vitality, meaning, and possibility. This is merely Glissant's observation of Caribbean cultural history, seen outside the frame of the colonial. The Caribbean is *already* rhizomatic and functions according to a *rhizomatic imaginary.* The word "rhizome," in Glissant's hands, is therefore at once a proper noun (the rhizome), adjective (rhizomatic), and verb (rhizomes), *entangled* with pursued, unexpected, and even haunting senses of the Other.

Entanglement means everything here, and I want to conclude with a final remark on the imperative to think Levinas across borders. What Levinas calls Europe is famously composed of "the Bible and the Greeks." That formulation of European identity, however, is as peculiar as it is common. For, though the Greek-Christian and Judaic elements of European culture certainly describe and account for much of what we call "Europe," there is also the now over five centuries of entanglement of Europe with the Americas—and indeed with the globe as such. What is Europe without this entanglement? How much entanglement is necessary before the object of entanglement—here, of conquest and domination—becomes part of identity? Part of what is entailed in these questions is the difficult matter of responsibility, as well as the meaning of historical experience. But what I want to underscore here in conclusion is how the question of beginning after catastrophe in Glissant's work is situated in the same entangled—even *rhizomatic,* perhaps—historical experience as that of Levinas. Césaire's remark is important, of course, noting the continuity of Europe in its very violence. And there is also simply the sense in which the history of the Caribbean is immanent to the meaning of Europe, which implicates catastrophe across the spectrum of historical experience. Beginning after catastrophe, from the ashes or the abyss, is therefore a matter for all thinking of beginning, even those sites of beginning that most put in question notions of fecundity, paternity, fraternity, and the name.

The implications, 50 years later, are clear for me—two-fold. First, we need to begin rereading a periodized *Totality and Infinity*. That is a very different book. Levinas did not write from his cramped office in some neighborhood or at the university. He wrote from the world. That world was writing, too, and under the same tone and tenor of catastrophe, memory, and beginning. The world had fallen apart for so many hundreds of millions of people, who then faced the future because time is obstinate and uncooperative. *Beginning again imposes itself.* Under that imposition, there is the urgent question of the logic of reproduction and production. Let us then read *Totality and Infinity* as a period piece, but, as better readers, without the fantasized insularity of its author and without the casual, unproblematized generalizing rhetoric of *the* Other, *the* Ethical, and *the* Future. That means expanding our literacy and troubling our habits of writing and thinking: *to, and then from, the Other!*

Second, we need to begin rereading *Totality and Infinity*—and indeed Levinas's work as a whole—in terms of a more generalized philosophical methodology.[14] Once we give up the casual generalizing language of Levinasian *thinking*—that is, *after* the task of exposition and *into* the task of thinking with or from alterity—the epistemological and quasi-ontological aspects of his work come into clearer focus. With that clearer focus, Levinas is less an oracle and an immovable text (an approach that has dominated so much scholarship, even when putting Levinas into conversation with others), and more a method for reckoning with the problem of difference in a wider sense. This wider sense disrupts so much. Namely, it raises questions for Levinasian thinking regarding the relevance of, or even insistence on, historical experience, transnational contact, and the remnants of colonial hegemony. Where are those remnants in Levinas's work? For those of us moved by the Levinasian account of the Other, this means loosening our thinking and buying a lot of new books, producing a very Levinasian openness to instruction from the other Other, and, to use Glissant's term, *creolizing* philosophical methodology in response to an expanded literacy. Why have we Levinasians kept such a narrow scope when thinking about the Other? What would it mean to think in a Levinasian register with those other accounts—there are so many!—of alterity, epistemological rupture, traumatic beginning, and production and reproduction? These are our questions, 50 years later. I do wonder, and even worry, how our scholarship will look in another 50 years. I offer here a plea for the transnational, other sites of trauma, other narratives of beginning, and so other ways in which we are called into question. We write from the world. Let us also write from other stories of loss, not just those we find most intimate and easy and familiar. Does not Levinas call us to the strange and the stranger? A critical, perhaps *decolonized* moment of the strange and the stranger requires a reduction—phenomenological *and* anticolonial—of the familiar, even when it gives us that small yet important comfort of the continuity of the name. In fact, such a reduction is *most* necessary in those moments. Eurocentrism is a bad habit.

Totality and Infinity was written in interesting times—let us reread it with interesting times as our frames. Pulled back into its moment in history, we see so much of the possibility in Levinas's work. We also see how the moment in time puts so much of that possibility in question. Would the Levinas of *Totality and Infinity* have wanted it any other way?

TWELVE

Levinas's Ethical Critique of Levinasian Ethics

Robert Bernasconi

THE RECEPTION OF TOTALITY AND INFINITY

Since its appearance in 1961, Levinas's *Totality and Infinity* has largely been promoted as a book about ethics, but important though ethics already was for him, the question of ethics was not the primary question guiding his philosophical endeavors at that time. The tendency of commentators to focus on the ethical import of the book has opened Levinas up to a number of criticisms: he is seen as moralistic; his ethics is divorced from politics; and above all, it is tied to a notion of infinite responsibility that is so burdensome that it would be impossible to live by. However, it is not possible to determine how telling these criticisms are in the absence of an account of the book's overall argument. If the construction of an ethics in the conventional sense was not the dominant purpose of *Totality and Infinity*—for example, if the account of ethics is not normative but descriptive—then the status of these criticisms would need to be reassessed. This is part of what I attempt in this essay.

The remainder will be directed to clarifying the book's over-all argument in an effort to correct what I show to be partial readings.

There has been no shortage of attempts to show that eth-ics is not the guiding thread of Levinas's *Totality and Infinity*. Etienne Feron made the case already in 1992 that Levinas's own description of his book as a defense of subjectivity should be accepted.[1] Even earlier, Bernard Forthomme argued that it is the idea of transcendence rather than that of ethics that guides Levinas's whole *corpus,* including *Totality and Infinity*.[2] But in the popular mind Levinas is reduced to being primar-ily the philosopher of the face-to-face as an ethical relation, with the other themes he addresses being largely ignored, including the place that the face-to-face is given in his over-all argument. To the extent that these attempts to present Levinas's philosophy as other than primarily ethical have so far proved unpersuasive, it is because they have not been accom-panied by a full account of how that argument is supposed to work. Although a detailed line by line commentary of the kind other philosophical classics have received would be the only truly compelling way to make that case, I will attempt another strategy and suggest that Levinas already saw, more clearly than his commentators have, the limits of the ethics of the face devel-oped in the book's third section, when read in isolation. I will show that he tried to address those problems in the pages that followed. If one means by "Levinasian ethics" the tendency of commentators to present the ethics of the face in isolation from the rest of Levinas's argument, then I believe it is legiti-mate to talk of Levinas's critique of Levinasian ethics before the fact.

I will begin by trying to give the phrase "Levinasian ethics" some precision, as it could mean a number of different things. By that phrase I am not referring here to the attempts to popu-larize Levinas's thought by identifying him as the proponent of an ethics of the stranger, the poor and the hungry. On that interpretation Levinas is understood to have said that we *should* respond to the face of the Other which demands from me food, comfort, and other assistance. But for the most part, Levinas was careful to avoid telling us what we ought to be doing. He was not preaching, but describing what happens (*DF* 171). That is why, in a series of interviews he gave to Philippe Nemo, he distanced himself from attempts to construct an ethics on the basis of an account of the face of the Other and insisted that he conceived his own task to be that of finding "the meaning (*sens*)" of ethics (*EI* 90). Levinas's remark on this occasion that it would be possible to construct an ethics on the basis of his ideas seems, however, to be somewhat disingenuous, given the fact that one of the features of the ethical relation to the Other to which Levinas repeatedly returns in *Totality and Infinity* and elsewhere is that the Other puts me in question and that this sets off a process of self-questioning. But this questioning also embraces ethics itself. If one can talk about *an* ethics in Levinas, it would have to be characterized as an "ethics of suspicion," that is to say, an ethics that puts in question any certainty one might have, before or after acting, that one ever knows for sure the right action in any given situation or the entire story about one's reason for doing what one does.[3] But Levinas also excludes the possibility of having a good conscience by insisting that one can never do enough and that no limits can be placed on one's responsibility. What Levinas says about the ethical relation thus issues a challenge to conventional morality. This is why some of his ideas are appropriate resources for anyone wanting to address the kinds of problems that philosophical ethics as it is found in the tradition finds intractable, such as world hunger.[4] But this is not the guiding theme of Levinas's philosophy.

I also want to separate my discussion here of Levinasian ethics from attempts to shape his account into a narrative. It is true that the temptation to present Levinas in this light is strong when introducing him to someone for the first time. But such a narrative, reminiscent of the accounts of individuals coming together to form society that one finds in social contract theory, does not do justice to the way that Levinas interweaves motifs from transcendental philosophy alongside the description of the experience of the Other in an effort to disrupt any such naïve reading.[5] The difficulty of loosening the hold on Levinas scholarship of this narrative of an atheist separated I who suddenly is surprised to encounter an Other that puts that I morally in question may be the biggest obstacle to generating a philosophically rich reading of Levinas. To be sure, such an encounter can sometimes happen, and as a philosopher Levinas must be able to account for its possibility, which he subsequently attempted to do in *Otherwise than Being or Beyond Essence*. But in addition to feeding into naïve ideas of radical individualism, the narrative reading can make it seem that the ethical and the political cannot subsist together, whereas Levinas separated them only because the political sometimes dominates to the point where the ethical gets lost (*EN* 100–01). However, in the ordinary course of things they belong together: "The presence of the face, the infinity of the other, is a destituteness, a presence of the third party (that is, of the whole of humanity which looks at us)" (*TI* 213). The relation of politics to ethics in Levinas cannot be reduced to a story.

However, these ways of presenting Levinas are not my target on this occasion. Under the label "Levinasian ethics" I am here putting in question a series of interpretations that has already gone beyond these simplifications of his thought, but which nevertheless still exhibits the double tendency within the secondary literature, first to locate the core of his thought in the ethics of the face and, secondly, to treat it as if it could stand alone.[6] The results can be seen in the number of books and articles on Levinas's ethics that have tended to ignore the whole of the fourth section of *Totality and Infinity* on eros and fecundity.[7] To be sure, these pages have been the subject of some brilliant readings, largely by feminist philosophers, but these interpretations have not usually been concerned to clarify the place of this section within the book as a whole.[8]

Beyond the Face

What guides Levinas's thought is the quest for what he calls "modes of metaphysical transcendence" (*TI* 29). The fourth and final section of *Totality and Infinity* has the title "Beyond the Face." This presents a problem for the standard reading, which presents the face of the Other as the privileged site of transcendence. "Beyond the Face" must mean that there is a transcendence more transcendent than the face of the Other, so that although the face is a site of transcendence, it cannot be the privileged site of transcendence.[9] Levinas announced this explicitly when he wrote that the plane of eros and fecundity, "where the I bears itself beyond death and recovers also from its return to itself," is "a plane both presupposing and transcending the epiphany of the Other in the face" (253). So how does the turn to eros and fecundity modify the standard understanding of the ethics of the face? What is the relation of this plane to both the ethical and the ontological planes? Is there an ethics of fecundity or does fecundity displace ethics?

In order to address these questions, it is necessary first to recall the grounds on which Levinas introduced the ethical relation to the Other in *Totality and Infinity*. Two separate arguments can be identified. The first is that the face of the Other exhibits the formal structure of exteriority and so answers to the quest for transcendence. The second is that my encounter with the face of the Other which puts me in question has priority within philosophy because it sets in motion all subsequent questioning and reasoning. I will take these in turn as a prelude to showing that the relation of the face of the Other to fecundity is not restricted to their representing two different forms of transcendence. They are integrated as ethical. That is why I refer to this critique of the Levinasian ethics of some of his commentators as an ethical critique. Fecundity and the face-to-face are joined not only as modes of transcendence, but also through their relation to ethics. It is this conjunction that serves to unite the various parts of the book and establishes transcendence as a resource against a totalitarianism which drew strength from the dominance of the concept of totality within Western philosophical thought, a thought that identifies being with war (*TI* 21). It is because the ethics of the face-to-face in isolation from the ethics of fecundity is incomplete that one can say that Levinas already foresaw the deficiencies of the reading to which *Totality and Infinity* has predominantly been submitted.

Levinas seems to have taken it for granted that philosophy is the quest for transcendence. This is what he understood by the word "metaphysics" and why he kept returning to Plato's phrase "the good beyond being" and Descartes's idea of the infinite. It is in the context of this assumption about philosophy that he engaged in an ongoing polemic against those who maintain a mystical, otherworldly, ecstatic conception of transcendence in which one loses oneself in the beyond. In *On Escape* in 1935 Levinas introduced the neologism *excendence* to distinguish his attempt to find a way out by a new path from the conventional other-worldly conception of transcendence.[10] He renewed this attempt in 1947 when he described excendence as a departure from being that retains a foothold in being (*EE* xxvii). And in the same year, in *Time and the Other*, Levinas persisted with the attempt to identify where and how excendence is accomplished, albeit he abandoned that term and reverted to talk of transcendence. After considering a number of candidates, his focus came to rest on fecundity. It answers the question: "How in the alterity of a you, can I remain I, without being absorbed or losing myself in that you?" (*TO* 91). That is to say, in paternity the ego becomes other to itself.

In *Totality and Infinity*, Levinas continued the task of examining various modes of transcendence in an effort to find which of them approximated most closely to what he had previously called "excendence." The continuity between how he thought of the issue in the 1940s and how he thought of it in 1961 is already suggested by the fact that under the title

"Transcendence and Fecundity" he included in *Totality and Infinity,* with only minor changes, an essay first published in 1948 under the title "Pluralism and Transcendence." Both versions include the same fundamental argument in which he rejects the conventional notion of transcendence: "The idea of transcendence is in a certain sense contradictory. The subject that transcends is swept away in its transcendence; it does not transcend itself."[11]

Levinas already approached transcendence as a formal structure in *Time and the Other,* but by the time of *Totality and Infinity* he had refined his method. He now stipulated that the meaning of transcendence as a formal structure lay in its concretization or deformalization. He writes, "The method practiced here does indeed consist in seeking the condition of empirical situations, but it leaves to the development called empirical, in which the conditioning possibility is accomplished—it leaves to the *concretization*—an ontological role that specifies the meaning of the fundamental possibility, a meaning invisible in that condition" (*TI* 173).[12] This establishes the significance of the question of where transcendence is produced. The standard answer locates it in the ethical relation to the face of the Other and this is not wrong. But it is not the whole truth because it does not take into account fecundity as a plane transcending the face-to-face.

Against Plato, Levinas claimed that goodness is produced in the relation with the face, such that "The exteriority of being is morality itself" (*TI* 302). In the penultimate section of the conclusions, he repeated the point: "The ethical, beyond vision and certitude, delineates the structure of exteriority as such" (304). But he also believed that fecundity, understood initially as the parents' relation to the child, is, like the face of the Other, also a concretization of transcendence (*TO* 89–91). For example, he wrote, "In fecundity the I transcends the world of light—not to dissolve into the anonymity of the *there is,* but in order to go further than the light, to go *elsewhere*" (*TI* 268). These two concretizations of transcendence are not presented in *Totality and Infinity* as competing candidates. We should understand fecundity as the fulfillment of the ethical relation insofar as it establishes a relation that goes beyond it: "Transcendence, the for the Other, the goodness correlative of the face, founds a more profound relation: the goodness of goodness. Fecundity engendering fecundity accomplishes goodness: above and beyond the sacrifice that imposes a gift, the gift of the power of giving, the conception of the child" (269). Fecundity is the gift that keeps on giving.

Levinas rethought fecundity in such a way that it is already seen as ethical, as it was not in *Time and the Other*. But the relation of fecundity to eros in *Time and the Other* is not unlike that between fecundity and the ethical relation to the face of the Other in *Totality and Infinity*. Commentators have picked up on the fact that Levinas explicitly identified eros as a relation of transcendence, but have focused less on how the culmination of that relation arises in fecundity, where the relation to the future only anticipated in eros is accomplished in the relation to the son. Commentators can also be faulted for anticipating Levinas's decision to drop his focus on fecundity. It is surprising how many discussions of *Totality and Infinity* bypass this whole section, and Levinas himself did so in the *précis* of the book that he wrote to accompany its presentation to the University of Paris as his principle thesis. He did not even mention the word "fecundity" or indicate the contents of this fourth section, in spite of the fact that the word "fecundity" is mentioned almost as frequently in *Totality and Infinity* as the word "ethics."[13] However, once one attends to the formal structure of fecundity in reading *Totality and Infinity* it can be seen to approximate to what Levinas meant by excendence more closely than the face-to-face relation of the I to the absolute Other does. Paternity is "the way of being other while being oneself" (*TI* 282). Levinas's explanation of the claim is as follows: "My child is a stranger (Isaiah 49) who is not only mine (*à moi*), for *he is* me. He is me stranger to myself (*à soi*)" (267). This seems to have been formulated to meet the objection he leveled against false ideas of transcendence which did not conform to the model of transcendence.

ETHICS AS FIRST PHILOSOPHY

It is not because the ethical relation exhibits transcendence that Levinas first turned to it, but for another reason. Opinions differ as to when Levinas began to be concerned with ethics, but it was in 1951 in "Is Ontology Fundamental?" that Levinas first raised what would become one of the major questions addressed in *Totality and Infinity*. The main thrust of the essay was to challenge the idea that ontology is fundamental on the grounds that the relation to the other is not ontology and could not be accounted for by it. This led to the question of "how the encounter of the face could be described as a condition of consciousness" (*EN* 11; translation modified).

Ten years later in *Totality and Infinity* the role of the encounter as the condition of consciousness was described in the formulation: ethics is first philosophy. However, Levinas did not mean thereby that a subdiscipline within philosophy should be raised to the highest rank. His point was that one of the places where metaphysics, understood as our relation to the beyond being, happens is in my relation to the face of the Other (*TI* 78). It is not practical philosophy that is primary. Nor is it even the practical action that follows on from the demand made on me by the Other. It is moral conscience, consciousness in the face of the Other, as it takes precedence over self-consciousness and indeed drives self-consciousness and the quest for truth. Hence Levinas in the name of the face-to-face describes *Totality and Infinity* as opposing "a whole tradition of philosophy that says that being is produced as a panorama" (305).

All of this is clearly spelled out in the best known pages of the book, the subsection "Ethics and the Face," on which the proponents of Levinasian ethics rely: "Preexisting the disclosure of being in general taken as basis of knowledge and as meaning of being is the relation with the existent that expresses himself: preexisting the plane of ontology is the ethical plane" (*TI* 201). The full meaning of these lines is lost if one does not attend to the argument that prepares the way for it. We are told that the primordial expression "You shall not commit murder" is not reducible to the standard moral imperative that employs the same words. Killing, we are told, means here the absolute renunciation of comprehension (198–99). The words are said silently by the face of the Other, but to respond to this demand is, echoing a point already made in "Is Ontology Fundamental?", to enter into discourse (*EN* 7). The prohibition announced in the face introduces the "discourse rationalism prays for" and "thus founds the true universality of reason" (*TI* 201).

However, Levinas repeatedly employed an additional argument to arrive at the same conclusion. He claimed that "as critique precedes dogmatism, metaphysics precedes ontology," where critique is understood as the ability to put oneself in question, but where one can put oneself in question only because the other has already put one in question ethically (*TI* 43; 85).[14] The claim is stated more clearly in "Transcendence and Height" a year later. He wrote there, "And because moral consciousness is auto-critical, i.e. because it produces its own critique in its forward movement anterior to the movement of reflection, which, as second intention, would already be dogmatic, moral consciousness is primary and the source of first philosophy" (*BPW* 20). The face of the Other, by putting my freedom in question, makes good conscience impossible and in the process makes possible critique in its more usual philosophical sense: "Morality thus presides over the work of truth" (*TI* 304).

I have already quoted a sentence from the penultimate section of the conclusions where Levinas asserted the ethical meaning of transcendence: "The ethical, beyond vision and certitude, delineates the structure of exteriority as such." He immediately followed it with a sentence in which he reiterated the claim about the primacy of ethics by identifying metaphysics with morality: "Morality is not a branch of philosophy but first philosophy" (*TI* 304). Levinas here brought together his claims about the ethical relation as exteriority and as first philosophy, albeit the basis for doing so lay in the methodological assertion that the "beyond the totality" is reflected within the totality, such that we can "proceed from the experience of the totality back to a situation where the totality breaks up" (24).

Nevertheless, if these two theses about ethics were alone sufficient for Levinas, then one could not explain why there are four sections to *Totality and Infinity* and not just the first three. In "The Infinity of Time," the final part of the fourth section of *Totality and Infinity*, he began the task of integrating his understanding of ethics with his understanding of fecundity. He here opposed to Heidegger's account of the finitude of being as the essence of time a claim about the infinity of time. It took the form of an account of temporality which embraces both a rupture of continuity and continuation across the rupture, the upshot of which was that the definitive is not definitive. This account of time is not organized around regret for what might have been, but around forgiveness, which is understood to act upon the past and conserve it purified in "the strange happiness of reconciliations" among irreconcilable parties (*TI*, 281–83). The infinity of time makes it possible for the attitude that clings to the past to give way to one that repairs it (282).[15] This not only gave fecundity an ethical meaning it did not have in *Time and the Other*, but also has a political dimension, even if it was not spelled out at that point of the book. But for the circle in which Levinas moved, the question of forgiveness could not be raised without evoking the holocaust.[16] And the political dimension of forgiveness becomes clearer in the final paragraph of the book where fecundity is presented as a radical alternative to the virile virtues promoted by the state, thereby adding a further dimension to the opposition to virility set out in *Time and the Other* (*TI* 306; *TO* 70).[17]

The main part of the book thus ends with an attempt to use the notion of fecundity to connect ethics with a refusal of totalitarian politics. At the beginning of "The Infinity of Time," we are told that the structure of temporality results from the refusal of totalization, which is produced "as the welcoming of alterity—concretely as presentation of the face" (*TI* 281). At the end of the section, time is referred to fecundity in the sense of multiplicity and discontinuity. In between, he took up the account of the death and resurrection of the instant set out in detail in *Existence and Existents* and identified in *Totality and Infinity* as a formal structure (*EE* 94–96). There he writes, "But such a formal structure presupposes the relation of the I *(Moi)* with the Other and at its basis, fecundity across the discontinuous which constitutes time" (*TI* 284). Here, within the quasi-transcendental register Levinas sometimes employed, we learn that fecundity lies beneath or behind the relation to the Other. But, of course, this is only one part of the relation, for, as he had already explained, the plane of fecundity not only transcends the ethical relation with the Other but also presupposes it (253).

By associating fecundity with infinite time, Levinas gave it a more general meaning than simply paternity (with or without maternity, which is given a single reference and is not given prominence until *Otherwise than Being*) (*TI* 278). Indeed, in the penultimate paragraph of the conclusions he tried to release the account of fecundity from biology, although there are serious questions as to whether he succeeds in doing so.[18] But at the same time he was engaged in a polemic against totalitarian politics: "fecundity in general as a relation between man and man and between the I and itself (*relation du Moi avec soi*) not resembling the structures constitutive of the State." Fecundity happens in teaching, it happens in forgiveness, but its concretization is the family.[19] He writes, "The situation in which the I thus posits itself before truth in placing its subjective morality in the infinite time of its fecundity—a situation in which the instant of eroticism and the infinity of paternity are conjoined—is concretized in the marvel of the family." This shows how eroticism is separated from fecundity as the instant is separated from the infinity of time, but the overall point being made in the final pages of the book is that the concretization of fecundity in the family has a political meaning. This emerges in the penultimate paragraph: "The family does not only result from a rational relation of animality; it does not simply mark a step toward the anonymous universality of the State. It identifies itself outside of the State, even if the State reserves a framework for it" (306). That Levinas, by giving the family a place within and outside the State, is here opposing Hegel is clear. But the main point is that the family is to be understood as a bulwark against totalitarianism. This idea, which he left undeveloped, may not be particularly satisfying in terms of practical politics, but it has some merit as a diagnosis: Levinas's recognition that totalitarianism has no place for the private resembles Hannah Arendt's observation that totalitarianism destroys private life.[20]

Totality and Infinity was written against the philosophical roots of the totalitarianism of the State, as Levinas understood them, whether it be the State of Plato, Hegel, or Heidegger in the mid-1930s. That is why the book ends with a paragraph that questions "the heroic being that the State produces by its virile virtue" which is how Levinas read Heidegger's being-toward-death. But in the book's remarkable final sentence Levinas associated this virile soul produced by the State with an isolated soul seeking its own personal salvation (*TI* 307). The implication is that because the virtues on which totalitarianism thrives can be reconciled with the morality of personal fulfillment in eternal life, then that morality cannot be relied upon as a defense against totalitarianism.

LEVINAS'S PROBLEMS WITH THE RECEPTION OF "TOTALITY AND INFINITY"

It should now be clear why Levinas had a sufficiently severe problem with the reception of his work, and especially of *Totality and Infinity,* that he felt obliged to caution against the widespread image of him as a philosopher of ethics. So, for example, in an interview given in 1986 he announced that he preferred to talk of the holiness of the face or the holiness of obligation rather than of ethics.[21] This does not constitute a denial that he was concerned with ethics but it does amount to a warning against assuming that his work could be reduced to an ethical philosophy.

At the beginning of this essay I identified certain criticisms of Levinas and I believe that they can now be better understood as criticisms of what I have been calling "Levinasian ethics," rather than of Levinas's philosophy as such. These criticisms include charges that his philosophy is moralistic, neglects politics, and fails to supply appropriate limits to the notion of responsibility. I have already addressed the first two criticisms, and in his discussion of the infinity of time Levinas also addressed the third. In the course of explicating how true temporality is a release from regret, he explained, "It is not a question of complacency in some romanticism of the possibles, but of escaping the crushing responsibility of existence that veers into fate, of resuming the adventure of existence so as to be to the infinite" (*TI* 282). This does not diminish the responsibility, but clarifies its meaning, which is directed not to correcting the past but to opening up another future. The truly burdensome responsibility is the one that normally goes under the name of accountability and is construed on a legal model. Levinas opened the way to a form of responsibility where the emphasis is not on the past, but where there is still time to be for the Other in a future that is not mine. This is Levinas's answer ahead of time to those critics who subsequently characterized his philosophy of responsibility as excessively burdensome—from the perspective of infinite time, responsibility is not a burden, as existence is for Heidegger.[22]

However, the most serious question Levinas would have wanted to pose against a Levinasian ethics was raised by him in the preface to *Totality and Infinity* and answered only at its end. In other words, it serves to frame the book. In the very first sentence, Levinas issued a challenge: "Everyone will readily agree that it is of the highest importance to know whether or not we are duped by morality" (*TI* 21). Levinas addressed this concern at the end of the fourth section where he announced that "goodness would be subjectivity and folly" were it not for "the infinite time of triumph" (280). Furthermore, Levinas reminded us in the conclusions that the convergence of morality and reality is assured in "an infinite time which through fecundity is its time" (306). Infinite time does not mean time without end. It does not mean that eventually morality and reality will converge. Infinite time is the reflection of the infinite within time as it takes place in a forgiveness that remakes the world. A reading of *Totality and Infinity* that stops short of the account of the infinity of time and of fecundity leaves this possible objection unanswered.

Levinas also warned in the preface that "a proclamation of morality based on the pure subjectivism of the I is refuted by war, the totality it reveals, and objective necessities" (*TI* 25). This is an indication that there is a problem with attempts like that of Feron to reduce Levinas to a defender of subjectivity that stop short of a reading of the fourth section, because they miss the moment when in fecundity subjectivity departs from Being while retaining its foothold there: "The fecundity of subjectivity by which the I survives itself, is a condition required for the truth of subjectivity" (247). By the same token, one also cannot characterize him as writing a philosophy of desire, and not only because desire for the Other is not deaf to the Other's needs, which is why one does not approach the Other with empty hands, but with hands that maintain a grasp on what exists (172). Although Levinas had earlier presented the concretization of the idea of the infinite as desire, as when he wrote that the infinite within the finite is produced as desire, he moved beyond desire in the final section of the conclusions when he wrote that "The discontinuity of generations, death and fecundity, releases Desire from the prison of its own subjectivity and puts an end to the monotony of its identity" (304).

Levinasian ethics is not only deprived of some of the best resources Levinas himself provided to meet these objections, but is two-dimensional insofar as it is confined to the ontological and ethical planes, and neglects the third plane of eros and fecundity. My thesis that any account of the argument of *Totality and Infinity* is radically incomplete if it does not embrace the discussion of fecundity should hardly be surprising. If it would appear to be news to many Levinas commentators, it is perhaps because the temptation to ignore fecundity is too strong on account of the embarrassment at the sexist language Levinas employed there. It helps that the word "fecundity" virtually disappears from his lexicon in the immediate aftermath of the book's publication.

It is important to understand in closing that certain aspects of fecundity are retained albeit under a different title. In particular, the formal structure of fecundity as excendence that is reflected in the formulation "I am my child" is retained in the "je est autre" of substitution (*TI* 277).[23] Indeed, it is easier to understand substitution as at the basis of the face-to-face relation with the Other in which I am put in question, than it is in the case of fecundity even though Levinas made the same claim about both of them. Substitution directly addresses the question of what kind of being one must be in order that the Other can put me in question. But if the introduction of substitution clarified the place of ethics in Levinas's thought, it obscured the political dimension that fecundity had highlighted, thereby serving to justify the complaints sometimes leveled against Levinas on that score, until he introduced his account of the rights of the Other.[24]

It may at first sight seem paradoxical, but even though for Levinas ethics has a certain primacy in the sense of being first philosophy, it was never his starting-point. He returned always to the formal structure of transcendence and it was only as the result of a lengthy journey that he recognized ethics as its concretization. To put it another way, he was not concerned with ethics for its own sake, and this is why he explored objections to

Levinasian ethics in the way he did and also why what he wrote about ethics as the meaning of transcendence will not satisfy those looking for an ethical theory of a conventional kind. He was not attempting to meet those standards.

If there is a practical aim behind the book, it is to show that much of the Western philosophical tradition is implicated in totalitarianism by virtue of its failure to recognize transcendence as excendence, a critique which was strengthened by the reference of transcendence to the ethical relation to be found both in the face and in the family. The aim of the present essay has not been to support that claim but simply to highlight how the ethical relation appears within *Totality and Infinity* as part of an argument about transcendence. Failure to understand this explains why so many readers appear to have stopped short of the final section of the book, with the result that they have not fully understood that Levinas's ethics of the face was supported in *Totality and Infinity* by an ethics of fecundity that is directed to the future.

NOTES TO INTRODUCTION / DAVIDSON AND PERPICH

1. Salomon Malka, *Emmanuel Levinas: His Life and Legacy,* trans. Michael Kigel and Sonja M. Embree (Pittsburgh: Duquesne University Press, 2006), 267.

2. Levinas earned his *Doctorat d'Université* from the University of Strasbourg in 1930 for a single thesis on *The Theory of Intuition in Husserl's Philosophy.* The more prestigious *Doctorat ès Letters* required the submission of two theses and qualified the recipient for a teaching position in a French university. By the 1950s, the *Doctorat ès Lettres* was renamed the *Doctorat d'Etat,* with little change in the work required except that by then it had become more acceptable for a significant body of work comprised of several essays or articles to replace one of the theses.

3. As an *émigré* from Lithuania, Levinas did not come up through the unique set of academic institutions that typically produced France's philosophical elite. He did not take the entrance examination that would have qualified him to study at the École Normale Supérieure or the Sorbonne, nor, after his getting his *Diplômes d'études supérieures* (the equivalent of an American bachelor's degree) at Strasbourg, did he sit for the *Agrégation* exam that would have qualified him to teach in a French *lycée* or high school. In the introduction to *The Cambridge Companion to Levinas* (Cambridge: Cambridge University Press, 2002), Simon Critchley notes, "In private conversation, Levinas admitted that his ignorance of Greek prevented him from sitting the *Agrégation*" (xvii–xviii). This is somewhat puzzling since Greek became optional for the *Agrégation* in 1911 and Levinas could have substituted German. Nonetheless, it is worth noting that Alexandre Koyré and Alexander Kojève, both Jewish *émigrés* like Levinas, did not sit the exam either. For an excellent account of the *Agrégation* exam and its role in shaping French philosophy, see Alan D. Schrift, "The Effects of the Agrégation de Philosophie on Twentieth Century French Philosophy," *Journal of the History of Philosophy* 46, no. 3 (July 2008): 449–72. There is no better account of the impact of France's academic institutions, many of which have no exact counterpart in either the American, British, or German systems of education, than Schrift's *Twentieth-Century French Philosophy: Key Themes and Thinkers* (Oxford: Blackwell Publishing Ltd., 2006).

4. Merleau-Ponty was 53 at the time of his death, thus two years Levinas's junior. Paul Ricoeur, who attended the defense, was seven years younger than

Levinas and Blin more than ten years younger. Blin was responsible for publishing Levinas's early work *Existence and Existents* in the years immediately after the war.

5. Malka, *Emmanuel Levinas,* 153.

6. Marie-Anne Lescourret, *Emmanuel Levinas* (Paris: Flammarion, 1994), 218.

7. Xavier Tilliette, in attendance at the lectures that would become *Time and the Other* (1947), said of Levinas at that time, "No one would have thought that he would write such important books and that he would become one of the glories of French philosophy." Levinas's speaking style was apparently rather dry, his voice "small," and his presentation style "brittle." The evident originality and brilliance of the analyses pursued in *Totality and Infinity* were thus all the more striking for those who knew Levinas only as a quiet figure on the margins of the Parisian intellectual scene. See Malka, *Emmanuel Levinas,* 152–53.

8. Levinas remained the director of the École Normale Israélite Orientale (ENIO) throughout his university career, though he delegated more and more of the administrative tasks to others.

9. See Adriaan Peperzak's review of Salomon Malka, *Emmanuel Levinas: His Life and Legacy, Contintal Philosophy Review* 40, no. 3 (2007): 349–52. Peperzak helpfully corrects a number of errors in Malka's account. See Roger Burggraeve's *Emmanuel Levinas: Une bibliographie primaire et secondaire (1925–1985)* (Leuven: Peeters Verlag, 1986). Burggraeve's bibliography lists some 39 theses (10 for the doctorate, the remainder for the *licence* degree) devoted to Levinas's thought between 1963 and 1976. Almost all of these were generated by students at either the Katholieke Universiteit or at the Université catholique de Louvain (Louvain-la-neuve).

10. When *Totality and Infinity* was published, phenomenologically-oriented French philosophy was dominated by the influence of Sartre and Merleau-Ponty. Levinas's religious commitments and his relative distance from Marxist political thought (a result, perhaps, of having lived through the Russian revolution and its aftermath) meant that he was of relatively little interest to Sartre and his circle. Explaining Levinas's outsider status, in *French Philosophy in the Twentieth Century* (Cambridge: Cambridge University Press, 2001), Gary Gutting notes that despite having first encountered Husserl and the phenomenological tradition through Levinas's work, Sartre nonetheless "did not welcome religious believers with no interest in Marxist politics" (354). Gutting also astutely points out that while later "poststructuralists of difference were quite sympathetic to Levinas's critique of the same and his emphasis on radical alterity," they were less sympathetic to "the central place he gives to subjectivity and, especially, to a religiously oriented ethics" (363). Levinas thus continued to remain at the margins of French philosophy even during the sixties and seventies when he was officially a member of the French university system.

11. Richard Cohen, ed., *Face to Face with Levinas* (Albany: State University of New York Press, 1985).

12. Robert Bernasconi and Simon Critchley, eds., *Re-Reading Levinas* (Bloomington: Indiana University Press, 1991), xii.

Notes to Chapter 1 / Benso

1. On Levinas's relation to Plato, see Stella Sanford, *The Metaphysics of Love* (London: The Athlone Press, 2000); Sarah Allen, *The Philosophical Sense of Transcendence: Levinas and Plato on Loving Beyond Being* (Pittsburgh: Duquesne University Press, 2009); and Tanja Staehler, *Plato and Levinas: The Ambiguous Out-Side of Ethics* (London: Routledge, 2010). On Levinas's confrontation with the Greek philosophical tradition, see the essays contained in *Levinas and the Ancients,* ed. Silvia Benso and Brian Schroeder (Bloomington: Indiana University Press, 2008). See also Jean-Marc Narbonne, *Levinas and the Greek Heritage* (Leuven: Peters, 2006). In the collection *Levinas and the Ancients,* more sympathetic readings of Plato than the one presented here are offered in the essays by Deborah Achtenberg and Francisco Gonzalez.

2. Emmanuel Levinas and Richard Kearney, "Dialogue with Emmanuel Levinas," in *Face to Face with Levinas,* ed. Richard Cohen (Albany: State University of New York Press, 1986), 22.

3. Plato, *Theaetetus* 155d.

4. Aristotle, *Metaphysics* 982b.

5. Immanuel Kant, "Critique of Practical Reason," in *Practical Philosophy,* trans. Mary J. Gregor (Cambridge: Cambridge University Press, 1996).

6. Martin Heidegger, *An Introduction to Metaphysics,* trans. Ralph Manheim (New Haven: Yale University Press, 1987), 1.

7. Friedrich Nietzsche, *Human, All Too Human,* trans. R. J. Hollingdale (Cambridge: Cambridge University Press, 1996), vol. 1, part 1, section 2.

8. A masterful analysis of boredom is presented also by Martin Heidegger in *The Fundamental Concepts of Metaphysics,* trans. W. McNeill and N. Walker (Bloomington: Indiana University Press, 1995). Despite Heidegger's treatment of profound boredom (*tiefe Langeweile*) as one of Dasein's fundamental modes of attunement, intellectual boredom does not seem properly to belong to Dasein. On the contrary, for Heidegger, wonder is part and parcel of the event of being. In *What is Philosophy?* (trans. Jean T. Wilde and William Kluback [New Haven: College and University Press, 1959]), Dasein's wonder comes from the very fact of its being the being in which being itself is at stake. "Being in being [*Seiendes im Sein*]: that became the most astonishing thing [*das Erstaunlichste*] for the Greeks" (49), Heidegger remarks—it became most astonishing for the Greeks, for whom "astonishment is the tuning with which the Greek philosophers were granted the correspondence to the being of beings" (85), but also for authentic Dasein, for which the question of being still retains all its ontological primacy and importance. That is, wonder is an ontological dimension of Dasein. Philosophical questioning, that is, the way in which wonder configures itself for Heidegger, is dictated by being itself. Dasein is subjected to being, it obeys being in its very being. In this sense, Dasein can do nothing except wonder. Boredom does not belong to the questioning Dasein (that is, to the Dasein that corresponds to the call of being), but to the Dasein who does not question, that is, who is not authentic and therefore, in a sense, is not—not appropriated by being, that is. Wonder is for being, and as such, it is essential to the very being Dasein is.

Wonder is of Dasein's *esse*. It would remain to be seen, however, whether, on a Levinasian reading, Heidegger's wonder is truly wondrous or rather it is a case of boring wonder, like Plato's.

9. Søren Kierkegaard, *Either/Or*, vol. 1, trans. David F. Swenson and Lillian Marvin Swenson (Princeton: Princeton University Press, 1959), 36.

10. Kierkegaard, *Either/Or*, 287.

11. Too proud or full of themselves to admit their ignorance, both the dialogical figure of Alcibiades in the *Symposium* and the historical character of Dionysius in the *Seventh Letter* are incapable of wonder, and therefore, of philosophizing.

12. Plato, *Republic*, 518d–e. A few centuries later, Augustine will reformulate most clearly the Socratic pedagogical principle in the formula "*rede in te: in interiore homine habitat veritas.*"

13. This is true in the case of Euthyphro, Crito in the *Phaedo*, and Alcibiades in the *Symposium*.

14. Plato, *Symposium*, 215b, 217a, and 221e–d.

15. See Plato, *Phaedrus*, 245c–246e. Although some have more difficulties than others to actualize their longing, all souls yearn for "the plain of truth," for the meadow where "the fitting pasturage for the best part of the soul is" (*Phaedrus*, 248b–c).

16. In the *Phaedo* (79d), Plato reasserts the kinship existing between the soul and what is pure, ever existing, immortal, and unchanging.

17. Heidegger, *Fundamental Concepts of Metaphysics*, 5.

18. Plato, *Symposium*, 203d–204b.

19. Immortality is the teleological goal toward which the Platonic philosopher is directed. See Plato, *Symposium*, 207a–208b.

20. See for example Plato, *Phaedo*, 72e–73a.

21. Kierkegaard, *Either/Or*, 281.

22. The egoistic contentment of fulfillment is described in the section of *Totality and Infinity* devoted to "Interiority and Economy."

23. Plato, *Symposium*, 223d.

24. Levinas, "Preface to the German Edition," in *TI* iv.

25. Martin Heidegger, "Letter on Humanism," trans. Frank A. Capuzzi, in *Basic Writings* (New York: Harper & Row, 1977), 217.

NOTES TO CHAPTER 2 / BAUTISTA AND PEPERZAK

1. Levinas's efforts are clearly made in response to Hegel's and Heidegger's version of the Western tradition, and draw explicitly on themes from Plato, Descartes, Husserl, and Rosenzweig.

2. The work is, of course, more than a defense of subjectivity, as we have noted already; but it is this particular goal and aspect of *Totality and Infinity* that gives us our focus.

3. If we say "both at once," however, we must immediately qualify this remark: given the thrust of his analyses and his emphasis on the importance

of separation, Levinas could never countenance a simultaneity that ended by *confusing* or *merging* God and the other. If I am related to both at once, then both God and the other person must signify and found my subjectivity, *but differently.*

4. This is why Levinas says "the idea of the infinite": the idea of the infinite is only produced as *a relationship with the infinite,* where alone the infinite reveals itself and the term "infinite" gains a meaning. See *TI* 26–27. Ultimately, then, if I am founded in the idea of the infinite, I am founded in relation to the infinite whose idea it is. The mathematical infinite is never encompassed in Levinas's use of the term "infinite."

5. That Levinas construes ipseity as a synonym for "separation," rather than as simply linked closely to it, is itself problematic, since then there is not only an overlap between them but an identity that forces ipseity to remain at all times separate from others. At this point, however, we are concerned to follow Levinas's analysis, not yet to challenge it.

6. Only in a few places have we found it appropriate to depart in any significant way from Alphons Lingis's translation of the French. Where the translation departs from the standard English translation, the citation is noted as modified or it will refer to the English page numbers for comparison (e.g., cf. *TI*).

7. "To be me, is to have identity as content, beyond every individuation that one can owe to a system of references" (cf. *TI* 36). The upshot of this way of conceiving the subject as separate means that even though the subject is not a moment of totality, it does not oppose it, either in the usual sense of the word, or in the Hegelian sense of opposition.

8. "Possession through enjoyment is confused [*confond*] with enjoyment. No activity precedes sensibility. But to possess by enjoying is also to be possessed and to be delivered to the fathomless depth, the disquieting future of the element" (*TI* 158; translation modified).

9. What is the context that explains the use of "assume" and "unassumed"? Levinas couples "assume" with the antonym "refuse," which suggests that he has in mind some form of choosing of the relationship between myself and other beings. If "choice" presupposes or means that I begin in a position of original freedom, out of which I assume relationships to beings by choosing these beings and relationships, then, as has already been suggested above, I have no choice with respect to my original relationship with beings. Likewise, if "choice" presupposes that there is an alternative to this relationship with beings, then I have no choice — I am *always* related to them, even if I kill myself at some later point in my life. That Levinas refuses to take either of these positions does not mean, however, that the Levinasian subject cannot affirm and will the relationship it is always already living, but this "choosing" should not be confused with the previous two definitions of choice. All of this is of a piece with Levinas's argument against the idea that the subject is essentially a *freedom* first of all, and that its dignity lies strictly in its freedom — ideas that suggest his target is existentialism. See Levinas's criticism of existentialist philosophies at *TI* 145–46, which argues against the idea that to live, as an unchosen or unassumed relationship (initially at

least), is fundamentally to be alienated and abandoned. They fail to see, Levinas, argues, that the negative and oppositional mode of relation is derivative of an initial agreement, and in fact targets the indeterminateness of the future and the pain that is in fact intrinsic to labor. Rejection and opposition target aspects of a being's relationship with me, but fail to touch the initial being-in-relation, which is itself a *yes* or an *affirmation* of this fundamental condition of existence.

10. See *TI* 59, 62, 88, 94, 112, 114, 118, 134, 135, 147, 148.

11. See *TI* 60, 115, 118, 119, 208, 217, 268, 277, 278, 280.

12. A similar, but not identical, difficulty attends relating this absolutely independent ipseity to the infinite who is God. In this case, we suffer the additional difficulty of having somehow to say both how God's infinity is not the infinity of the human other, and yet how God's infinity is at the same time inseparably present with the infinity of the Other, *without confusing the two.*

13. *TI* 33–35, 42–43, 49–50. The qualification of *TI* as a metaphysical study can be illustrated by Levinas's frequent use of the word "*métaphysique*," e.g., on the following pages: *TI* 29 (five times), 33–34 (five times), 35 (six times), 38, 41, 42, 43, 47, 50, 53, 55, 62, 64, 65, 77–78, 80, 82, 87, 88, 102, 109, 114, 148, 149, 172, 220, 261, 291, 292, 297, 299, 300, 303, 304. After *TI*, however, his use of "metaphysics" and "metaphysical" almost completely disappears.

14. "[Alterity] is understood as alterity of the Other [*Autrui*] and of the Most-High [*le Très-Haut*]" (*TI* 34).

15. "Il va raconter comment l'infini se produit dans la relation du Même avec l'Autre....Le terme de production indique et l'effectuation de l'être (l'événement 'se produit', une automobile 'se produit') et sa mise en lumière ou son exposition (un argument 'se produit', un acteur 'se produit'). L'ambiguïté de ce verbe traduit l'ambiguïté essentielle de l'opération par laquelle, à la fois, s'évertue l'être d'une entité et par laquelle il se révèle" Levinas, *Totalité et infini: Essai sur l'extériorité* [La Haye: Martinus Nijhoff, 1961], xiv; cf. *TI* 26). The exact translation of "*se produire*" ("showing up" or "performing"— *not* "making") is extremely difficult to render in English. Lingis's translation says only "production" and he suggests two meanings of "produce" found in the *Shorter Oxford Dictionary,* one of which means to present something ("produce your cause, saith the Lord"), the other of which ("Art may make a Suit of Clothes, But Nature must produce a Man"), if "produce" contrasts with "make," effectively gives no meaning beyond that of the first example. If, on the other hand, it is taken as a synonym for "make," then we have production as making. Recourse to *Le Petit Robert* dictionary does not show that contemporary French includes in the meanings of "*se produire*" anything like "making," however.

16. *TI* 25, 26–28, 48–52. For a more detailed analysis of Levinas's handling of the idea of the Infinite, see also Adriaan Peperzak, *To The Other: An Introduction to the Philosophy of Emmanuel Levinas* (West Lafayette: Purdue University Press, 1993), 55–72.

17. "[Metaphysics] is turned toward the 'elsewhere,' and the 'otherwise,' and the 'other.' For in the most general form it has assumed in the history of thought it appears as a movement going forth from a world familiar to us...toward a

foreign [*étranger*] outside-of-oneself, toward an over there [*là-bas*]" (*TI* 33; translation modified). Metaphysics and desire are closely related: one might say that "metaphysical desire" is either a pleonasm for Levinas, or else it marks an equivocal use of desire, if one wishes to use desire of both enjoyable, impersonal beings and the infinite, personal other. Elsewhere, desire is used equivocally, with metaphysical marking a sharp difference between desire for worldly beings and desire for the personal other: "Desire without satisfaction which, precisely, *intends* the distancing [*entend l'éloignement*], the alterity and the exteriority of the Other [*l'Autre*]" (34; translation modified).

18. Although it must seem evident that the analysis of the facing relationship is to be seen as concretizing the opening, and rather formal, analyses of desire in *Totality and Infinity;* in fact, Levinas himself rarely invokes desire after the opening sections of the book. The experience of desire as such is not dwelt on in terms that recall the fact that we are dealing with an affect. Instead the analysis emphasizes the exceptionality of the other and the other's commanding height in a way that is hard to reconcile with the experience of desire in the absence of efforts explicitly to connect affection by desire, the imperative of the other, and a certain humiliation of the self.

19. While acknowledging the standard translation of this difficult phrase (Lingis translates it as "my ability for power"), we would like tentatively to suggest "power of powers" as a translation, along the lines of "song of songs" and "king of kings," which are Hebraic modes of expressing a superlative. As my power of powers, my life is identified as the ultimate capacity of any individual power I may assert.

To avoid misunderstanding, generosity here is clearly not to be understood as a supererogatory virtue. It is rather that I cannot respect the Other's dignity and ethical height, if I do not care for his or her needs. Levinas cites Rabbi Yochanan, who writes: "To leave men without food is a fault that no circumstance attenuates; the distinction between the voluntary and the involuntary does not apply" (*TI* 201). Food symbolizes here all other needs, such as shelter, medicine, water, clothes etc., but must also encompass the social institutions of justice, since Levinas acknowledges Hegel's great insight that human freedom and right do not exist without these. Thus, need can encompass, if perhaps not in the first instance, elaborate social institutions.

20. *TI* 199–200, 213, 215. Nothing is said about whether or not the fact that I am moved by desire for the infinite other is itself desirable in a way that is comparable to the desirability of the other.

21. Even if we read Levinas's insistence upon calling ipseity ego*ism* throughout the abstract analysis of interiority as the deliberate reminder of the concrete situation of the subject founded in the idea of the infinite, still, we have no careful delineation between ego*ism* and a justified egocentricity that would render ipseity as having a clear moment of desirousness that would solicit respect or counter Levinas's fear of a dyadic union outside of all justice.

22. Levinas does not supply an argument for knowing myself to be an other like the others until *Otherwise than Being.*

23. See Levinas's analysis of "the I, as other" (le je, comme autre) (*TI* 36–37). Here, he is concerned to show that indeed, "je, comme autre" does not signify the sort of alterity that is ethically absolute.

24. Moreover, the child's more universal perspective does not eliminate our sexed existence: to be the child of parents encompasses relations to male and female parents, as well as relations arising from male and female perspectives.

25. All economic forms of empowerment, cultivation, housing, familiarizing, etc., can be included here.

26. Levinas claims that the other's language is "a silent language, an understanding without words, an expression in the secret" (*TI* 155). This language holds in reserve the *Vous* of ethical height, speaking familiarly, intimately, arranging hospitable welcome.

27. Here, we mean "egoist" in the sense of *egoism proper*. We do this not to say that only egoist enjoyment is possible, but to acknowledge that this is the major concern we should have over the character of parental love, but also that we have, as yet, no clear sense of what it would mean to say that the parents' love is egocentric without being egoist. We have, in other words, no account from Levinas of what a justified enjoyment of one's child might be like.

28. Such a claim is contentious, and we unfortunately have no time to construct an argument for it. We must rely here on the experience of children's dependency and the trials of their education as a *prima facie* warrant for this claim.

29. Some interpreters, perhaps following in the wake of Derrida, have interpreted the Other's demands as violence leveled against me. Here we can only point to the fact that Levinas's self-understanding in *Totality and Infinity* does not agree with his critics': for him, the ethical relationship is *peace* and so nonviolence (*TI* 22–25, 202–04). That the relationship of persons does not present the other to me as an originary violation or violence against me is an abiding theme of Levinas's work, and cannot be adduced as an example of my-being-violated.

30. See the subsections "Ethics and the Face" (*TI* 197–201); "Commerce, the Historical Relation and the Face" (226–32); and "The Truth of the Will" (240–47).

31. "Violence" occurs more frequently, but is generally used to discuss how the face elicits a response that always contains the possibility of violence. See, for example, "Ethics and the Face" (*TI* 197–201).

32. "L'intégration dans un monde économique, n'engage pas l'intériorité dont les oeuvres procèdent" (*Totalité et infini,* 151; cf. *TI* 176). Lingis's translation differs from ours: he reads "engage" in the sense of "commit," and emphasizes the interiority's reservation toward the economic order; we read "engage" in the sense of "take on," and emphasize the way in which the economic order and the state ignore or do not respond to the interiority whose products they integrate into a quasi-system.

33. Levinas's use of the term "violate" in relation to maieutic education is likewise an application with little in the way of description. There, the term clearly refers to the question of whether an education that relies on dependency

and an unchosen relationship, in which what is taught is not an idea originally present in both student and teacher, violates the mind [*esprit*] or descends into irrationality by imposing limits on the freedom of the student—both of which charges Levinas denies. See *TI* 171, 203–04.

34. The last lines of this passage are the only place where it appears that the subject of torture is me. One might, however, split this hair: Levinas speaks here of being before death, which is always my death. Earlier, he had spoken of the phenomenology of being toward my death, specifically (*TI* 232–36); it could be that he uses these passages on torture to contextualize my death *generally* (and not specifically death by torture, which had been at issue).

35. "The privileged situation where the ever future evil becomes present...is reached in the suffering called physical" (*TI* 238).

36. See, for example, some of the stories of survivors collected in Jennifer K. Harbury's *Truth, Torture, and the American Way: The History and Consequences of U.S. Involvement in Torture* (Boston: Beacon Press, 2005). This work is intended to demonstrate both the evidence for U.S. involvement in torture regimes, particularly in the Latin American context, and the level of that involvement, working through the evidence given by survivors of torture regimes who had direct contact with American personnel, as well as the testimony of former members of death squads who eventually left and tried to tell their stories. In assembling the evidence, Harbury recounts the stories of these survivors, and also of those who did not survive but who were of special interest to survivors or to relatives of the disappeared. See especially the stories of Sister Dianna Ortiz (65–69) and of María Guardado (73–74).

37. As in Aristotle's *De anima*, we come to know our own soul by observing our activities and their outcomes, products, and results. I see in the responses of others to my existence and acts *how* I am experienced by them.

Notes to Chapter 3 / Horowitz

1. Perhaps this has been due, on the one hand, to the way in which Levinas has been assimilated to discussions within liberalism concerning the relation between ethics and politics, and on the other hand, to the at best ambivalent attitude of Marxists toward any abstract ethics or metaethics. Early on, Edith Wyschogrod referred to Levinas's sympathies with Marx in her *Emmanuel Levinas: The Problem of Ethical Metaphysics* (New York: Fordham University Press, 2000), 6, 26n7. Robert Gibbs, *Correlations in Rosenzweig and Levinas* (Princeton: Princeton University Press, 1992), 229–54, went considerably further in suggesting that the sense of Levinasian ethics could be brought into the concrete world of the political inasmuch as both Levinas and Marx are thinkers of the social. Enrique Dussel's *Philosophy of Liberation,* trans. Aquilina Martinez and Christine Morkovsky (Maryknoll: Orbis Books, 1985), also depends on a certain mapping of some Marxian and Levinasian categories onto each other. But these indications of a potentially fruitful interrelation have been largely ignored in favour of other seemingly more direct political preoccupations having to do

with law, the state and revolution, identity and violence, aporia and messianicity, and so on.

2. The term "social ontology" was, to the best of my knowledge, introduced by George Lukacs and used to excellent effect by Carol Gould in her *Marx's Social Ontology: Individuality and Community in Marx's Theory of Social Reality* (Cambridge, Mass.: MIT Press, 1978), xi, xv. My own usage overlaps with hers, but is more restricted in the context of this essay, not extending here to the being of historical social structures.

3. Although there are earlier statements of this in the book on Husserl, the clearest and most forceful indication is at *TIH* 155–57.

4. There is a brief suggestion in "Meaning and Sense", written shortly after *Totality and Infinity,* that Levinas might have been open to bridging the gap between goodness and works. See *BPW* 48–51.

5. Karl Marx, *Theses on Feuerbach,* in *Karl Marx: Selected Writings,* ed. Lawrence H. Simon (Indianapolis: Hackett, 1994), 100.

6. Karl Marx, *Economic and Philosophical Manuscripts* in *Karl Marx: Early Writings,* ed. Quentin Hoare, trans. Rodney Livingstone and Gregor Benton (New York: Vintage Books, 1975), 374; hereafter cited as *EPM.*

7. Karl Marx, "Excerpt Notes of 1844," in *Karl Marx: Selected Writings,* 43–44; hereafter cited as ExN.

8. For excellent analyses of the sense of having compared to unalienated human sense, see Kevin M. Brien, *Marx, Reason and the Art of Freedom* (Amherst: Humanity Books, 2006), 165–78, and John Maguire, *Marx's Paris Writings: An Analysis* (Dublin: Gil and Macmillan, 1972), 75–78.

9. Stephen Mulhall, "Species-Being, Teleology and Individuality, Part I: Marx on Species-Being," *Angelaki* 3, no. 1 (1998): 9–27, esp. 21. Mulhall gives an excellent account of particularly this aspect of species-being, while at the same time almost entirely abstracting it from what I have called the human-to-human aspect. A similarly one-sided approach to the concept is to be found in other recent treatments, good examples of which would be Sean Sayers, "Creative Activity and Alienation in Hegel and Marx," *Historical Materialism* 11, no. 1 (2003): 107–28, and Nick Dyer-Witherford, "Species-Being Resurgent," *Constellations* 11, no. 4 (2004): 476–91. In such cases the ethical dimension of Marx's conception of species-being is truncated to its emphasis on the development of the powers and capacities of individuals, considered severally and in functional relation with each other. A much less mono-egological understanding of species-being, closer to the one developed here, may be found in an earlier piece: Paul Santilli, "Marx on Species-Being and Social Essence," *Studies in Soviet Thought* 13, no. 1–2 (June 1973): 76–88.

10. Herbert Marcuse, "The Foundations of Historical Materialism [1932]," in Herbert Marcuse, *Studies in Critical Philosophy,* trans. Joris de Pres (Boston: Beacon Press, 1972), 18.

11. Marcuse, "Foundations of Historical Materialism," 37–38.

12. Mulhall points out that Marx borrows not only the term, but also elements of the concept of species-being from Feuerbach, for whom it meant a

particular form of consciousness aware of itself not only as an individual, but also as a member of a species (Mulhall, "Species-Being," 14). At first glance this might appear to imply a co-arising of the human-to-human with the human-to-itself; closer inspection recognizes it as a subordination of the human-to-human to the effects of the human-to-itself. The priority of the former over the latter, correlated with the priority of the sensible over the intellective, will remain one of the most important theses of *Totality and Infinity*.

13. Karl Marx, *Grundrisse: Introduction to the Critique of Political Economy*, trans. Martin Nicolaus (New York: Vintage Books, 1973), 488.

14. Terry Eagleton, "Self-Realization, Ethics and Socialism," *New Left Review* 237 (1999): 158.

15. This is not the place for a fuller discussion, but it should be pointed out that totalization is not in and of itself totalitarian, that it lends itself, quite literally, to conservatism, liberalism, socialism and more often than not, anarchism.

16. Marcuse, "Foundations of Historical Materialism," 4, 19–20.

17. Ibid., 13.

18. Is it distressing that most—nearly all—of the time Marxists are unable to see or move beyond *bourgeois* morality? That when pressed on the question of Marx and ethics they revert to forms of eudaemonism (in which Hegel might be included), utilitarianism or Kantian ethics? Thus, for example, Gould (*Marx's Social Ontology*, 162–76) advances a mixed form of Kantian-utilitarian ethics; Eagleton ("Self-Realization," 155, 160) invokes both a modernist Aristotelianism in seeing a Marxian ethic as pointing to "an abundance of life" and an inversion of the harm principle of Millian liberalism. Even the early Horkheimer in "Materialism and Morality" will see a future ethic in terms of a fusion of duty and interest. See *Critical Theory: The Essential Readings*, ed. David Ingram and Julia Simon Ingram (New York: Paragon House, 1991), 176–202.

19. Robert Gibbs made the intriguing suggestion, without really following it up, that *both* Marx and Levinas suffer from too much Hegel even in opposing him. Gibbs, *Correlations*, 251.

NOTES TO CHAPTER 4 / MORGAN

1. Cavell also takes Emerson and Thoreau to be predecessors in this regard.

2. The ordinary or everyday world is the domain in which moral or Emersonian perfectionism is worked out, the domain in which one seeks to be true to oneself, to care for oneself, and it is the locale for "marriage" and those human relationships in which the "confrontations and conversations" of life that are the mechanisms of such a working out of our selfhood occur.

3. Cavell's understanding of modernist thinking was forged in early discussions with Michael Fried. See Stanley Cavell, *The Senses of Walden* (New York: Viking Press, 1972); Stanley Cavell, *Must We Mean What We Say?* (Cambridge: Cambridge University Press, 1969); and Michael Fried, *Art and Objecthood* (Chicago: University of Chicago Press, 1998).

4. Stanley Cavell, *Contesting Tears: The Hollywood Melodrama of the Unknown Woman* (Chicago: University of Chicago Press, 1996), 38–45; hereafter cited as *CT*. The essay originally appeared in *Languages of the Unsayable*, ed. Sanford Budick and Wolfgang Iser (New York: Columbia University Press, 1989).

5. Cavell treats these as roughly the same. Being true to oneself is being authentically what one is as a self; caring for oneself, in the Socratic sense, is to be invested in living well, removing obstacles to such a life, and cultivating those character traits (Socrates, like many ancients, called them *aretai* or virtues) that enhance this project. Who we are, for Cavell, is a project worked out in relationship with others.

6. Cavell's collective quotation draws on Brooks, *The Melodramatic Imagination* (New Haven: Yale University Press, 1985), 4, 5, 11, 16, 22, and 202; hereafter cited as *MI*.

7. See *MI* 20–21: "what we have called the 'moral occult' [is] the domain of spiritual forces and imperatives that is not clearly visible within reality, but which they [viz., Balzac and James] believe to be operative there, and which demands to be uncovered, registered, articulated. In the absence of a true Sacred (and in the absence indeed of any specific religious belief of their own) they continue to believe that what is most important in a man's life is his ethical drama and the ethical implications of his psychic drama."

8. See Franz Rosenzweig, "The New Thinking" (1925), in *Philosophical and Theological Writings,* ed. and trans. Paul W. Franks and Michael L. Morgan (Indianapolis: Hackett, 2000).

9. See *TI* 251: "The Other qua Other is situated in a dimension of height and of abasement—glorious abasement; he has the face of the poor, the widow, and the orphan, and, at the same time, of the master called to invest and justify my freedom."

10. For the expression "primary sociality," see *TI* 304.

11. See, for instance, *TI* 64, 67, 73, 75.

12. See also Levinas, "A Religion for Adults," in *DF* 17.

13. Levinas uses the word "height" to indicate that the other person has a status above the subject, akin to that of a king or ruler; the face speaks "up" to the subject as the poor, widow or orphan, and speaks "down" to the subject as a ruler or monarch. The term "height" therefore means something like the authority or normative force of the face-to-face; it is introduced very early in *TI* 34–35.

14. Levinas describes the project of the book this way: "We propose to describe, within the unfolding of terrestrial existence, of economic existence (as we shall call it), a relationship with the other that does not result in a divine or human totality, that is not a totalization of history but the idea of infinity. Such a relationship is the metaphysical itself" (*TI* 52).

15. Toril Moi, *Henrik Ibsen and the Birth of Modernism: Art, Theater, Philosophy* (Oxford: Oxford University Press, 2006), 89.

16. Cavell discusses two "genres" of Hollywood film, what he calls the "comedies of remarriage" and the "melodramas of the unknown woman," as expressing

this attitude of moral perfectionism and the primacy of the ordinary. See *Pursuits of Happiness* and *Contesting Tears*. Also, one should look at the collection of Cavell's work on Shakespeare, *Disowning Knowledge*.

17. In *Totality and Infinity*, Levinas shows that he appreciates his understanding of transcendence or the infinite to stand between a rejection of transcendence altogether—a capitulation to totality—and a return to an old view, a traditional theism. Later, in works such as "Meaning and Sense," "Phenomenon and Enigma," and "God and Philosophy" this awareness becomes even more explicit. See Michael L. Morgan, *Discovering Levinas* (Cambridge: Cambridge University Press, 2007), chap. 7.

Notes to Chapter 5 / Bertram

The following considerations occur in the context of further considerations leading to an explication of the problem of normativity as an essential aspect of language, mind, and world. Commentaries by Anna Krewani, David Lauer, Andreas Niederberger, and audience members at a DFG colloquium on Deconstruction in Potsdam and at the seventh international French-German Philosophy Colloquium in Evian have helped this exposition reach the level of precision, which it attains, in the best of cases, in the following form.

1. The solutions offered by Levinas have gone through several changes over time. Not until his later texts does Levinas trace the "ethical or meta-ontological transcendence," from which the present considerations begin. Before that, one can characterize the solution with the concept of "erotic transcendence." See Wolfgang Nikolaus Krewani, *Emmanuel Levinas. Denker des Anderen* (Freiburg: Alber, 1992).

2. Axel Honneth, "Das Andere der Gerechtigkeit," in *Das Andere der Gerechtigkeit* (Frankfurt: Suhrkamp), 133–70.

3. See Simon Critchley, *The Ethics of Deconstruction: Derrida and Levinas* (Oxford: Blackwell, 1992).

4. In the context of Levinas's philosophy, it is common to talk about metaethics or the ethicity of ethics. See for example, Jacques Derrida, *Adieu. To Emmanuel Levinas,* trans. Pascale-Anne Brault and Michael Naas (Palo Alto: Stanford University Press, 1999), 50; and Derrida, "Violence and Metaphysics," in *Writing and Difference,* trans. Alan Bass (Chicago: University of Chicago Press, 1978), 111. Even Levinas helped to push the course of his philosophy's reception in this direction; see Levinas, *Ethics and Infinity: Conversations with Philippe Nemo,* trans. Richard Cohen (Pittsburgh: Duquesne University Press, 1985), 90.

5. It is helpful in interpreting Levinas to consider that in postanalytic philosophy a movement has come about that one can understand as the "normative turn," see Sebastian Knell, "Die normatistische Wende der analytischen Philosophie," *Allgemeine Zeitschrift für die Philosophie* 25 (2000): 225–45. Authors such as Wilfrid Sellars and Robert Brandom developed a normative theory of mind and sought to determine the core of normativity as well. These works (which incidentally connect with Kant's thought) offer a framework in

which Levinas's fundamental idea becomes comprehensible. See, on the question of normativity, Christine M. Korsgaard, *The Sources of Normativity* (Cambridge: Cambridge University Press, 1996).

6. Thus reads, among other places, the title of the closing section in the programmatic essay: "Philosophy and the Idea of Infinity," in *CPP* 47–59, esp. 57–59.

7. See, for example, Edmund Husserl, *Ideen zu einer reinen Phänomenologie und phänomenologischen Philosophie*, Husserliana, vol. 3 (Den Haag: Nijhof, 1950), § 97.

8. See ibid., § 24.

9. The abstract diagnosis that such a consciousness of the other is not to be grasped in concepts of intentionality is one that Levinas shares with Sartre, *Being and Nothingness*, trans. H. Barnes (New York: Washington Square Press, 1984), 341. Along with Sartre, Levinas is also in agreement about the basic thesis that the relation to the other is not a form of knowing, but rather is to be grasped as a special form of experience.

10. The thought that such a demand, in the context of our confrontation with others, has a special status can be pursued back to Fichte, who in this sense speaks of a "calling" (*Aufforderung*). See J. G. Fichte, *Grundlage des Naturrechts nach Principien der Wissenschaftslehre 1796*, in *Werke*, vol. 3, ed. I. H. Fichte (Berlin: de Gruyter, 1971), 33.

11. Levinas, "The Trace of the Other," in *Deconstruction in Context: Literature and Philosophy*, ed. Mark C. Taylor (Chicago: University of Chicago Press, 1986), 353.

12. Levinas, "Philosophy and the Idea of Infinity," 59.

13. Levinas, "The Trace of the Other," 352.

14. In the following I will continue to speak with Levinas of moral consciousness, even if I will reject many of the implications of this concept. The concept is thus solely to be understood as the title for the specific relationship that Levinas thematizes.

15. See the corresponding passage in Levinas, "The Trace of the Other," 347–50.

16. Levinas developed a concept for the nonobjectivity of this form of consciousness. He speaks of the "nakedness of the face." In its nakedness the face is nonobjective, that is, not reachable as an object that initiates the consciousness of the demand. See "The Trace of the Other," 352.

17. I am of the view that the two dimensions just considered do not suffice for reconstructing consciousness, that is, the determinate content of convictions. I trace the other dimensions that come into play and how they interact in Georg W. Bertram, *Die Sprache und das Ganze. Entwurf einer antireduktionistischen Sprachphilosophie* (Weilerwist: Velbrück Verlag, 2006).

18. Derrida takes up these considerations of Levinas in the context of questions of laws and their applicability and thus indirectly paves the way for an interpretation of the philosophy of Levinas as a contribution to explaining normativity. See Jacques Derrida, "The Force of Law," *Cardozo Law Review* 11 (1990): 920–1045.

19. One can consider this Levinasian result as confirmation of the analyses of Kripke. He namely concludes from the lack of a factical ground of determination in the case of rules—quite in opposition to Levinas—that there are not normative relations in any authentic sense. See Saul Kripke, *Wittgenstein on rules and Private Language* (Cambridge: Cambridge University Press, 1982).

20. Compare this to a reconstruction that is oriented in this direction: Axel Honneth, "Das Andere der Gerechtigkeit," in *Das Andere der Gechtigkeit* (Frankfurt am Main: Suhrkamp, 2000), 159. The following comment by Honneth clarifies the perspective on the other as an exceptional object: "The core of [the philosophical work of Levinas] must naturally consist in a phenomenological demonstration that in the encounter with other persons we have just such a moral experience that can be interpreted as the inner-worldly place-holder for infinity" (161).

21. See for example, Bernhard Waldenfels, *Antwortregister* (Frankfurt am Main: Suhrkamp, 1994), 333.

22. See Wilfrid Sellars, *Empiricism and the Philosophy of Mind* (Cambridge, Mass.: Harvard University Press, 1997); and Robert Brandom, *Making It Explicit: Reasoning, Representing, and Discursive Commitment* (Cambridge, Mass.: Harvard University Press, 1994).

23. In passing, I want to hold on to the notion that both Levinas and Brandom introduce the concept of freedom in the context of fundamental normative concepts. The common factor of both philosophies rests in the thought that freedom arises out of normative bonds, that such bonds cannot be understood as something that limits freedom. Cf. *TI* 84; Levinas, "Philosophy and the Idea of Infinity," 55–56; Robert Brandom, "Freedom and Constraint by Norms," *American Philosophical Quarterly* 16 (1979): 187–96.

NOTES TO CHAPTER 6 / PERPICH

1. Karen Jensen and Leif Lahn, "The Binding Role of Knowledge: An Analysis of Nursing Students' Knowledge Ties," *Journal of Education and Work* 18, no. 3 (September 2005): 305–20.

2. Kathleen Theresa Galvin and Les Todres, "Embodying Nursing Openheartedness: An Existential Perspective," *Journal of Holistic Nursing* 27, no. 2 (2009): 141–49.

3. This point is made by a number of theorists. See Mireille Lavoie, Thomas De Koninck, and Daninelle Blondeau, "The Nature of Care in the Light of Emmanuel Levinas," *Nursing Philosophy* 7 (2006): 225; Chris Gastmans, Bernadette Dierckx de Casterle, and Paul Schotsmans, "Nursing Considered as Moral Practice: A Philosophical-Ethical Interpretation of Nursing," *Kennedy Institute of Ethics Journal* 8, no. 1 (1998): 43; and Per Nortvedt, "Sensitive Judgement: An Inquiry into the Foundations of Nursing Ethics," *Nursing Ethics* 5, no. 5 (1998): 385–92.

4. Galvin and Todres, "Embodying Nursing Openheartedness," 141.

5. Per Nortvedt, "Levinas, Justice and Health Care," *Medicine, Health Care and Philosophy* 6 (2003): 27.

6. Nortvedt, "Levinas, Justice and Health Care," 27; emphasis mine.

7. Anne Clancy and Tommy Svennson, "Faced with Responsibility: Levinasian Ethics and the Challenges of Responsibility in Norwegian Public Health Nursing," *Nursing Philosophy* 8 (2007): 158, 165.

8. Byung-Hye Kong, "Levinas's Ethics of Caring: Implications and Limits in Nursing," *Asian Nursing Research* 2, no. 4 (December 2008): 209.

9. Lavoie et al., "The Nature of Care," 228.

10. Gastmans et al., "Nursing Considered as Moral Practice," 7.

11. As one essay notes: "A first obvious observation is the extent to which we owe our presence in the world to our body." Lavoie et al., "The Nature of Care," 226.

12. Gastmans et al., "Nursing Considered as Moral Practice," 10.

13. Stanley Cavell, "Knowing and Acknowledging," in *Must We Mean What We Say? A Book of Essays* (Cambridge: Cambridge University Press, 1976), 263.

14. Kong, "Levinas's Ethics of Caring," 210.

15. Galvin and Todres, "Embodying Nursing Openheartedness," 146.

16. Clancy and Svennson, "Faced with Responsibility," 160.

17. Ibid., 166.

18. Kong, "Levinas's Ethics of Caring," 210.

19. Lavoie et al., "The Nature of Care," 228.

20. Edwin E. Gantt and Richard N. Williams, "Pursuing Psychology as Science of the Ethical: Contributions of the Work of Emmanuel Levinas," in *Psychology for the Other: Levinas, Ethics, and the Practice of Psychology,* ed. Edwin E. Gantt and Richard N. Williams (Pittsburgh: Duquesne University Press, 2002), 10.

21. Gantt and Williams, "Pursuing Psychology," 11.

22. Richard N. Williams, "Self-Betraying Emotions and the Psychology of Heteronomy," *European Journal of Psychotherapy, Counseling and Health* 7, no. 1–2 (March–June 2005): 9.

23. Williams, "Self-Betraying Emotions," 9.

24. Edwin E. Gantt, "Levinas, Psychotherapy, and the Ethics of Suffering," *Journal of Humanistic Psychology,* 40, no. 3 (Summer 2000): 12.

25. Ibid., 23.

26. Ibid., 22.

27. Ibid., 20.

28. Williams, "Self-Betraying Emotions," 7.

29. Ibid., 12; Williams, "On Being for the Other: Freedom as Investiture," in Gantt and Williams, *Psychology for the Other,* 155.

30. Williams, "Self-Betraying Emotions," 7.

31. Ibid., 13, 14, 13.

32. Gantt and Williams, *Psychology for the Other,* 30.

33. George Kunz, "Simplicity, Humility, Patience," in Gantt and Williams, *Psychology for the Other,* 131.

34. For a fuller argument against these three points see Perpich, *The Ethics of Emmanuel Levinas* (Stanford: Stanford University Press, 2008), esp. chapters 2–4.

35. Kong, "Levinas's Ethics of Caring," 210.

36. See Perpich, "Normativity without Norms," *Ethics of Emmanuel Levinas,* 124–49.

37. See Perpich, *The Ethics of Emmanuel Levinas,* chapter 3.

38. See Rorty's exchange with Simon Critchley in chapters 2–4 of Chantal Mouffe, ed., *Deconstruction and Pragmatism* (London: Routledge, 1996).

39. Alasdair MacIntyre, "Danish Ethical Demands and French Common Goods: Two Moral Philosophies," *European Journal of Philosophy* 18, no. 1 (March 2010): 14, 5.

40. It is in this context that we need to read the section on "Time and the Will" in *Totality and Infinity.* What Levinas offers there is a telling critique of reason as a ground for action. When he writes that hunger and deprivation can so distort our vision that we no longer see them, but see *from them,* he is pointing precisely to the false confidence in reason that pervades Kantian accounts.

41. Nortvedt, "Levinas, Justice and Health Care," 31.

42. Ibid., 31.

43. For a good example using Levinas in practical fields, see Per Nortvedt, "Subjectivity and Vulnerability: Reflections on the Foundation of Ethical Sensibility," *Nursing Philosophy* 4 (2003): 222–30.

NOTES TO CHAPTER 7 / MANDERSON

1. *Donoghue v. Stevenson* (1932), AC 562.

2. Desmond Manderson, ed., *Essays on Levinas and Law: A Mosaic* (New York: Palgrave Macmillan, 2009). The arguments of this chapter are developed in much more detail in Desmond Manderson, *Proximity, Levinas and the Soul of Law* (Montreal: McGill-Queen's University Press, 2006). An earlier version of the material in this chapter was previously published as "Proximity—the law of ethics and the ethics of law," *UNSW Law Journal* 28 (2005): 697–720. See also "The Ethics of Proximity: An essay for William Deane," *Griffith Law Review* 14 (2005): 295–329.

3. Antony Gormley, *Field for the British Isles,* sculpture, 8 x 26 cm, British Museum, London (1993).

4. Jacques Derrida, " 'Violence and Metaphysics: An Essay on the Thought of Emmanuel Levinas," in *Writing and Difference,* trans. Alan Bass (London: Routledge, 1978), 125–26.

5. See Alphonso Lingis, "Translator's Introduction." in *OB* xxxiii.

6. See Emmanuel Levinas, *Le visage de l'autre,* illustrations by Martin tom Dieck (Paris: Editions Seuil, 2001). For a recent discussion see Diane Moira Duncan, *The Pre-Text of Ethics* (New York: Peter Land, 2001), 41.

7. This theme is evoked in *Otherwise than Being,* in particular.

8. Jacques Derrida, *The Gift of Death,* trans. David Wills (Chicago: University of Chicago Press, 1995), 68–70.

9. See Derrida, *Gift of Death,* chap. 4.

10. See Derrida, "Violence and Metaphysics," and Simon Critchley, *The Ethics of Deconstruction* (Oxford: Blackwell, 1992), 96–98. Further, see Jacques

Derrida, "Force of Law: The Mystical Foundation of Authority," *Cardozo Law Review* 11 (1990): 920, 947.

11. Derrida, "Violence and Metaphysics," 79.

12. See Emmanuel Levinas, "Wholly Otherwise," in *Re-Reading Levinas,* ed. Robert Bernasconi and Simon Critchley (Bloomington: Indiana University Press, 1982), chap. 1.

13. See also *DF* 18.

14. Critchley, *Ethics of Deconstruction,* 231.

15. Derrida, "Violence and Metaphysics," 185.

16. *United States v. Carroll Towing* (1947), 159 F. 2d 173.

17. See Mason J. in *Wyong Shire Council v. Shirt* (1980), 146 CLR 40 at 47–48.

18. *Carroll Towing* (1947), 159 F. 2d 173 per Learned Hand J.

19. John Wild, "Introduction," in *TI* 14.

20. Mark Dowie, "Pinto Madness," *Mother Jones* (Sept./Oct.1977): 18–32.

21. Ibid. See also Douglas Birsch and John Fielder, eds., *The Ford Pinto Case: A Study in Applied Ethics, Business, and Technology* (Albany: State University of New York Press, 1994).

22. *Grimshaw v. Ford* (1981), 119 Ca. 3rd 757.

23. *Romeo v. Conservation Commission of the Northern Territory* (1998), 192 CLR 431.

24. Ibid., 431.

25. *Mercer v. Commissioner of Road Transport & Tramways (NSW)* (1936), 56 CLR 580, per Rich, Evatt & McTiernan JJ.

26. See Emmanuel Levinas, "Martin Buber and the Theory of Knowledge," in *PN.*

27. See Levinas, "Ethics and Spirit," in *DF* 3–10.

28. The failure to understand the difference, and thus the failure to appreciate what Levinas means by infinity, lies at the heart of the some of the most careless criticism of his work, as I trust I have elsewhere shown.

29. See, for example, *Perre v. Apand* (1999), 198 CLR 180 per McHugh J.

30. See Manderson, *Proximity and the Soul of Law,* chap. 5.

31. Ibid., 216.

32. *Leigh & Sullivan v. Aliakmon Shipping* (1985), AB 350, 397 per Robert Goff LJ; *Caparo v. Dickman* (1990), 2 AC 605, 618 per Lord Bridge.

33. *Pyrenees Shire Council v. Day* (1998), 192 CLR 330.

34. See William Simmons, "The Third: Levinas's Theoretical Move from An-archical Ethics to the Realm of Justice and Politics," *Philosophy and Social Criticism* 25 (1999): 83, 93–97.

35. Sarah Roberts, "Rethinking Justice: Levinas and Asymmetrical Responsibility," *Philosophy in the Contemporary World* 7 (2000): 5.

36. Derrida, "Violence and Metaphysics," 157–59, 181–85.

37. Derrida, "Force of Law," 919.

38. Ibid., 961.

39. See Diane Perpich, "A Singular Justice: Ethics and Politics between Levinas and Derrida," *Philosophy Today* 42, supplement (1998): 59–70.

40. Simmons, "The Third," 84; see also Roberts, "Rethinking Justice," 7–8.

41. Derrida, "Force of Law," 955.

42. For further on contemporary theories of legislative drafting, see Nicholas Horn, "Black letters: epistolary rhetoric and plain English laws" *Griffith Law Review* 9 (2000): 7.

43. Levinas writes: "The discourse that suppresses the interruptions of discourse by relating them maintain the discontinuity under the knots with which the thread is tied again" (*OB* 170).

44. For examples, see *Romeo v. Conservation Commission of the Northern Territory* (1998), 192 CLR 431; *Pyrenees Shire Council v. Day* (1998), 192 CLR 330; *Modbury Triangle Shopping Centre v. Anzil* (2000), 176 ALR 411; *Perre v. Apand Pty. Ltd.* (1999), 198 CLR 180.

45. See Levinas, "A Religion for Adults," in *DF* 11–23, esp. 19–21. See the critique of positivism as "infantile" in Jerome Frank, *Law and the Modern Mind* (New York: Brentano's, 1930).

46. For further on these themes see Marinos Diamantides, "Ethics in Law: Death Marks on a Still Life," *Law and Critique* 6 (1995): 209–28.

47. See H. L. A. Hart, *The Concept of Law* (Oxford: Clarendon Press, 1960); Ronald Dworkin, *Law's Empire* (Cambridge, Mass.: Belknap Pres, 1986); William Lucy, *Understanding and Explaining Adjudication* (Oxford: Oxford University Press, 1999).

48. Derrida, "Violence and Metaphysics," 195.

Notes to Chapter 8 / Davidson

1. Several recent efforts, however, have been directed toward a recovery of this important theme in Levinas's thought, including: Roger Burggraeve, *The Wisdom of Love in the Service of Love: Emmanuel Levinas on Justice, Peace and Human Rights,* trans. Jeffrey Bloechl (Milwaukee: Marquette University, 2002 [1985]); Thaddée Ncayizigiye, *Réexamen éthique des droits de l'homme sous l'éclairage de la pensée d'Emmanuel Lévinas* (Boston: Peter Lang, 1997); Robert Bernasconi, "Extra-Territoriality: Outside the State, Outside the Subject," in *Levinas Studies: An Annual Review,* vol. 3, ed. Jeffrey Bloechl, 61–77 (Pittsburgh: Duquesne University Press, 2008); Stephen Minister, "From Perpetual Peace to the Face of the Other: A Levinasian Reframing of Human Rights," *Philosophy in the Contemporary World* 14, no. 2 (Fall 2007): 143–52.

2. As Robert Bernasconi has noted, the debate over human rights is already reflected in Levinas's 1933 essay, "Reflections on the Philosophy of Hitlerism," trans. Sean Hand, *Critical Inquiry* 17, no. 1 (Autumn 1990): 62–71.

3. The four essays on human rights are: "The Rights of Man and the Rights of the Other," "The Prohibition against Representation and 'The Rights of Man,'" "The Rights of the Other Man," and "The Rights of Man and Good Will."

4. Karl Marx, "On the Jewish Question," in *Selected Writings,* ed. Lawrence H. Simon (Indianapolis: Hackett, 1994), 17.

5. See Hannah Arendt, *The Origins of Totalitarianism* (New York: Harcourt, 1973). And, for a more recent treatment of this issue, see Seyla Benhabib, The Rights of Others: Aliens, Residents, Citizens (Cambridge: Cambridge University Press, 2004).

6. I take this term from C. B. MacPherson's *The Political Theory of Possessive Individualism: From Hobbes to Locke* (London: Oxford University Press, 1962). An interesting variation of the treatment of this notion can be found in Etienne Balibar, "Possessive Individualism Reversed: From Locke to Derrida," *Constellations* 9, no. 3 (2002): 299–317.

7. One example of a similar, but much more detailed, account of the violence against the individual present equally in totalitarian systems and market-based systems can be found in Michel Henry, *La Barbarie* (Paris: Grasset, 1998).

8. David Gauthier, *Morals by Agreement* (Oxford: Clarendon, 1986).

9. A purported comparison between Kant and Levinas forms the basis of Stephen Minister's "From Perpetual Peace to the Face of the Other: A Levinasian Reframing of Human Rights," *Philosophy in the Contemporary World* 14, no. 2 (Fall 2007): 143–52. Much more extensive treatments of the relation between Kant and Levinas can be found in Catherine Chalier, *What Ought I to Do? Morality in Kant and Levinas,* trans. Jane Marie Todd (Ithaca: Cornell University Press, 2002); and Diane Perpich, "Freedom Called into Question: Levinas's Defence of Heteronomy," in *In Proximity: Emmanuel Levinas and the Eighteenth Century,* ed. Melvyn New, Robert Bernasconi, and Richard A. Cohen (Lubbock: Texas Tech University Press, 2001), 303–25.

10. See Alan Gewirth, *Human Rights: Essays on Justification and Application* (Chicago: University of Chicago Press, 1982); Alan Gewirth, *The Community of Rights* (Chicago: University of Chicago Press, 1996).

11. On this point, Levinas resembles recent critics of the Rawlsian theory of justice such as Jürgen Habermas and Axel Honneth who question whether Rawls's proceduralism can genuinely prevent all preexisting prejudices and inequalities from entering into the veil of ignorance.

12. Of particular interest is his discussion of the possible connection between Levinas and Moses Mendelssohn. See Bernasconi, "Extra-territoriality."

13. Bernasconi, "Extra-territoriality," 73.

14. For this reason, Deleuze and Guattari's chapter "Year Zero: Faciality," which is implicitly aimed against Levinas's notion of the face, misses the target. Deleuze and Guattari point to the way in which the face takes over and becomes visible in everything, for example, heads, hands, stomachs, and so on. The face, in their view, is impersonal; it is the product of power/knowledge. There is thus no room for any comparison between Levinas's notion of the face and Deleuze and Guattari's "faciality." Whereas for the former the face transcends all power and knowledge, for the latter it enforces power/knowledge. See Gilles Deleuze and Felix Guattari, *A Thousand Plateaus,* trans. Brian Massumi (London: Athlone Press, 1988), 167–91.

15. With regard to the extraterritoriality of human rights, Levinas interestingly observes that "the defense of human rights corresponds to a vocation

outside the state, disposing, in a political society of a kind of extraterritoriality.... The capacity to guarantee that extraterritoriality and that independence defines the liberal state and describes the modality according to which the conjunction of politics and ethics is intrinsically possible" (*OS* 123).

16. On this point, Levinas clearly seeks a way out of the skepticism expressed by thinkers like Hannah Arendt, who take the problem of stateless persons to demonstrate the futility of human rights discourse. Instead of taking this phenomenon to be the refutation of human rights, what Levinas seeks to do here, as I take it, is to show that such situations are precisely the meaning of human rights discourse.

17. For example, Levinas writes: "They [the difference between the self and the other] are due to the I-Other conjuncture, to the inevitable orientation of being 'starting from oneself' toward 'the Other'" (*TI* 215).

18. Note also that in the same paragraph he says, "the epiphany of the face *qua* face opens humanity" (*TI* 213). What I take these observations to mean is that the face is neither simply individual nor universal, instead it preserves a tension between these two in which the universal is opened up by the absolutely unique.

19. On this point, Levinas notes, "There does indeed exist a human race as a biological genus, and the common function men may exercise in the world as a totality permits the applying to them of a common concept. But the human community instituted by language, where the interlocutors remain separate, does not constitute the unity of a genus" (*TI* 213–14).

20. The story of Deucalion is drawn from Greek mythology. Similar to the story of Noah's ark, Deucalion and his wife survived a flood that destroyed the human race. Afterwards, Deucalion was granted his wish to repopulate the earth. They were told that they could do so by throwing their mother's bones over their shoulders. He and his wife, Pyrrha, solved this riddle by figuring out this was a reference to mother Earth and so they cast stones from the Earth over their shoulders. The stones cast by him produced men, while those cast by her produced women. The myth is cited at *TI* 214.

21. W. N. Hohfeld, *Fundamental Legal Conceptions Applied to Judicial Reasoning* (New Haven: Yale University Press, 1919). Joel Feinberg, "The Nature and Value of Rights," *Journal of Value Inquiry* 1 (1970/71): 243–57.

22. The background history, however, indicates that this article was taken quite seriously, undergoing many drafts and extended discussion. For more detail, see *The Universal Declaration of Human Rights: A Commentary*, ed. Abjorn Eide et al. (Oslo: Scandinavian University Press, 1992); and, The International Council on Human Rights Policy, *Taking Duties Seriously: Individual Duties in International Human Rights Law — A Commentary* (Versoix, Switzerland: SADAG, 1999).

23. The fascinating history behind the drafting of this article indicates that the role of duties was taken very seriously by the framers of the UDHR. Indeed, with an earlier draft in 1947, the article referring to duties was placed in article 2, but then was placed at the end of the document in the subsequent 1948 draft.

24. The full text of article 29.2 states: "In the exercise of his rights and freedoms, everyone shall be subject only to such limitation as are determined by law solely for the purpose of securing due recognition and respect for the rights and freedoms of others and of meeting the just requirements of morality, public order and the general welfare in a democratic society."

25. The question of whether to include a list of specific duties to the communities was itself a point of much debate. Note, however, that there are several other rights documents that do specify such duties, including the following: The American Declaration of the Rights and Duties of Man (1948), The African Charter on Human and Peoples' Rights (1981), and the InterAction Council's draft of The Universal Declaration of Human Responsibilities (1999). These documents, which codify human duties, offer reveal a number of deficiencies but nevertheless offer an interesting basis for thinking through the implications of this project.

Notes to Chapter 9 / Hansel

1. Note that the term "metaphysical asymmetry" is used at *TI* 53.

2. This critique of the autarchy of the self is developed by Levinas from his early writings, notably in *On Escape*. On this topic, see Joëlle Hansel, " 'L'être est' et 'Il y a': autarchie et anonymat de l'être dans les premiers écrits d'Emmanuel Levinas," *Les Etudes phénoménologiques* (2006): 43–44.

3. The critique of "aesthetic sufficiency" that occurs in art is the indication of a connection betweeen "La transcendance des mots" and "La réalité et son ombre." The latter article was published by Levinas in 1948 in *Les Temps modernes* and was reprinted in *Les imprévus de l'histoire*. See "Reality and its Shadow" in *Unforeseen History*, trans. Nidra Poller (Urbana: University of Illinois Press, 2004), 76–91.

4. See Levinas, "The Meaning of Religious Practice," trans. Peter Atterton, Matthew Calarco, and Joëlle Hansel, *Levinas Studies* 5 (2010): 1–4.

5. We are inspired here by the position taken by Levinas in a conversation with Rabbi Josy Eisenberg shown on French television on the show "La source de vie" on March 26, 1978. "Morality in the Laboratory: An Interview with Emmanuel Levinas by Josy Eisenberg," trans. Peter Atterton and Joëlle Hansel, *Levinas Studies* 6 (2011): 1–7.

6. Cf. "Is Ontology Fundamental?" in *BPW*.

7. Contrary to what some commentators suggest, there are not "two Platos" for Levinas, the one of epistemology and the other of ethics, but only one!

8. Immanuel Kant, *Critique of Pure Reason*, trans. Werner S. Pluhar (Indianapolis: Hackett, 1996), 106.

9. Kant, *Critique of Pure Reason*, 72; italics mine.

10. This passage is repeated almost word for word at *TI* 44.

11. Plato, *Phaedrus*, 275e–76a.

12. Ibid., 272a.

13. The figure of the other as an "interlocutor" appeared already in the essay "Is Ontology Fundamental?"

14. See *Babylonian Talmud*, Treatise Horaiot 17a and Berakhot 67a.

15. Maimonides, *Mishneh Torah*, chap. 1, par. 9. In Hebrew: *ma'atikei ha shemu'a*. They are those who transmit the tradition by listening, as indicated by the talmudic expression "*ish mi pi ish*," which literally means "the one from the mouth of an other."

16. The term "Pharisee" in Hebrew is *perushim*, literally meaning "separated." It refers to those who, unlike the Sadducees who hold to the letter of the *Pentateuch*, "admit alongside the written text of the Torah the authority of an oral tradition (the *Torah she be al pei*), which is received, transmitted, and deepend by those who are called the *hakhamim*, the 'wise'"—these are the Sages of the Talmud and those who study it and extend it. Georges Hansel, *Explorations talmudiques* (Paris: Odile Jacob, 1998), 28.

Notes to Chapter 10 / Katz

1. Howard Caygill, "The Prison Notebooks," *Radical Philosophy* 160 (March/Apr. 2010), http://www.radicalphilosophy.com/default.asp?channel_id=2188&editorial_id=28975; accessed July 27, 2010.

2. Salomon Malka, *Emmanuel Levinas: His Life and Legacy* (Pittsburgh: Duquesne University Press, 2006), 84.

3. Emmanuel Levinas, *Levinas: Philosophe et pédagogue* (Paris: Les Editions du Nadir, 1998).

4. Ady Steg, "A Fable," in *Levinas: Philosophe et pédagogue*, 7; my translation.

5. For two instances where Levinas's ethical project has been examined in relationship to Judaism and also education, see Richard A. Cohen, *Ethics, Exegesis and Philosophy: Interpretation after Levinas* (Cambridge: Cambridge University Press, 2001). And Robert Gibbs, *Why Ethics: Signs of Responsibilities* (Princeton: Princeton University Press, 2000). See also Denise Eg-Kuehne, ed., *Levinas and Education: At the Intersection of Faith and Reason* (New York: Routledge, 2008). This edited collection brings together 18 essays engaging Levinas's work with themes important to educational theory and practice. The book is important for alerting scholars and practitioners to this connection. However, with the exception of the first essay which was translated from *Levinas: Philosophe et pédagogue*, none of the essays written for this collection engage Levinas's own essays on education and only the essay by Gert Biesta makes any mention of these essays whatsoever.

6. Grinberg (sometimes spelled "Greenberg") was a member of the Labor Zionist movement. He was also part of the Zionist organization that helped found the network of Tarbut Hebrew schools, which were also secular, that were developed in Eastern European countries before the Holocaust. For more information, see "Zionism and Zionist Parties" on the YIVO Web site: http://www.yivoinstitute.org/index.php?tid=109&aid=534; accessed July 20, 2010.

7. Robert Bernasconi recently argued that this final section of *Totality and Infinity*, "Beyond the Face," which includes the discussions of eros and fecundity, is a holdover from *Time and the Other*, a discussion that Levinas drops in his later

work because it reads too much like a family structure. For the full argument, see Robert Bernasconi, "No Exit: Levinas' Aporetic Account of Transcendence," *Research in Phenomenology* 35 (2005): 101–17. Bernasconi might be right that Levinas had personal reasons to include and philosophical reasons to discard it. However, one could also argue that inclusion of this section was less about something idiosyncratically personal and more about how the ethical subject is formed. In this regard, Levinas's description calls us to think about what it means to be a parent who is responsible for raising a child. While it is not the case that we are all Jewish and therefore we would not respond to Levinas's call to participate in Jewish education, it is the case that being a parent is an experience that transcends religious, among other, categories. Thus, Levinas can offer a mechanism for explaining how the ethical subject comes into being—by the way in which the child obligates the parent to respond by providing food, clothing, and care. The parent is called to respond to the child but in so doing one could argue that the parent is part of the cultivation of that child to respond to other others.

8. One criticism in particular stands out: Luce Irigaray's essay, "The Fecundity of the Caress," in *Ethics of Sexual Difference,* trans. Carolyn Burke and Gillian Gill (Ithaca: Cornell University Press, 1993), 185–217. For a response to Irigaray, see Claire Katz, *Levinas, Judaism, and the Feminine: The Silent Footsteps of Rebecca* (Bloomington: Indiana University Press, 2003) and Claire Katz, "'For Love is as Strong as Death': Taking Another Look at Levinas on Love," *Philosophy Today* 45, no. 5 (July 2002): 124–32.

9. Levinas's emphasis on fecundity underscores the importance of asymmetrical responsibility that is unique to the parent/child relation. It should be noted that Robert Gibbs disagrees with characterizing this relationship as *strictly* asymmetrical and which is not a characteristic of the erotic relationship that Levinas describes in the preceding section (See, Gibbs, *Why Ethics*). Nonetheless, Levinas describes love as bringing us out of ourselves through the desire that cannot be fulfilled, but that longs for eternity. The birth of the son represents this eternity. The parent's responsibility for the child is joined to the child's role as the parent's teacher. Insofar as the child is unique, the child teaches the parent, instructs her to be attentive to the child's own growth. And it is in turn the parent's responsibility to help the child become responsible for others. And so our hope that our children will be responsible to others opens onto the hope that others will be responsible for other others. This movement from love to fecundity opens finally into fraternity, as the first microcommunity, and then to a larger community.

10. Cf. Emmanuel Levinas, *Humanism of the Other,* trans. Nidra Poller (Urbana: University of Illinois Press, 2006).

11. Levinas's talmudic reading, "The Temptation of Temptation," references the acceptance of the covenant at Sinai. I believe this is what he has in mind when he thinks about what his ethics means in reality and for a community, but it remains an open question as to how this covenant translates outside the Jewish community.

12. One anonymous reader suggested that in fact we do—we read Levinas's books and then become more Levinasian. My point is not to rule out the possibility that people might become more reflective about their individual actions,

the way they live their lives, or the choices that they make. My point is more fundamental—while it might be the case that minds are changed, I do not believe that hearts are changed simply by reading. My claim is not meant to be anti-intellectual, but rather the opposite. By circumscribing what the intellect can and cannot do, we actually give it the power it deserves.

NOTES TO CHAPTER 11 / DRABINSKI

1. Claude Lanzmann, *Shoah: The Complete Text of the Acclaimed Holocaust Film* (New York: Da Capo Press, 1995), 185.

2. Cf. Emmanuel Levinas, "The Trace of the Other," trans. Alphonso Lingis, in *Deconstruction in Context: Literature and Philosophy*, ed. Mark C. Taylor (Chicago: University of Chicago Press, 1986), 345–59.

3. Consider, for example, Jean-Paul Sartre's famous essay "Black Orpheus" in 1948 (a preface to Léopold Senghor's collection of poetry from the black global south) and then his controversial, influential introduction to Fanon's *Wretched of the Earth* in 1961. Both Sartre pieces bookend an incredibly productive period in Levinas's work, and yet the growing awareness about France's place in the rapidly decolonizing world remain absent from the pages of Levinas's work.

4. Édouard Glissant, *Poetics of Relation*, trans. Betsy Wing (Ann Arbor: University of Michigan Press, 1997), 6.

5. Glissant, *Poetics of Relation*, 6.

6. On the abyss, memory, and the break from European models of trauma, see my "What Is Trauma to the Future? On Glissant's Poetics," *Qui Parle* 18, no. 2 (Spring/Summer 2010): 291–307.

7. Glissant, *Poetics of Relation*, 7.

8. Ibid., 6.

9. Ibid., 154–55.

10. Ibid., 155.

11. Ibid., 1.

12. Ibid., 8.

13. Ibid., 9.

14. This is the argument of the first chapter of my *Levinas and the Postcolonial: Race, Nation, Other* (Edinburgh: Edinburgh University Press, 2011).

NOTES TO CHAPTER 12 / BERNASCONI

1. Etienne Feron, *De l'idée de transcendance à la question du langage* (Paris: Jerome Millon, 1992), 7. Levinas himself described his book in these terms; see *TI* 26.

2. Bernard Forthomme, *Une philosophie de la transcendance* (Paris: La Pensée Universelle, 1979), 7.

3. Robert Bernasconi, "The Ethics of Suspicion," *Research in Phenomenology* 20 (1990): 3–18.

4. See Robert Bernasconi, "Globalization and World Hunger: Levinas and Kant" in *Radicalizing Levinas*, ed. Peter Atterton and Matthew Calarco (Albany:

State University of New York Press, 2010), 69–84. See also "Before Whom, and for What?" in *Difficulties of Ethical Life,* ed. Shannon W. Sullivan and Dennis J. Schmidt (New York: Fordham University Press, 2008), 131–46.

5. I challenged this reading first in "Rereading *Totality and Infinity,*" in *The Question of the Other,* ed. Arleen B. Dallery and Charles E. Scott (Albany: State University of New York Press, 1989), 23–34.

6. The best statement of this position that I am aware of has been formulated by Diane Perpich, *The Ethics of Emmanuel Levinas* (Stanford: Stanford University Press, 2008), but I should make it clear that this essay is directed more against a tendency within Levinas scholarship than any specific interpretation of it. I should also be clear that, even though from time to time I cite some of my own writings in support of the interpretation presented here, I do not exempt myself from having on occasion advocated "Levinasian ethics" in the past.

7. This is true of even Levinas's best readers. See, for example, the minimal attention given to these themes within the 500 pages of Michael Morgan's *Discovering Levinas* (Cambridge: Cambridge University Press, 2007). But one could cite many other examples. For a reading that, by contrast, insists on the importance of fecundity for the whole work, see Jean-Luc Thayse, *Eros et fécondité chez le jeune Levinas* (Paris: L'Harmattan, 1998), 220. For my own treatment of this issue in more detail, see "Levinas and the Transcendence of Fecundity," in *MonoKL* (Istanbul), forthcoming.

8. For some excellent observations on Luce Irigaray's reading, see Tina Chanter, *Ethics of Eros* (London: Routledge, 1995), 214–24.

9. For a treatment of the title that explores some of the issues raised here, see Elisabeth Louise Thomas, *Emmanuel Levinas: Ethics, Justice, and the Human beyond Being* (New York: Routledge, 2004), 98–99.

10. *OE* 54. My discussion of Levinas's thinking of transcendence is somewhat curtailed as I have given a fuller account in "No Exit: Levinas's Aporetic Account of Transcendence," *Research in Phenomenology* 35 (2005): 101–17.

11. Emmanuel Levinas, "Pluralisme et transcendance," *Proceedings of the Tenth International Congress of Philosophy,* vol. 1, ed. E. W. Beth and H. J. Pos (Amsterdam: North-Holland, 1948), 381. The passage can be found with minor changes at *TI* 274.

12. Levinas's account of the concretization of formal structure risks being dismissed as arbitrary. However, the fact that one can draw parallels between these concretizations and what Levinas highlights in his confessional or Jewish writings suggests that one needs to understand this aspect of his thought to be culturally conditioned in some positive sense. See, for example, Levinas's discussions of the feminine in *DF* 30–38. This returns us to the complex question of the sense in which Levinas must be understood as a Jewish philosopher.

13. Emmanuel Levinas, "Resumé de *Totalité et Infini,*" *Annales de l'Université de Paris* 3 (July–September 1961): 385–86. There are 63 occurrences of the word *éthique* compared with 55 occurrences of *fécondité* according to *Levinas Concordance,* ed. Cristian Ciocan and Georges Hansel (Dordrecht: Springer, 2005), 273, 309.

14. See Peter Atterton, "Levinas's Skeptical Critique of Metaphysics and *Anti*-Humanism," *Philosophy Today* 41, no. 4 (1997): 491–506.

15. There is a remarkable proximity to Hegel here. See Robert Bernasconi, "Hegel and Levinas: The Possibility of Forgiveness and Reconciliation," *Archivio di Filosofia* 54 (1986): 325–46.

16. See, for example, *La conscience juive face à l'histoire: Le pardon,* ed. Eliane Amado Lévy-Valensi and Jean Halperin (Paris: Presses Universitaires de France, 1965). The task of forgiveness is easier for future generations. This is one of the roles Levinas assigned to youth. See *TI* 284.

17. On the political resources of the discussion of fecundity, see Mielle Chandler, "Hemorrhage and Filiality: Towards a Fecundation of the Political," in *Difficult Justice,* ed. Asher Horowitz and Gad Horowitz (Toronto: University of Toronto Press, 2006), 97–110.

18. Stella Sanford has made the case for the difficulty of separating biology from fecundity, which would appear to undercut Levinas's attempt to see the family as an alternative to the nation. See *The Metaphysics of Love* (London: Athlone Press, 2000). For the alternative view, see Adriaan Peperzak, *To the Other* (West Lafayette: Purdue University Press, 1993), 195.

19. On broader conceptions of fecundity, see Paul Davies, "Asymmetry and Transcendence: On Skepticism and First Philosophy," *Research in Phenomenology* 35 (2005): 119.

20. Hannah Arendt, *The Origins of Totalitarianism* (New York: Harcourt Brace, 1979), 475. For an indication of the difficulties here, see Bettina Bergo, *Levinas Between Ethics and Politics* (Dordrecht: Kluwer, 1999), 127. In the context of *Totality and Infinity* the idea seems to be an afterthought, but Levinas subsequently turned to an account of the rights of the Other in order to provide an alternative way of establishing an "outside the state." See Robert Bernasconi, "Extra-Territoriality: Outside the State, Outside the Subject," in *Levinas Studies,* vol. 3, ed. Jeffrey Bloechl (Pittsburgh: Duquesne University Press, 2008), 61–77.

21. Francois Poirié, *Emmanuel Levinas: Qui etes-vous?* (Lyon: La Manufacture, 1987), 95; trans. Jill Robbins as *Is It Righteous to Be?* (Stanford: Stanford University Press, 2001), 49.

22. Martin Heidegger, *Being and Time,* trans. Joan Stanbaugh and revised by Dennis J. Schmidt (Albany: State University of New York Press, 2010), 131.

23. See Emmanuel Levinas, "Substitution," trans. Peter Atherton, Simon Critchley, and Graham Noctor in *BPW* 92. See further, Robert Bernasconi, "What is the Question to which 'Substitution' is the answer?" in *Cambridge Companion to Levinas,* ed. Simon Critchley and Robert Bernasconi (Cambridge: Cambridge University Press, 2002), 234–51.

24. See Emmanuel Levinas, "The Rights of Man and the Rights of the Other," in *OS* 116–25.

Stacy Bautista recently earned her Ph.D. from Loyola University Chicago by writing on the shift from ontological to social evil in Levinas's phenomenology. She has presented papers on the problematic significance of the gendered other at the heart of *Totality and Infinity,* on Levinas and ideological critique, and plans to pursue an analysis on the possibility (and necessity) of a politically viable plural subjectivity ("we") in Levinas's work.

Silvia Benso is professor of philosophy at Rochester Institute of Technology, where she works in the areas of contemporary European philosophy, Italian philosophy, and ancient philosophy. She is the author of *Pensare dopo Auschwitz: Etica filosofica e teodicea ebraica, The Face of Things: A Different Side of Ethics.* With Brian Schroeder, she is also the coeditor of *Contemporary Italian Philosophy: Crossing the Borders of Ethics, Politics, and Religion; Levinas and the Ancients;* and *Between Nihilism and Politics: The Hermeneutics of Gianni Vattimo.* She has translated from Italian Carlo Sini, *Ethics of Writing,* and Ugo Perone, *The Possible Present.* She is the coeditor, with Brian Schroeder, of the SUNY Series in Contemporary Italian Philosophy.

Robert Bernasconi is Edwin Erle Sparks Professor of Philosophy at Penn State University. He is a coeditor of *The Provocation of Levinas; Re-Reading Levinas; Levinas: Basic Philosophical Writings; In Proximity: Emmanuel Levinas and the Eighteenth Century;* and *The Cambridge Companion to Levinas.* He is the author of more than 30 articles on Levinas. He also publishes on Hegel, Heidegger, Sartre, Derrida, and in critical philosophy of race and political philosophy.

Georg W. Bertram is associate professor of philosophy at the Free University of Berlin. His recent books include: *Die Sprache und das Ganze. Entwurf einer antireduktionistischen Sprachphilosophie* (*Language and the Whole: Outline of an Antireductionist Philosophy of Language*); and *Kunst. Eine philosophische Einführung* (*Art: A Philosophical Introduction*).

Scott Davidson is associate professor and chair of the philosophy department at Oklahoma City University. He is the editor of *Ricoeur Across the Disciplines* and co-editor of two journals, *Ricoeur Studies* and *Journal of French and Francophone Philosophy*. He is also the translator of three books by Michel Henry, *Barbarism, Seeing the Invisible,* and *Material Phenomenology.*

John Drabinski, in addition to over three dozen essays in European and Africana critical theory, has published *Sensibility and Singularity; Godard between Identity and Difference;* and *Levinas and the Postcolonial: Race, Nation, Other.* He is editor (with Eric S. Nelson) of *Between Levinas and Heidegger,* an issue of Journal of French and Francophone Philosophy on Godard and Philosophy, an issue of *The C. L. R. James Journal* (with Marisa Parham) on Édouard Glissant, and (with Jill Stauffer, Ozlem Biner, and Sharika Thiranagama) a special double issue of *Humanity* on reconciliation. Drabinski's current research includes a recently completed manuscript entitled *Abyssal Beginnings: Glissant, Philosophy, and the Middle Passage* and the beginnings of a book-length study of James Baldwin and black Atlantic critical theory. He and Scott Davidson edit the *Journal of French and Francophone Philosophy.*

Joëlle Hansel is the director of the Raissa and Emmanuel Levinas Center, Jerusalem and a board member of SIREL (Société

Internationale de recherches Emmanuel Levinas, Paris). She is the author of a number of books including: *M. H. Luzzatto: Kabbale et philosophie; Emmanuel Levinas: De l'Etre à l'Autre;* and *Levinas in Jerusalem*. She has also published numerous articles on Levinas, Jankélévitch, Bergson, Luzzatto, and the revival of Jewish thought in France after the Shoah. She is the author of *Vladimir Jankélévitch: Une philosophie du charme* (2012).

Asher Horowitz is professor of political science at York University in Toronto. He is the author of a number of works on modern political thought and recently of articles and books having to do with the relation of Levinas to political thought and critical theory, including *Difficult Justice: Commentaries on Levinas and Politics,* edited with G. Horowitz; and *Ethics at a Standstill: History and Subjectivity in Levinas and the Frankfurt School*.

Claire Katz is an associate professor of philosophy and women's and gender studies at Texas A&M University. She is the author of *Levinas, Judaism, and the Feminine: The Silent Footsteps of Rebecca,* and the editor, with Lara Trout, of *Emmanuel Levinas: Critical Assessments*. She has also published essays on Rousseau, Kant, Kierkegaard, and Merleau-Ponty, and on themes including philosophy of education, philosophy of religion, Jewish philosophy, and feminist theory. Her forthcoming book, *Levinas and the Crisis of Humanism,* considers the relationship between Levinas's essays on Jewish education and the overall structure of his philosophical project.

Desmond Manderson is professor and Future Fellow in the College of Law and the Research School of Humanities and the Arts at Australian National University. From 2002 to 2011 he held the Canada Research Chair in Law and Discourse at McGill University, where he was founding director of the Institute for the Public Life of Arts and Ideas. His books include

From Mr. Sin to Mr. Big; Songs without Music: Aesthetic Dimensions of Law and Justice; Proximity, Levinas, and the Soul of Law; Essays on Levinas and Law; and *Kangaroo Courts and the Rule of Law — The Legacy of Modernism.*

Michael L. Morgan is Emeritus Chancellor's Professor of Philosophy and Jewish Studies at Indiana University (Bloomington). He has held visiting appointments at Yale University, Northwestern University, and the University of Toronto. His most recent books include *Discovering Levinas; The Cambridge Companion to Modern Jewish Philosophy,* which is edited with Peter Eli Gordon; and *On Shame.* He is currently working on *The Cambridge Introduction to Emmanuel Levinas* and *Modern Jewish Philosophy,* with Paul Franks.

Adriaan Peperzak is the Arthur J. Schmitt Professor in Philosophy at Loyola University Chicago. His most recent books are *Modern Freedom: Hegel's Moral, Legal, and Political Philosophy; Philosophy between Faith and Theology;* and *Thinking.*

Diane Perpich is associate professor of philosophy and director of women's studies at Clemson University. She is the author of *The Ethics of Emmanuel Levinas,* and of articles on phenomenology, French feminism, and ethics.